Climate Economics and Finance

Climate change and its mitigation has become one of the most pressing challenges facing our societies. Shocks and phenomena related to climate change cause important economic losses due to damages to property infrastructure, disruptions to supply chains, lower productivity, and migration. *Climate Economics and Finance* offers a comprehensive analysis of how climate change impacts economies and financial systems. Focusing on the economic and financial implications of climate change, it addresses critical yet often overlooked areas such as greenflation, public and private financing of the transition process, and the challenges faced by central banks and supervisors in preventing and managing associated risks. The work delves into the challenges that emerging and developing economies face in accessing climate finance, highlighting innovative financial and de-risking solutions. Synthesizing state-of-the-art research and ongoing policy discussions, this book offers a clear and accessible entry point into the intersection of climate and finance.

STÉPHANE DEES is Head of the Climate Economics Unit at the Banque de France and Associate Professor at the Bordeaux School of Economics. He spent a majority of his career at the European Central Bank. His research, which has been published in top academic journals, covers various topics in financial and international macroeconomics, financial stability, and climate change.

SELIN OZYURT-MILLER is a climate and country risk economist at the Economics and Market Research Department of the International Finance Corporation (World Bank Group). She holds a PhD from the University of Paris Dauphine and has lectured at top universities and published extensively on trade spillovers and climate change. Selin's insights are featured in leading academic journals, media outlets, and her online platforms.

Climate Economics and Finance

STÉPHANE DEES
Banque de France and Bordeaux School of Economics

SELIN OZYURT-MILLER
International Finance Corporation

Shaftesbury Road, Cambridge CB2 8EA, United Kingdom

One Liberty Plaza, 20th Floor, New York, NY 10006, USA

477 Williamstown Road, Port Melbourne, VIC 3207, Australia

314–321, 3rd Floor, Plot 3, Splendor Forum, Jasola District Centre, New Delhi – 110025, India

103 Penang Road, #05–06/07, Visioncrest Commercial, Singapore 238467

Cambridge University Press is part of Cambridge University Press & Assessment, a department of the University of Cambridge.

We share the University's mission to contribute to society through the pursuit of education, learning and research at the highest international levels of excellence.

www.cambridge.org
Information on this title: www.cambridge.org/9781009628631
DOI: 10.1017/9781009628617

© Stéphane Dees and Selin Ozyurt-Miller 2026

This publication is in copyright. Subject to statutory exception and to the provisions of relevant collective licensing agreements, no reproduction of any part may take place without the written permission of Cambridge University Press & Assessment.

When citing this work, please include a reference to the DOI 10.1017/9781009628617

First published 2026

Cover image: Hurricane Sandy aftermath, flooded tunnel, West Street, Lower Manhattan, NYC – JayLazarin / Editorial RF / Getty Images

A catalogue record for this publication is available from the British Library

A Cataloging-in-Publication data record for this book is available from the Library of Congress

ISBN 978-1-009-62866-2 Hardback
ISBN 978-1-009-62863-1 Paperback

Cambridge University Press & Assessment has no responsibility for the persistence or accuracy of URLs for external or third-party internet websites referred to in this publication and does not guarantee that any content on such websites is, or will remain, accurate or appropriate.

For EU product safety concerns, contact us at Calle de José Abascal, 56, 1°, 28003 Madrid, Spain, or email eugpsr@cambridge.org

Contents

List of Figures		*page* vi
List of Tables		ix
General Introduction		1
1	Climate Change and Its Economic Impacts	4
2	The Economics of Climate Change Mitigation	46
3	The Macroeconomic Effects of Mitigation Policies	93
4	Climate Finance and Main Instruments	129
5	Central Banks, Climate Change, and Price Stability	169
6	Risks to Financial Stability and Prudential Policy	211
7	Challenges in EMDEs and Ways to Overcome Them	253
References		300
Index		321

Figures

1.1	GHG emissions and by type	*page* 9
1.2	Global surface temperature change relative to 1850–1900 (in °C) in IPCC scenarios	13
1.3	NGFS scenarios	17
1.4	Frequency of natural disasters (number of disasters per year)	23
1.5	Growth in global natural catastrophe insured losses (2022 USD billion)	24
1.6	The articulation between hazards, exposure, and vulnerability	35
1.7	Damage functions	41
1.8	Global GDP impact by climate risk source	44
2.1	Implication in terms of global temperature rise of various policies and targets (°C above preindustrial average)	50
2.2	Carbon emissions to date and carbon budget remaining by G20 nations in Gt of CO_2	52
2.3	Cost-benefit approach vs. cost-effectiveness approach	55
2.4	Carbon price in NGFS scenarios (in USD per tonne of CO_2)	60
2.5	Transition phases	89
2.6	Evolution of policy adoption – number of adopted policies, 2010–2022, OECD average	90
3.1	Causal links involved in the Porter Hypothesis	96
3.2	Historical investment in energy benchmarked against needs in the IEA scenario in 2030	103
3.3	Energy demand reduction effects	104

3.4	Ownership chain of stranded assets by OECD/non-OECD geography and major institutional categories (USD trillion)	107
3.5	Reduction potential in global GHG emissions of final consumption sectors in 2050 through demand	109
3.6	Variations in annualized growth rates in GDP and welfare (full-income) due to climate change mitigation (annualized difference in growth rate between GHG 50 percent reduction and BAU, in percentage points)	117
3.7	Country-level comprehensive carbon price by country (2019 USD per tonne of CO_2 emissions)	122
4.1	Global investment in renewable energy and fossil fuels (USD billion)	131
4.2	Sustainable/ESG finance subcomponents	133
4.3	The scope of sustainable/ESG, low carbon, green, and climate finance	133
4.4	The typology of climate finance	134
4.5	Public versus private climate finance by region (USD billion, 2021/2022 annual average)	138
4.6	Breakdown of global finance for adaptation and mitigation (USD billion)	140
4.7	Breakdown of global climate finance by instruments (USD billion)	141
4.8	Typology of GSS+ financial instruments	151
4.9	Breakdown of green bonds by region and issuer (USD billion)	153
4.10	GSS+ issuance by category (USD billion)	161
4.11	Regional and issuer currency distribution of the GSS+ deals in 2023	163
5.1	Food price indices (2014–2016 = 100)	174
5.2	Climate transition: a wide diversity of shocks, which can coexist	179

5.3	Climate risks, macroeconomic variables, and challenges for monetary policy	182
5.4	Monetary policy transmission under climate change strains	183
5.5	Dominant negative supply shock	189
5.6	Negative demand shock	195
6.1	Channels and spillovers for materialization of physical and transition risks	213
6.2	Bridging the climate data gap	217
6.3	CRISK and marginal CRISK for World Financials	224
6.4	Protection gap	228
6.5	Dispersion of risk cost across institutions and correlation with the share of sensitive sectors in portfolios	240
6.6	Integrating climate-related risks into micro- and macro-prudential policies	248
6.7	A ladder approach to catastrophe insurance	251
7.1	Investment needs for climate and sustainable development (USD billion per year by 2030)	256
7.2	Blended finance structure	278
7.3	Sources of financing to climate blended finance (USD billion)	281
7.4	Climate blended finance deals by regional breakdown (%)	282
7.5	Breakdown of private sector investor commitments by instrument type (%)	283
7.6	Carbon removal versus avoidance solutions	288

Tables

1.1	GHG, lifetime, and global warming potential	page 8
1.2	Top twenty costliest climate-related disasters	25
1.3	Channels of impacts	30
2.1	Timeline of UN climate talks since 1992	47
2.2	Overview of policy instruments to mitigate climate change	74
2.3	Assessment of policy instruments	86
3.1	Distribution of decarbonization effort by demand through sufficiency and energy efficiency, and median share of emissions avoided in the sector by 2050	111
4.1	Estimated climate financing needs for EMDEs to meet the GHG emission reduction targets	130
4.2	Breakdown of global climate finance by public and private sources (USD billion, biannual averages)	139
4.3	TCFD recommendations	145
4.4	Sustainable fixed-income market 2023 – GSS+	152
5.1	Inflationary impact of climate-related risks	172
5.2	Climate change and natural interest rate	186
5.3	Comparative assessment of policy options	206
6.1	Assessing impacts of acute physical climate risk	219
6.2	Climate change impacts on insurance products	226
6.3	Potential negative consequences of physical climate change risk on the nonlife insurance business	228
6.4	The specificities of climate scenarios	232
6.5	Overview of short-term scenario narratives	235
7.1	Investment needs estimates in EMDEs to align with climate targets	258
7.2	Types of investors and return expectations	264
7.3	Blended finance instruments	277
7.4	Voluntary versus compliance carbon markets	287

General Introduction

Climate change, driven by human activities, is significantly transforming global economic and financial systems. Increased extreme weather events, such as intense storms, heat waves, and shifting precipitation patterns, are causing widespread economic disruptions. These phenomena lead to substantial economic losses by damaging infrastructure, disrupting supply chains, reducing agricultural productivity, and forcing migration. Furthermore, the transition toward a low-carbon economy, necessary to mitigate further climate change, presents its own economic challenges and financial risks. This transition requires massive investments in green technologies and infrastructure, which, while costly initially, promise long-term benefits like reduced environmental damage, enhanced energy efficiency, and improved public health due to less pollution.

Actions of central banks and financial institutions are crucial in addressing these climate-related risks. Both climate change and the policies needed to mitigate it can lead to "greenflation" – inflation driven by higher costs in transitioning industries, particularly in energy and agriculture. The financial sector must also manage the risk of "stranded assets," where investments in carbon-intensive industries become obsolete or lose value due to regulatory changes and shifts in market demand. This highlights the need for comprehensive risk assessments and strategic policy responses to safeguard financial stability.

The climate-related challenge is especially acute in emerging markets and developing economies (EMDEs). These regions are disproportionately vulnerable to the impacts of climate change, including severe weather events and disruptions to critical sectors like agriculture and water supply, despite having contributed relatively little to global greenhouse gas emissions. EMDEs often face significant financial constraints, including limited fiscal capacity and high sovereign credit risks, which hinder their ability to invest in necessary adaptation and mitigation measures. To address these challenges, innovative financial mechanisms such as blended finance are being explored. These mechanisms aim to attract private sector investment by combining it with concessional funds, thereby reducing the risk and making sustainable projects more viable. International financial institutions and multilateral development banks are pivotal in providing the necessary funding, expertise, and risk mitigation strategies to support these efforts.

Addressing climate change requires prompt and decisive action from governments worldwide. Policy tools like carbon taxes, regulations, and subsidies for sustainable activities are essential for transitioning to a low-carbon economy. Moreover, the concept of climate justice needs to be central to these efforts, ensuring that the burdens and benefits of climate policies are equitably distributed. This involves addressing inequalities both within countries – preventing vulnerable populations from bearing the brunt of climate impacts – and between countries, recognizing the differing capacities and responsibilities in addressing climate-related challenges.

The book aims to provide an in-depth, comprehensive analysis of these critical issues, focusing particularly on the economic and financial aspects of climate change, which are often overlooked in other discussions. It explores the complexities of financing the green transition, the challenges posed by high indebtedness and climate risks in EMDEs, and the broader implications of climate-related shocks on global economic and financial systems. Through state-of-the-art research and engagement with ongoing policy debates, the book seeks to offer such an in-depth analysis across Chapters 1–7. The work begins with a detailed exploration of the science behind climate change, examining the greenhouse effect, human contributions, future projections, and the concept of tipping points. It highlights the economic implications through historical trends and the channels through which climate events affect economies. The second chapter focuses on the economics of climate change mitigation, discussing the concept of a carbon budget, the costs of climate policies, and various policy instruments for reducing greenhouse gas emissions.

The book then explores the macroeconomic effects of mitigation policies, including their impact on economic growth, capital markets, and consumption behaviors, while addressing international competitiveness issues like carbon leakage. A comprehensive overview of climate finance follows, detailing recent trends, the role of green capital markets, and the various financial instruments available to support sustainable development. Central banks' role in maintaining price stability amid climate-related risks is thoroughly examined, highlighting the challenges and strategic implications for monetary policy. The sixth chapter discusses the risks to financial stability, focusing on how climate-related shocks can affect financial systems, including the insurance and re-insurance sectors.

Finally, the book addresses the specific climate finance challenges faced by EMDEs. It explores the intersection of climate change and development, the importance of climate justice, and strategies for overcoming barriers to climate investment. This includes the critical role of concessional finance, blended finance, and other innovative mechanisms to mobilize resources for climate action in these vulnerable regions.

Overall, this book aims to provide a comprehensive framework for understanding the multifaceted economic and financial aspects of climate change, offering valuable insights for policymakers, financial professionals, and scholars.

Disclaimer: This book is a personal initiative reflecting the opinions of the authors and do not necessarily express the views of the Banque de France or the International Finance Corporation and the World Bank Group.

1 Climate Change and Its Economic Impacts

1.1 INTRODUCTION

Human activity has caused unprecedented and widespread changes in the climate system that increase the frequency and severity of extreme weather events and threaten ecosystems (IPCC, 2022; Quilcaille et al., 2025).[1] Changes in the climate system in direct relation to global warming include increases in the frequency and intensity of hot extremes, marine heat waves, heavy precipitation, and, in some regions, agricultural and ecological droughts; an increase in the proportion of intense tropical cyclones; and reductions in Arctic sea ice, snow cover, and permafrost (IPCC, 2021). These changes occurred in the past years at a speed and magnitude that has never been observed over the past 100,000 years.

Global warming poses a range of dangers at different temperature thresholds. Even a modest increase of 1°C–2°C above preindustrial levels can lead to more frequent heat waves, droughts, and extreme weather events. At this level, ecosystems face significant disruption, with coral reefs, polar ice caps, and vulnerable species particularly at risk. As temperatures rise further, reaching 2°C or 3°C, the consequences become increasingly severe, with a more pronounced impact on food security, water availability, and human health. Sea-level rise accelerates, posing threats to coastal communities and infrastructure. Beyond 3°C, the risks escalate dramatically,

---

[1] Quilcaille et al. (2025) show that CO_2 emissions from fossil-fuel and cement production account for 0.67 °C of the 1.3 °C temperature rise since 1850–1900 – roughly half of the observed warming. Their findings also reveal that these producers have driven not only long-term global warming but also the occurrence and severity of specific climate extremes, such as heat waves.

with the potential widespread ecological collapse, mass displacement, and irreversible damage to global ecosystems.

Urgent action is therefore required to limit global warming and safeguard the well-being of present and future generations. Awareness of the potential impacts of greenhouse gas (GHG) began to increase in the late twentieth century and led to establishing the Intergovernmental Panel on Climate Change (IPCC) in 1988. The United Nations Framework Convention on Climate Change in 1992 laid the groundwork for international cooperation to address climate change. The Kyoto Protocol, adopted in 1997, marked the first significant international agreement to reduce GHG emissions, setting binding targets for developed countries. However, its effectiveness was limited by the lack of participation from major emitters such as the United States and China.

Climate change and extreme weather events – what we call *physical risks* – can profoundly impact economic systems in several ways. First, they can disrupt agricultural production, leading to crop failures, reduced yields, and increased food prices. This not only affects farmers' incomes but also creates food shortages and inflationary pressures in the broader economy. Second, extreme weather events such as hurricanes, floods, and wildfires can damage critical infrastructure, including roads, bridges, and power lines, disrupting supply chains and causing costly repairs. Third, rising sea levels pose a threat to coastal communities and industries, leading to property damage, loss of land, and the need for costly adaptation measures. Moreover, climate-related disasters can also cause loss of life, displacement of populations, and increased healthcare costs, further straining economic resources.

However, quantitatively assessing the economic impacts of climate change and extreme weather events poses significant challenges, largely due to the complex and nonlinear nature of the interactions between climatic variables and economic systems. Factors such as the timing, intensity, and geographic location of extreme events can vary widely, making it difficult to predict their precise economic consequences. Additionally, indirect effects, such as changes in consumer behavior, investor sentiment, and government policy responses, further complicate the analysis. Moreover, economic models often struggle to account for the full range of feedback loops and dynamic interactions inherent in these systems. Despite these challenges, efforts are underway to improve the accuracy and robustness of economic impact assessments through interdisciplinary research, enhanced data collection and analysis techniques, and the development of more sophisticated modeling approaches.

1.2 THE SCIENCE OF CLIMATE CHANGE

1.2.1 Greenhouse Effect and Climate Change

The physics of the greenhouse effect has been very well understood by scientists for a long time. The GHGs contribute to global warming by acting like an insulating blanket that absorbs the energy escaping from the Earth to space. Sunlight can go through the atmosphere, which is very transparent and allows it to reach Earth. In contrast, when Earth radiates this energy back to space, then the GHGs act as a blanket and prevents this energy from escaping, which warms the Earth. This mechanism is called the greenhouse effect. As GHGs accumulate in the atmosphere, the atmospheric *blanket* thickens, intensifying its warming effect. Although the greenhouse effect is well-understood by the laws of physics, there is great uncertainty regarding the response of the climate system to ongoing warming. For instance, the overall response of the clouds to a warmer climate in a specific region remains unclear. Depending on their type and altitude, the response of clouds could either magnify or dampen the greenhouse effect and the warming of the temperatures.

CO_2 is the most important GHG because it stays in the atmosphere for hundreds of thousands of years. From one tonne of CO_2 emitted, about 20 percent would remain in the atmosphere in the next 1,000 years, creating significant inertia for the climate system. Other gases, such as methane (CH_4), nitrous oxide, and fluorinated gases, also contribute to global warming. They also radically differ in their ability to absorb energy and how long they stay in the atmosphere. Methane, for instance, has a greater GHG effect than CO_2, but it stays shorter in the atmosphere.

Greater concentrations of CO_2 and other GHG, together with the increase in global surface temperatures, sea-level rises, and Muir Glacier retreats, are key developments that illustrate global warming at an unprecedented rate. The concentration of carbon dioxide (CO_2) in the atmosphere has been increasing since the preindustrial period, and it is currently at higher levels than in the last two million years. In parallel, the global surface temperature is already 1.1°C warmer than during the preindustrial period to reach the highest levels of the past 100 years. In fact, each of the last four decades has been successively warmer than any decade that preceded it since 1850. The rise of sea levels is another key symptom of global warming. Over the past century, around 20 cm of sea-level rise has been recorded, and this increase happened at the fastest pace in the past 2,000 years. At the same time, since the 1950s, most of the world's glaciers have retreated at an unprecedented speed. It is unequivocal that human influence has warmed the atmosphere, ocean, and land since 1750. Widespread and rapid changes in the atmosphere, ocean, cryosphere, and biosphere have occurred. Temperatures to date are very likely higher than at any time in the last 12,000 years, the period in which human civilization has developed, and the speed of the current increase is unmatched over the past 2,000 years.

Although it is difficult to attribute the cause of one extreme event (e.g., hurricane, flood, and wildfire) to climate change, it is scientifically proven that climate change increases the frequency of these disruptive weather events. Observed climate change of 1.1°C has already more than doubled both the global land area and the global population annually exposed to river floods, crop failure, tropical cyclones, wildfires, droughts, and heat waves (Lange et al., 2020).

1.2.2 The Role of Human Activity

Human activities have profoundly affected Earth's geology, landscape, limnology, ecosystems, and climate. The Anthropocene is a proposed geological epoch that dates from the commencement of significant human impact on Earth to the present day. The term *Anthropocene* combines *anthropo* (meaning *man*) and *cene* (meaning *new*). It highlights the mass extinctions of plant and animal species, ocean pollution, atmospheric alterations, and other lasting impacts caused by human activities. Human activities have significantly contributed to climate change through the emissions of GHG, deforestation, and other forms of environmental degradation. The burning of fossil fuels for energy production, transportation, and industrial processes is the largest source of anthropogenic GHG emissions, including carbon dioxide (CO_2), methane (CH_4), and nitrous oxide (N_2O). Because human activities have emitted much more CO_2 compared to any other gas, CO_2 accounts for about three-quarters of GHG emissions of human origin. Methane emissions, which account around one-fifth of total GHG emissions, also offer key opportunities for emission reduction. These GHG emissions come from a variety of sources, the most important one being the combustion of fossil fuels (e.g., coal, oil, and gas) used to produce electricity for transportation and heating (Figure 1.1).

To make it comprehensive and easy to compare, the metric of global warming potential is widely used (Table 1.1). It measures how much greenhouse effect one tonne of the gas would create over 100 years compared to one tonne of CO_2. For instance, methane emitted

Table 1.1 *GHG, lifetime, and global warming potential*

Greenhouse gas	Average lifetime in the atmosphere (years)	Global warming potential over 100 years (relative to CO_2 = 1)
Carbon dioxide	50–200	1
Methane	12	21
Nitrous oxide	120	310
CFC-12	100	10,600
CFC-11	45	4,600
HFC-134a	14.6	1,300
Sulfur hexafluoride	3,200	23,900

Source: IPCC

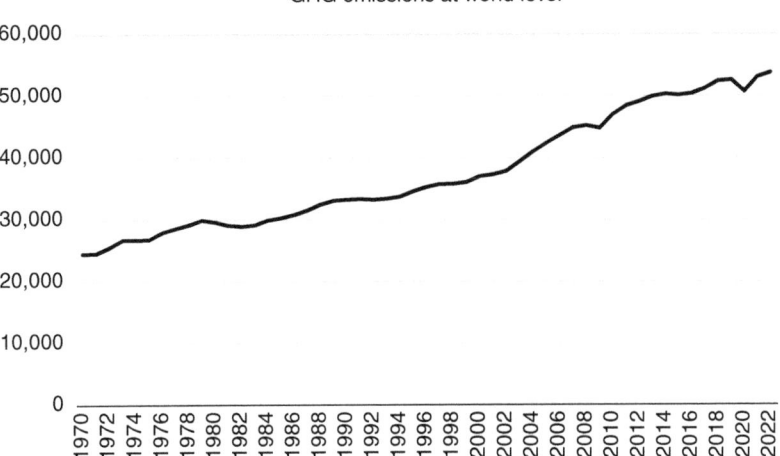
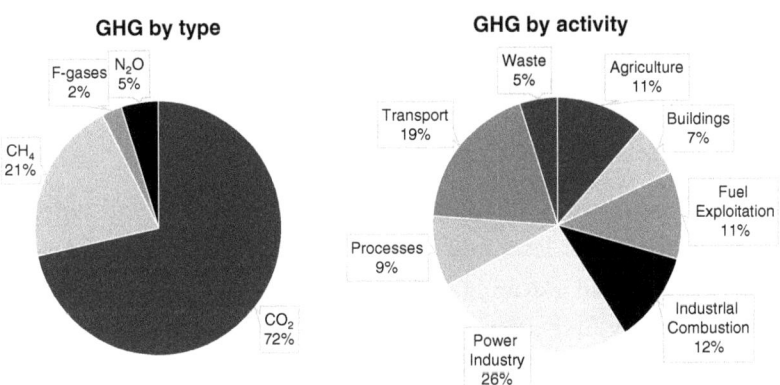

FIGURE I.I GHG emissions and by type
Source: https://edgar.jrc.ec.europa.eu/report_2023

today is expected to stay in the atmosphere for only about a decade, much shorter than CO_2. However, one molecule of methane has higher heat-trapping ability compared to one molecule of CO_2. When we combine how long it stays in the atmosphere and how efficient it is at absorbing energy, we find that 1 tonne of methane is equivalent to more than 20 tonnes of CO_2 in terms of the GHG effect.

Other major sources of emissions are linked to industrial processes that are not combustion (e.g., cement production), as well as to agricultural activities and forest management. Deforestation and land use changes also release CO_2 stored in forests and soils, further exacerbating global warming. This process is a large factor in emissions, as trees and plants remove CO_2 from the atmosphere as they grow and convert it into carbon stored in the branches, leaves, trunks, roots, and soil. When forests are cleared or burnt, the stored carbon is released into the atmosphere, mainly as carbon dioxide. Additionally, intensive agriculture, livestock farming, and waste management practices produce methane and nitrous oxide emissions.

These human-induced changes to the Earth's atmosphere have led to rising global temperatures, shifts in precipitation patterns, sea-level rise, and more frequent and intense extreme weather events. Addressing the root causes of climate change requires concerted efforts to reduce emissions, transition to renewable energy sources, promote sustainable land use practices, and adapt to the changing climate.

1.2.3 The Future of Climate Change

Climate experts project that global surface temperature will continue to increase until at least mid century under all global GHG emission scenarios. Global warming of 1.5°C and 2°C will be exceeded during the twenty-first century unless deep reductions in CO_2 and other GHG emissions occur in the coming decades (IPCC, 2021). Scientific evidence shows that recent dramatic changes in climate systems can be widely attributed to human activities (IPCC, 2021). Since the mid nineteenth century, human influence has been behind the observed increase in the concentration of CO_2 and other GHG, causing this unprecedented warming of the climate and change in global precipitation patterns. Human activities have also increased the frequency of compound extreme events since the 1950s, such as concurrent heat waves and droughts on a global scale. Climate scientists use climate models to simulate and reproduce the developments in the climate system. These models provide an accurate representation of the current state of the system only when considering human-induced emissions of GHG and human-induced changes in land use. If the effects of human activities are excluded, models fail to reproduce the current state of the climate system.

Scientists find that climate will continue to change in the future with overall higher temperatures and more intense and frequent extreme events, but also with irreversible changes in some systems. These future changes and risks remain highly uncertain, as they depend on the past but also on future emissions. These emissions, in turn, will be determined by human activity and adopted paths for socioeconomic and environmental policies. Climate scientists use models that represent Earth and human systems to explore these issues, and they use scenarios for the possible evolution of socioeconomic systems (e.g., technology, demography, economic growth, and land use) as well as the policies that would affect future emissions.

The IPCC scenarios below show diverse paths of evolution of global surface temperature under several scenarios. These scenarios are based on two main components: the shared socioeconomic pathways (SSP), which relate to the evolution of the economy and its demographics, and the representative concentration pathways (RCP), which represent the evolution of GHG in the atmosphere based on different policy choices impacting future emissions.

Five SSPs are envisaged:

- SSP1 (low adaptation challenge, low mitigation challenge) describes a world characterized by strong international cooperation, prioritizing sustainable development;
- SSP2 (medium adaptation challenge, medium mitigation challenge) describes a world where current trends continue;
- SSP3 (high adaptation challenge, high mitigation challenge) depicts a fragmented world affected by competition between countries, slow economic growth, security-focused policies, and industrial production with little regard for the environment;
- SSP4 (high adaptation challenge, low mitigation challenge) is a world marked by great inequalities between and within countries. In this scenario, a minority is responsible for the majority of GHG emissions,

making mitigation policies easier to implement, while most of the population remains poor and vulnerable to climate change;
- SSP5 (low adaptation challenge, high mitigation challenge) describes a world focused on traditional and rapid development in developing countries, based on high energy consumption and carbon-emitting technologies; the increase in living standards would enhance adaptation capacity, particularly by reducing extreme poverty.

The RCPs are scenarios that describe potential future changes in radiative forcing due to varying levels of GHG emissions. They are categorized by the radiative forcing level reached by the year 2100, expressed in watts per square meter (W/m^2). The scenarios range from RCP 8.5, which represents high GHG concentrations and continuously increasing radiative forcing, to RCP 2.6, which describes a peak in emissions followed by a decline. The radiative forcing value for the year 2022 was 2.92 W/m^2 relative to 1750.

These scenarios serve as crucial tools for climate research and policy development, helping to assess the range of potential outcomes based on different socioeconomic and technological pathways. By combining these two types of scenarios, economists analyze climate change and its impacts on the economic system and climate. The scenarios span a spectrum of emissions levels, from low to high, reflecting a variety of future development choices and policy interventions. By exploring these scenarios, scientists and policymakers gain insights into possible climate futures and the corresponding risks and opportunities for adaptation and mitigation. The socioeconomic dynamics, such as technology choices, investment, and policy decisions of today, will alter emissions and impact climate change in the future. Depending on these scenarios for the future, we see that the warming in 2100 can possibly range between 1.5°C and almost 5°C (Figure 1.2).

These overall average temperatures entail significant variations at the local level. For instance, warming is predicted to be more pronounced in higher latitudes and continents and less intense in the tropics and oceans. The same heterogeneity is expected for precipitations, global warming is set to cause more rainfall on average but in high latitudes and during the winter. Conversely, less

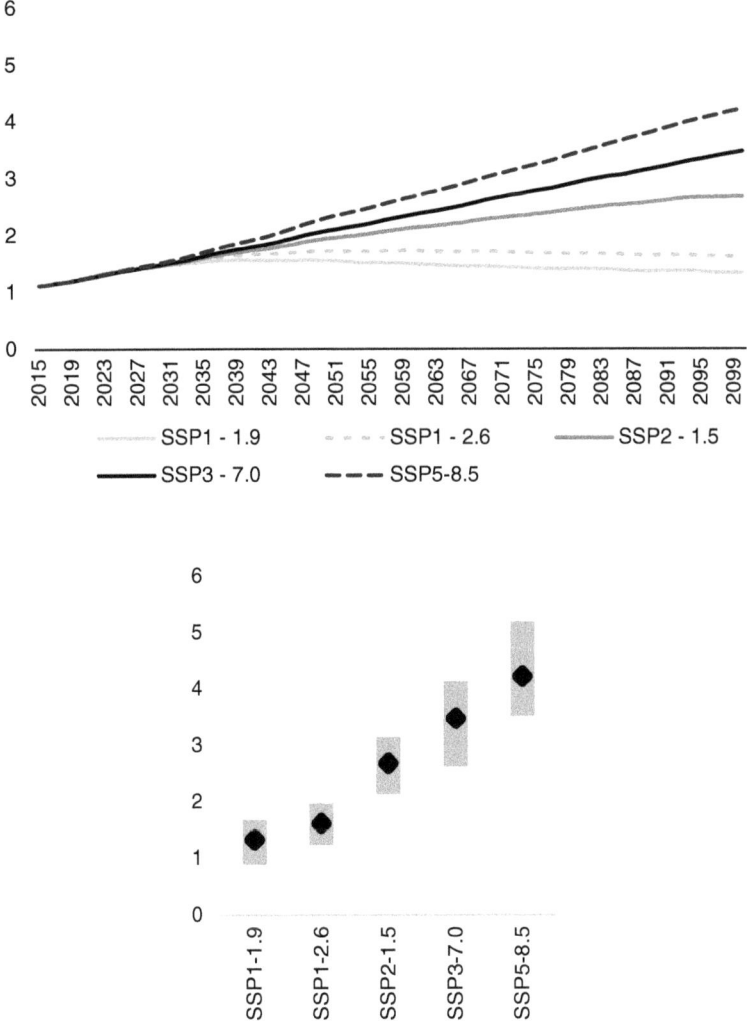

FIGURE 1.2 Global surface temperature change relative to 1850–1900 (in °C) in IPCC scenarios
Source: IPCC AR6 (2021)
Note: Projected median warming across global modeled pathways (top panel) and 5–95% 2,100 temperature outcomes – median as diamond – (bottom panel) for the five illustrative scenarios (SSPx-y).

rainfall is projected in the tropics and during the summer. All in all, the average temperature increase will exacerbate existing climate vulnerabilities, such as water scarcity or excess water, in the future.

1.2.4 Irreversibility and Tipping Points

Recent research shows that in response to CO_2 emissions, some regions of the world might experience irreversible climate change. This implies that even after removing emissions, the impact of emissions could last in some regions (Kim, S.-K. et al., 2022). Widespread irreversible changes in atmospheric variables could also induce irreversible changes in other subcomponents of the Earth's systems, such as mountain glaciers, sea ice, and rainforests. These climate irreversibility hotspots are mostly identified in coastal regions covered with ice, such as Antarctica, Greenland, Alaska, and the high mountain glacier region of the Himalayas, as well as monsoon areas, such as the African and South American monsoon regions.

Climate tipping points refer to the nonlinear response of extreme events to small changes in the climate. When the tipping points are reached, small changes may become significant enough to cause a larger, more critical change that can be abrupt, irreversible, and lead to cascading effects. The tipping points can create compound risks to natural and human systems. Overshooting the Paris Agreement warming targets would increase the risk of hitting tipping points and triggering irreversible changes in the system, like permafrost thawing or dieback of the Amazon rainforest. Triggering this tipping point would make it a lot more difficult, if not impossible, to get back below the 1.5°C target. The Greenland ice sheet, on the other hand, contains enough water to raise global sea levels by over 20 feet. Its melting has significantly accelerated since the 1990s and could reach a critical point beyond which its eventual collapse is irreversible for millennia.

Each small change in the average climate, temperatures, and precipitations causes major changes in the frequency and severity of the climate extremes. When we take the example of heat waves, an episode that occurred once every fifty years in the nineteenth century occurs five times more frequently today with +1°C of warming. In the case of the scenario with +1.5°C of warming, the event that occurred once in fifty years is expected to become common, occurring every five years (nine times more frequently). Considering the 4°C warming scenario, the frequency increases forty times. The heat waves that happened in the past once every fifty years would occur almost every year.

Deep uncertainty exists with regard to the biogeochemical processes potentially triggered by climate change. Climate scientists have shown not only that tipping points exist but remain difficult to estimate with precision, but also that they could generate tipping cascades on other biogeochemical processes. Evidence is now mounting that tipping points in the Earth system, such as the loss of the Amazon forest or the West Antarctic ice sheet, could occur more rapidly than was thought (Lenton et al., 2019).

Some research has proven the existence of a planetary threshold in the trajectory of the Earth System that, if crossed, could prevent stabilization in a range of intermediate temperature rises. The Late Quaternary (past 1.2 million years) has seen an alternation between glacial (cold) and interglacial (warm) periods. These cycles, known as Milankovitch cycles, are driven by changes in Earth's orbit and axial tilt. Not every cycle follows the same trajectory, but they share an overall pathway. The full glacial and interglacial states, along with approximately 100,000-year oscillations between them, constitute limit cycles. The Anthropocene marks a pivotal moment in Earth's history – a departure from the familiar glacial-interglacial cycles toward a new trajectory shaped by human influence. It represents a rapid shift away from the natural glacial interglacial rhythm propelled by human activities. Currently, over 1°C above preindustrial temperatures, the Earth is approaching the upper limit of interglacial conditions in the past 1.2 million years. Over the past half-century, our climate system has followed an accelerated path, and the Earth System may have already passed a critical juncture – a bifurcation – leading away from the next glaciation cycle (Ganopolski et al., 2016).

In contemplating the Earth's future, we encounter a multitude of potential trajectories. These pathways, often depicted by climate models, span a wide range of global temperature increases. Traditionally, these trajectories correlate closely with cumulative GHG – particularly carbon dioxide – released by human activities. However, beyond straightforward emissions, the Earth System's fate is influenced by intricate biogeophysical feedback, and these processes involve interactions between living organisms, land, oceans, and the atmosphere. They can amplify or dampen climate effects, affecting the overall trajectory. Steffen et al. (2018) claim that there is a significant risk that these dynamics, especially strong nonlinearities in feedback processes, could become a dominant factor in steering the trajectory that the Earth System actually follows over the coming centuries.

Physical climate risks may be far greater in magnitude and materialize much sooner than previously anticipated. The Earth is currently on a trajectory toward a *Hot house Earth* state with potentially irreversible impacts. This could be further accelerated by tipping points such as the loss of ice sheets, rainforest cover, and permafrost. Tipping elements in our planet's complex system can behave quite differently, showing abrupt shifts, when they cross their critical thresholds. For instance, the Amazon rainforest could suddenly convert to a savanna or a seasonally dry forest. This type of change could occur rapidly and dramatically. Other elements respond more gradually but persistently, like the large-scale loss of permafrost, which, once started, tends to continue. Such a gradual shift can have long-lasting effects.

1.2.5 *Macroeconomic and Financial Scenarios*

The IPCC scenarios that were referred to earlier focus on overall possible future trends in physical and socioeconomic pathways. Based on such analysis, the Network for Greening the Financial System (NGFS), a coalition of central banks and supervisory authorities,[2] has developed a set of reference scenarios to assess the impact of climate risks on a wide-ranging set of economic and financial variables (e.g., GDP, inflation, equity and bond prices, and loan valuations). The NGFS regularly

---

[2] The Central Banks and Supervisors Network for Greening the Financial System (NGFS) is an international network launched in December 2017 of 132 members and 21 observers, central banks, supervisors, and international organizations (as at December 2023) eager to share their best practices in the monitoring of climate-related financial risks and committed to working toward a more sustainable financial system.

publishes several reference scenarios characterizing four different situations (see Figure 1.3). The first family of scenarios refers to an *orderly* transition. In these scenarios, the transition begins immediately with the introduction of proactive mitigation policies, such as a carbon tax policy or measures to support renewable energies. It is also based on assumptions of transformations in the behavior of consumers and financial players, better aligned with the requirements of a low-carbon economy. Announced and anticipated, this structural transformation of the economy is taking place gradually and without major macroeconomic shocks. Compliance with climate commitments also reduces physical risks. The second family of scenarios describes the response to a *disorderly* transition, which may be delayed or sudden, in both

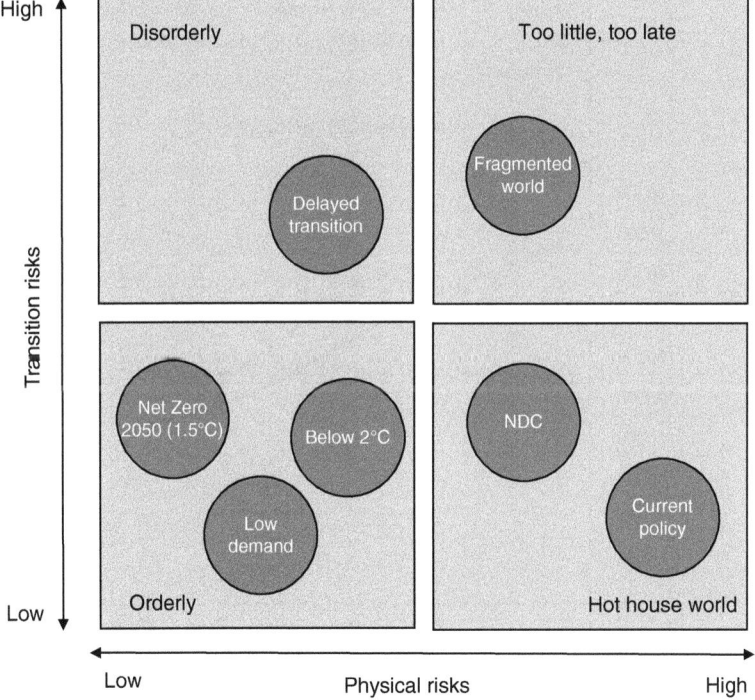

FIGURE 1.3 NGFS scenarios
Source: NGFS, www.ngfs.net/system/files/import/ngfs/medias/documents/ngfs_climate_scenarios_for_central_banks_and_supervisors_phase_iv.pdf

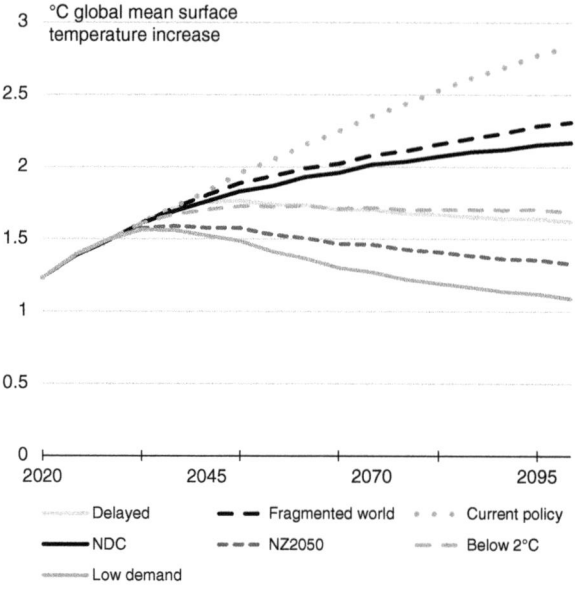
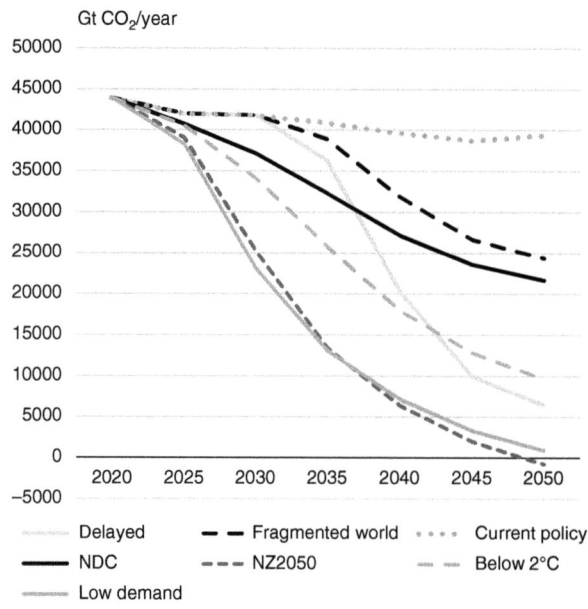

FIGURE 1.3 (cont.)

cases insufficiently anticipated and therefore abrupt. In the case of a delayed transition, new, more restrictive measures may, for example, be introduced, resulting in more disruptive adjustments depending on the sector. Households and businesses would then have to adjust their behavior rapidly, leading to major macroeconomic and sectoral disruptions. On the other hand, meeting climate targets limits physical risks. The third family of scenarios, *Hot house world*, corresponds to *Business as usual*. In this scenario, governments do not introduce any transition measures other than those already in place, and economic players do not change their behavior. GHG emissions, therefore, continue on past trends, causing temperatures to rise above 2°C, worsening chronic physical risks, and increasing the frequency and severity of extreme weather events. On the other hand, the risks of transition remain limited. Finally, the last family corresponds to *too-little, too-late* scenarios where mitigation actions remain insufficient to achieve temperature objectives, and the materialization of physical risk leads to a disorderly transition.

In the NGFS scenarios where climate goals are met, deep reductions in emissions are required to limit the rise in global mean temperatures to below 1.5°C or 2°C by the end of the century (Figure 1.3). This does not occur in the Current policies scenario, leading to a temperature rise exceeding 3°C and severe and irreversible impacts. Temperatures are increasing unevenly across the world with land warming faster than oceans and high latitudes experiencing higher warming. Temperature changes lead to chronic changes in living conditions affecting health, labor productivity, agriculture, ecosystems, and sea-level rise. It is also changing the frequency and severity of weather events such as heat waves, droughts, wildfires, tropical cyclones, and flooding.

1.2.6 Why Is Scenario Analysis So Important for Climate Economics and Finance?

The unique features of climate risks present a hurdle to traditional risk assessment methods. Climate risks unfold over extended timeframes accompanied by significant uncertainty regarding policy trajectory and socioeconomic influences. They manifest globally and across economies, with varying complexity across regions and industries. These distinctive attributes elude conventional risk assessment approaches, which rely on simplistic modeling and historical data, narrow scopes, and assumptions of static economic and financial structures. Scenario analysis emerges, therefore, as a crucial solution to address these challenges. It offers a dynamic framework for exploring potential future trajectories, allowing stakeholders to better grasp how climate-related factors may shape economic and financial landscapes. This tool proves, in particular, invaluable for central banks, supervisors, financial entities, businesses, and policymakers seeking deeper insights into the impact of climate dynamics.

A scenario is a description of a *possible future*, encompassing both quantitative and qualitative elements (Foster, 1993). Such a description requires "a story with plausible cause and effect links that connects a future condition with the present, while illustrating key decisions, events, and consequences throughout the narrative" (Glenn, 2009). Scenarios are not predictions but reflect experts' knowledge about probable future outcomes based on "internally consistent and challenging narrative descriptions of possible futures" (van der Heijden, 2005). In the case of climate scenarios, each individual narrative is, therefore, an alternative description of how the future may unfold associated with a combination of socioeconomic, policy, technological, and climate changes (Mallampalli et al., 2016) and their impact on the future state of the key climate and economic and financial variables.

Climate scenarios first require the specification of the time horizon, either short to span frequencies relevant to central banks and supervisors, that is, between 3 and 5 years, or long to describe structural changes that an economy could undertake and the climate impacts associated, that is, 50 or 100 years. Each narrative is based on selected key drivers, which can be either a policy decision (mitigation policy or adaptation), a change in economic agents' behavior (e.g., repricing of risks by financial investors and increased savings by households facing higher uncertainty), or a technological change (e.g., innovation in green technologies that fosters productivity).

Although primarily qualitative, the scenario description can also provide insights into the severity of events. For example, the assumption that a scenario remains consistent with climate targets induces some degree of policy action; conversely, deviating from climate targets affects the potential severity of weather events. Relying on multiple scenarios reflects not only the trade-off between transition and physical risks but also the different nature of the key drivers, some of which primarily affect the supply side of the economy (e.g., carbon taxation or technological innovation), while others may be associated with demand-side drivers (e.g., public spending on green infrastructures or reduced consumption due to uncertainty in transition policies). Such diversity covers multiple use cases and provides a range of macrofinancial outcomes that can be useful in assessing the macroeconomic and financial stability implications of climate-related risks.

Finally, it is worth noting that adopting climate-related scenario analysis remains nascent, with methodologies in a continual state of refinement. Key challenges include the incomplete amalgamation of physical risk, transition risk, and macrofinancial transmission channels; scarcity of accessible data and research to fine-tune scenarios and evaluate repercussions; and a deficiency in technical proficiency concerning climate science and environmental economics within the financial domain.

1.3 ASSESSING THE ECONOMIC IMPACTS OF CLIMATE CHANGE

As per our understanding of science progresses and we collectively witness the rise in extreme weather events and other climate-related phenomena, the dangers posed by climate change become increasingly apparent. For businesses, the repercussions of this changing climate can manifest in financial losses – through property damage and other asset depreciation, as well as disruptions to operations, supply chains, and the broader social and economic frameworks businesses rely on.

The escalating frequency and/or severity of climate-related hazards – including those related to temperature, water, oceans, land, and wind – are already inflicting financial harm. After briefly reviewing historical trends in climate-related disasters, we will provide a typology of climate-related shocks that can weigh on economic and financial systems. We will then analyze the different transmission channels of those shocks before presenting various methodologies to assess their effects on economic growth and welfare.

1.3.1 Historical Trends in the Frequency and Cost of Climate-Related Disasters

Data on climate-related disasters are difficult to collect. The International Disaster Database (EM-DAT, www.emdat.be/) stands out as the only freely available global disaster loss database, but its effectiveness is limited by a narrow pool of sources and gaps in reporting accuracy. Despite these shortcomings, EM-DAT remains an indispensable tool for understanding disaster occurrences and impacts. Figure 1.4 shows the increase in the frequency of events since 1980, broken down into different perils. Floods and storms represent the larger share of disasters, and their frequency has clearly increased over the last forty years. The number of events has been multiplied by 3–4 since 1980.

In terms of losses, reinsurers assess global costs every year. Munich Re – the world's largest reinsurer – has released its global disaster loss calculation for 2023, coming in at a total of USD 250 billion. This roughly equals the entire GDP of New Zealand or Portugal. It is also slightly lower than the previous estimate for 2022, which originally came in at USD 270 billion. For Swiss Re, in 2023, natural catastrophes resulted in economic losses of USD 280 billion, for 332 catastrophe events and 76,000 victims. Out of the

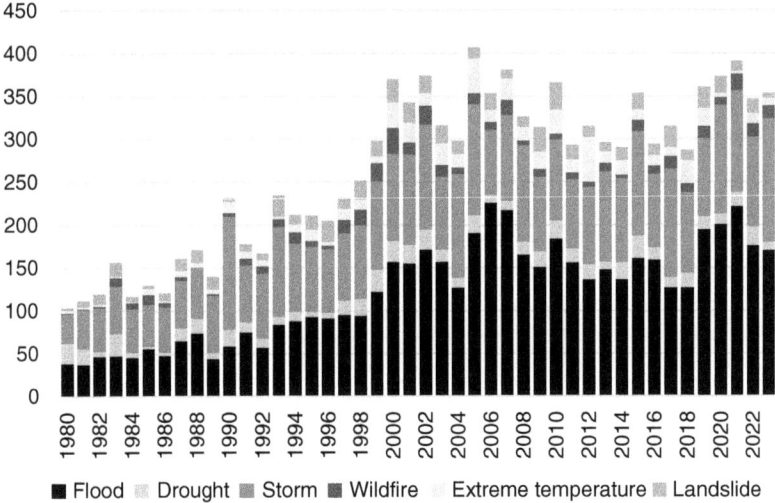

FIGURE 1.4 Frequency of natural disasters (number of disasters per year)
Source: EM-DAT, CRED/UC Louvain, Brussels, Belgium

USD 280 billion of total loss, USD 108 billion was insured. Insured losses (Figure 1.5) also increased over the last fifty years, and a clear upward trend is noticeable. Most of the losses are weather-related. These assessments offer only a fragmented view of the genuine magnitude of disasters, encompassing human casualties and economic, developmental, and social consequences. Many repercussions of disasters go unaccounted for in these evaluations. These include effects linked to gradual-onset and localized incidents, as well as the cascading consequences of disrupted supply chains, diminished productivity, compromised physical and mental well-being, and lasting disruptions to education. Together, these factors contribute to an unseen toll of disasters that far surpasses the economic estimates provided by insurers.

North America emerges as the region with the most significant economic repercussions, representing around 40 percent of the global losses. Typically, wealthier nations bear the brunt of financial losses from disasters due to their larger stock of more high-value assets, which are often insured. However, lower-income

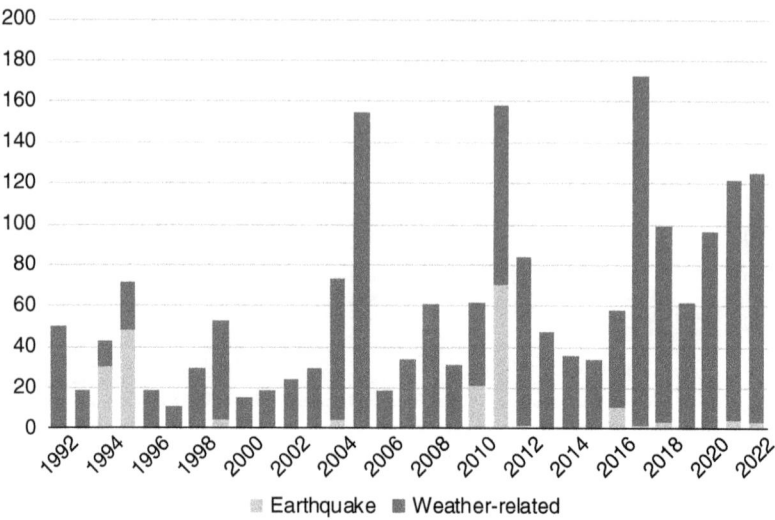

FIGURE 1.5 Growth in global natural catastrophe insured losses (2022 USD billion)
Source: Swiss Re Institute

countries shoulder a disproportionate economic burden relative to their overall wealth. While absolute dollar losses are higher in high-income nations, low-income and lower-middle-income countries record a notably larger share of economic loss compared to the global average. Additionally, poorer countries endure the most significant tolls in terms of both lives lost and disruptions experienced.

Furthermore, there exists a bias toward major events that receive widespread coverage, whereas lesser-known incidents, although infrequently reported, accumulate substantial losses. Table 1.2 includes the top twenty costliest climate-related events. Most of them were taking place in North America (US and Canada). Among the developing nations, Caribbean and South/Southeast Asian countries are the most exposed to severe disasters.

Although data collection extends beyond insurance companies (municipalities, national governments, international organizations, and nongovernmental organizations), these datasets often

Table 1.2 Top twenty costliest climate-related disasters

Event	Type	Year	Location	Financial losses (in billions USD)
Hurricane Katrina	Tropical cyclone	2005	United States	$125
Hurricane Harvey	Tropical cyclone	2017	United States	$125
Hurricane Ian	Tropical cyclone	2022	North America (United States, Cuba, Venezuela)	$113
2020 South Asian floods	Flood	2020	South Asia (India, Pakistan, Bangladesh)	$105
Hurricane Maria	Tropical cyclone	2017	North America (Puerto Rico, Dominica, Guadeloupe)	$91.6
Hurricane Ida	Tropical cyclone	2021	North America (United States, Cuba, Venezuela)	$75
2019–2020 Australian bushfires	Wildfire	2019–20	Australia	$70
Hurricane Sandy	Tropical cyclone	2012	North America (United States, Haiti, Cuba)	$68.7
Hurricane Irma	Tropical cyclone	2017	North America (United States, Sint Maarten, etc.)	$64.8
1988–1990 North American drought	Drought	1988–89	United States, Canada	$53.25

(continued)

Table 1.2 (cont.)

Event	Type	Year	Location	Financial losses (in billions USD)
2012–2013 North American drought	Drought	2012–13	United States, Canada	$49.6–$56.1
2011 Thailand floods	Flood	2011	Thailand	$45.7
2022 Pakistan floods	Flood	2022	Pakistan	$40
Hurricane Ike	Tropical cyclone	2008	North America (United States, Haiti, Cuba)	$38
2020 China floods	Flood	2020	China	$32
Typhoon Doksuri	Tropical cyclone	2023	Southeast Asia (China, Philippines, Taiwan, etc.)	$28.4
Hurricane Wilma	Tropical cyclone	2005	North America (United States, Mexico, Haiti, etc.)	$27.4
Hurricane Andrew	Tropical cyclone	1992	United States	$27.3
February 13–17, 2021 North American winter storm	Winter storm, Infrastructure failure (electric)	2021	North America (United States, Mexico, Canada)	$26.5
Hurricane Ivan	Tropical cyclone	2004	North America (United States, Grenada, Jamaica, etc.)	$26.1

Source: Wikipedia (https://en.wikipedia.org/wiki/List_of_disasters_by_cost)

lack comparability and may reflect inherent biases due to variations in collection methods and intended uses. For instance, recording a higher number of victims might influence aid allocation, while a lower count could mitigate authorities' accountability.

Overall, the complexities involved in recording, reporting, and compiling data on disaster impacts frequently yield fragmented, disjointed, or incomplete datasets, particularly within globally comprehensive databases (see UNDRR, 2023).

1.3.2 Climate Change, Weather, and Disasters

Up to this point, we have referred to the physical consequences of global warming in general terms – through climate change, weather conditions, and disaster frequency. To assess the economic consequences of such a complex phenomena, we need first to provide a clear terminology.

1.3.2.1 Climate

Climate refers to the long-term average of weather conditions in a specific region over an extended period (usually thirty years or more). It is characterized by the following:

- Stability: Climate is relatively stable and predictable over time.
- Patterns: It encompasses patterns of temperature, humidity, wind, precipitation, and other atmospheric conditions.
- Influence: Climate is influenced by factors such as latitude, altitude, ocean currents, and GHG concentrations.

Example: The tropical rainforest climate in the Amazon basin has high temperatures, heavy rainfall, and consistent humidity year-round.

1.3.2.2 Weather

Weather refers to the short-term atmospheric conditions (usually over hours to a few days) in a specific location. It is characterized by the following:

- Variability: Weather can change rapidly and is often unpredictable.

- Elements: It includes elements such as temperature, humidity, wind speed, cloud cover, and precipitation.
- Influence: Weather is influenced by local factors, such as air pressure systems, fronts, and seasonal variations.

Example: On May 6, 2024, BBC weather forecasts: "Tomorrow morning will be largely dry with plenty of sunshine. Variable cloud and a few scattered showers will develop through the afternoon, these largely dying out by evening."

1.3.2.3 Natural Hazards

These are extreme events caused by natural processes that can potentially result in significant harm to human life, property, and the environment. They are characterized by the following:

- Severity: These events are severe and have catastrophic consequences when they hit human communities.
- Types: Natural hazards include earthquakes, hurricanes, floods, droughts, wildfires, and volcanic eruptions.
- Impact: They can lead to loss of life, displacement, economic damage, and environmental degradation.

Example: In 2011, Thailand experienced its worst flooding in years, leaving more than 800 people dead and causing severe damage across.

The term *natural disaster* is commonly used to *describe* catastrophic events such as hurricanes, floods, earthquakes, or volcanic eruptions. However, this term can be misleading as it masks the role of human decisions and vulnerabilities. We prefer using the term *natural hazard*, which denotes a naturally occurring event such as earthquakes, hurricanes, or floods, capable of endangering human life, property, and the environment. As we focus only on weather-related events, we will therefore use *weather-related hazards/extreme events*. While the term *hazard* signifies the inherent risk associated with such phenomena, a natural disaster arises when a hazard materializes, resulting in notable damage, destruction, and loss. While a hazard presents a potential danger, a disaster represents its actual occurrence, underscoring widespread devastation and the imperative for response, recovery, and reconstruction efforts. In that sense, the adjective *natural* may be misleading because, while these phenomena stem from natural forces, their societal impact is deeply intertwined with human factors such as urbanization and infrastructure development. Categorizing such occurrences as *natural* can foster a perception of inevitability, overlooking the influence of societal choices on disaster risk.

In summary, climate represents long-term patterns, weather describes short-term conditions, and natural hazards are extreme events with potentially significant impacts. In what follows, we will distinguish physical risks into two broad categories:

- *Chronic risks* due to gradual global warming and the associated physical changes, such as rising sea levels or changing precipitation patterns; and
- *Acute risks* due to extreme weather events, such as tropical cyclones, storms, floods, and drought.

Though different in timing and immediate severity, both risks are dynamic, evolving over time and interacting with each other in a complex and nonlinear fashion.

1.3.3 Channels of Transmission to the Economy

The comprehensive examination presented in Table 1.3 provides a nuanced exploration of the multiple impacts of both chronic risks (gradual warming) and acute risks (extreme events) on the intricate structure of the economy. As temperatures steadily rise and climate patterns shift, the impacts are widespread and complex, permeating every facet of economic activity. From the agricultural sector grappling with declining yields and productivity losses due to changing climatic conditions, to labor markets facing disruptions from extreme heat waves and shifts in migration patterns, the effects of gradual warming are widespread and profound.

Global warming affects both the supply and demand sides of the macroeconomy. Concerning supply shocks, labor availability, and productivity might decrease due to factors such as heat stress, migration, and temporary incapacitation to work. The capital stock may diminish and undergo changes due to resource reallocation for adaptation

Table 1.3 *Channels of impacts*

Channels of impact	Chronic risks (gradual warming)	Acute risks (extreme events)
Food, energy and other input supply	Decline in agriculture productivity and yields.	Disruption to transport and production chains.
Labor supply	Loss of hours worked due to extreme temperatures. Increased international migration.	Destruction of workplaces, need to migrate (even if temporarily).
Capital stock	Diversion of resources from productive investment to adaptation capital.	Destruction due to extreme events.
Technology	Diversion of resources to reconstruction activity.	Diversion of resources to reconstruction activity.
Productivity	Lower labor productivity due to extreme heat waves and lower human capital accumulation (increased health issues and mortality).	Lower capital productivity due to (possibly permanent) capital and infrastructure destruction.
Energy demand	Increased demand for electricity in summer exceeds decreased demand in winter. Higher carbon tax leading to lower demand for fossil fuels.	Change in preferences toward more sustainable goods and services.
Investment	Change in preferences toward more sustainable goods and services. Uncertainty about climate events could delay investment.	Investment in reconstruction increases following events.
Consumption	Change in preferences toward more sustainable goods and services. If no insurance of household or firms, destruction could cause a permanent decrease in wealth and affect consumption.	Increased sustainability awareness and a shift toward greener consumption.

Trade	Disruption to trade routes due to geophysical changes (such as rising sea levels). Change in food prices and disruption to trade flows.	Risks of distortion from asymmetric or unilateral climate policies.
Aggregate Impact on Output	Lower labor productivity, investment being diverted to mitigation and arable land loss.	Physical destruction (crop failures, destruction of facilities and infrastructure, disruption of supply chains).
Wages	Downward pressures on wages from lower productivity. Unequal effects across sectors and economies.	Unequal effects across sectors and economies (reallocation of workers from one sector to another, increased training needs).
Inflation	Relative price changes due to shifting consumer demand or preferences and changes in comparative cost advantages.	Increased inflation volatility, particularly in food, housing, and energy prices.
Inflation Expectations	Climate-related shocks, for example, to food and energy prices, may affect inflation expectations. Inducing more homogeneous, sudden, and frequent revisions of expectations.	Formation of inflation expectations affected by policies.

Source: Drudi et al. (2021), adapted from Batten (2018)

purposes, while technology could suffer from diverted resources away from innovation and research toward reconstruction and adaptation efforts. This could lead to a slowdown in productivity growth, affecting future incomes and calling for higher savings to maintain future consumption levels. On the demand side, changes in energy demand may result from anticipated shifts in energy prices and consumer preferences. Additionally, investment dynamics may weaken due to increased uncertainty, although there could be a temporary boost in investment related to reconstruction needs. Changes in consumption patterns may emerge from shifts in preferences, increased precautionary savings, and enduring wealth losses for uninsured individuals.

At the same time, the looming threat of extreme events is becoming increasingly evident, heralding widespread devastation and upheaval in infrastructure networks, supply chains, and production systems. Hurricanes, floods, and wildfires leave a trail of destruction in their wake, compelling urgent efforts to rebuild and adapt while reshaping consumer preferences and investment strategies.

Similar to global warming, extreme weather events impact both the supply and demand sides of the economy. However, these effects vary in terms of timing and severity compared to those induced by global warming (as outlined in Table 1.3). Extreme weather events prompt immediate and significant economic repercussions on the supply side, damaging workplaces, depleting productive capital, disrupting production processes, impeding energy supply, and disrupting global value chains. Trade may also suffer due to disruptions in transportation links and shifts in relative prices. These macroeconomic impacts pose challenges for central banks in the short term, as they often lead to conflicting trends in output and inflation (see Chapter 5). As for demand side impacts, investment may stagnate due to heightened uncertainty, although short-term boosts may occur from reconstruction efforts. Consumption may suffer if uninsured agents face permanent wealth losses.

The consequences of these climate-related phenomena reverberate through the economy, triggering cascading effects across multiple dimensions. Capital investment is redirected toward resilience-building measures and infrastructure upgrades, while shifts in consumer demand force industries to adapt and innovate. Trade dynamics are reshaped as disruptions to global supply chains alter production and consumption patterns, creating both winners and losers in the global marketplace (Andersson et al., 2020).

Table 1.3 also highlights the inherent disparities and inequalities that underpin the distribution of climate risks and impacts. Vulnerable communities, particularly those in low-income regions and developing countries, bear a disproportionate burden of climate-related shocks and face increased risks of displacement, economic hardship, and social upheaval.

1.3.4 *Measuring the Economic Impacts of Physical Risks*

Traditionally, climate impact studies adopt a *top-down approach*, where different scenarios of GHG concentrations are simulated using Earth system models to provide broad-scale projections. Hydroclimatic variables relevant to specific hazards, such as floods or wildfires, are often downscaled either statistically or dynamically to match the spatiotemporal scale of these processes. Subsequently, societal impacts, characterized by losses pertinent to stakeholders, are determined based on the hazard, incorporating additional factors related to impact exposure and vulnerability. This assessment informs decision-making processes. Recently, there has been increasing interest in stakeholder-centered approaches, or *bottom-up approaches*. These approaches employ risk-based reasoning, beginning with an understanding of stakeholders' information needs, including key decision-making criteria, decision variable nature, impact domain, and spatial and temporal scales of climate and meteorological processes (Leonard et al., 2014).

The various hazards do not have the same scale, neither in terms of distance nor in terms of time. At the micro-scale (<2 km), numerous events occur, including lightning strikes initiating wildfires, wind eddies, hailstone, and rainfall formation. Within the

2–20 km range, thermal convection can lead to intense rainfall bursts, flash flooding, strong winds, or tornadoes. Cold fronts within the 20–200-km scale can generate individual or sequences of storm events lasting hours to days. Events spanning multiple days are often associated with synoptic weather patterns such as tropical cyclones and anti-cyclones (e.g., wildfires and heat waves). Natural climatic variability may induce periods of above or below-average occurrence rates of extreme events over years or decades. Ultimately, anthropogenic climate change may drive long-term trends such as increased temperatures or ocean levels, expected to unfold over centuries or longer (Leonard et al., 2014).

In this section, we will briefly review how weather-related hazards need to be assessed together with exposure and vulnerability to correctly assess risks. We will then look at bottom-up approaches, introducing the concept of damage function for each climate-related hazard, before presenting the aggregate damage functions used in top-down approaches.

1.3.4.1 Hazards, Exposure, and Vulnerability

The impact of climate and weather-related events on individuals and economic systems is shaped by hazard, exposure, and vulnerability (Figure 1.6). The hazard represents the likelihood of an extreme weather event occurring, exposure identifies the individuals or assets that could be impacted by the weather event, and vulnerability assesses the extent to which these individuals or assets may suffer adverse consequences. More precisely (IPCC, 2012):

- *Hazard*: The potential occurrence of a climate or weather-related event or trend that may cause loss of life, injury, or other health impacts, as well as damages and loss to property, infrastructure, livelihoods, service provision, ecosystems, and environmental resources.
- *Exposure*: The presence of people, livelihoods, species or ecosystems, environmental functions, services, and resources, and infrastructure. These, together with economic, social, or cultural assets, may be found in places and settings that could be adversely affected.

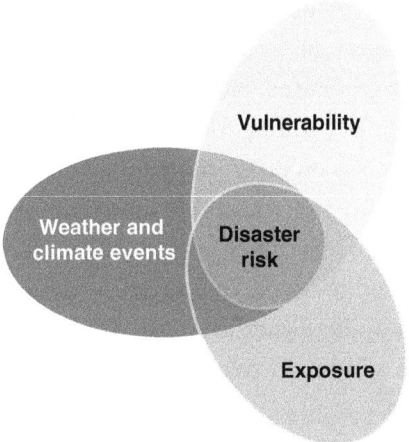

FIGURE 1.6 The articulation between hazards, exposure, and vulnerability
Source: IPCC (2012)

- *Vulnerability*: The propensity or predisposition to be adversely affected. Vulnerability encompasses a variety of concepts and elements, including sensitivity or susceptibility to harm and lack of capacity to cope and adapt.

When modeling risks, these three dimensions should be taken into account. The unit chosen to measure risk should be the most pertinent in a given decision context, which may not necessarily be monetary units. For instance, wildfire hazard could be quantified by burned area, exposure by population, and risk expressed as the number of affected individuals for evacuation planning or the repair cost of buildings for property insurance purposes. Risk, as defined by the International Organization for Standardization and the IPCC, reflects the potential for consequences when uncertainty surrounds objectives or values. It can be quantified by combining the probability of an outcome with its magnitude, often represented by a convolution of probability and severity distributions.

1.3.4.2 Damage Functions for Climate-Related Hazards

Damage functions are utilized in climate or weather-related hazard risk assessments to convert the severity of extreme events into measurable damage. A damage function is defined as the mathematical relation between the magnitude of a (natural) hazard and the average damage caused either on a single structure (microscale), for example, a building, or a portfolio of structures (macroscale). The emphasis is on direct monetary damage, but the findings can be generalized to any measurable quantity (Prahl et al., 2015, 2016). Microscale models can be empirical (i.e., statistically derived from data), engineering-based, or a mixture of both. On the macroscale, damages may be either aggregated from microscale models or obtained from statistical relationships based on empirical data (Merz et al., 2010).

We provide here two examples of damage functions at the macroscale that relate to the hazards of coastal flooding and wind storms.

1.3.4.2.1 Coastal Flooding

The analysis requires a detailed mapping of the geographical areas that could have possibly been flooded and the buildings affected. For example, Boettle et al. (2011) concentrate on a hypothetical storm surge occurrence in an area in Denmark, presuming that the seawater entirely submerges the landscape at the specified water level. To pinpoint the submerged area, they utilize a map incorporating elevation data, delineating areas susceptible to inundation with high precision. Subsequently, they ascertain which properties fall within the inundated zone and compute the extent of flooding for each building.

A diverse array of functional forms, including logarithmic, square-root, linear, and quadratic models (see Nascimento et al., 2007; Dutta et al., 2003; Buchele et al., 2006; Apel et al., 2009, and related literature) have been employed as building damage functions for flooding risks. Boettle et al. (2011) opt for a linear function represented as:

$$d_{\text{lin}}(e) = \begin{cases} 0 & \text{for } e < 0 \text{ m} \\ \dfrac{e}{3 \text{ m}} - 0.5 & \text{for } 0 \text{ m} \leq e \leq 3 \text{ m}, \\ 0.5 & \text{for } e > 3 \text{ m} \end{cases}$$

where e signifies the water level relative to the building's foundation base. This function is applied to all affected buildings, and the aggregate damage for the specified sea-level E is computed as follows:

$$D_{\text{lin}}(E) = \sum_i d_{\text{lin}}(e_i) V_i,$$

where e_i represents the flood height at building i and V_i denotes its value. $D(E)$ can be interpreted as an approximation of the total monetary damage incurred by a particular flood event of magnitude E affecting buildings across the entire study area. Adjusting the sea-level E in increments of 10 cm from 0 m to 3 m establishes a macroscopic damage function with zero loss up to 1 m and exponentially increases up to 400 million Danish krona when water reaches 3 m.

1.3.4.2.2 **Wind Storms** Klawa and Ulbrich (2003) developed a simple storm damage function based on a cubic power law term as a proxy for storm damage (Prahl et al., 2015).

$$D(v) = \begin{cases} \left(\dfrac{v - v_{98}}{v_{98}}\right)^3 & \text{if } v \geq v_{98} \\ 0 & \text{if } v < v_{98} \end{cases}.$$

The shape of the damage function is determined by the power law term, which is influenced only by the 98th wind gust percentile. The value of this threshold controls the shape and the steepness of the damage function. Leckebusch et al. (2007) amend this function by noting that damages depend on the amount of values in an affected area, and the population density (p) is used as a reasonable proxy. Thus, the applied damage function is given by the following:

$$D(v) = p \left(\dfrac{v}{v_{98}} - 1 \right)^3 \text{ for } v > v_{98}$$

Storm-damage functions are typically calibrated to insurance data. Jaison (2023) uses different damage functions, including the excess cubic one as detailed above, to assess windstorm damages for Norway using municipality-level insurance data and the high-resolution wind speed data for the period 1985–2020. Here again, there is no loss as long as wind speed is lower than 12 m/s and then losses increase up to 400 Norwegian krona/person when it is higher than 18 m/s.

Overall, empirical damage functions are generally challenging to derive due to insufficient observations for certain impacts or locations. Moreover, weak correlations between loss and explanatory variables could render loss estimates unreliable, amplifying uncertainty. This underscores the necessity for a comprehensive damage assessment to facilitate the quantification and comparison of impacts across different natural hazards and their interrelations (Kreibich et al., 2014).

1.3.4.3 Aggregate Climate Damage Functions
Bottom-up damage functions are used in catastrophe models of the insurance sector to correctly assess the risk of losses they could be exposed to. They are limited, however, to direct impacts, that is, the immediate harm inflicted upon assets (e.g., property) by a weather-related event, resulting in losses occurring either during or shortly after the event. However, the economic effects of physical risks should also include indirect impacts, which encompass alterations in economic activity post-disaster. These effects cover disruptions in economic operations and any positive repercussions stemming from production substitution and reconstruction demand. Indirect impacts encapsulate both short- and long-term economic setbacks in production and consumption, along with related pathways to economic recovery (Kousky, 2014). These indirect repercussions, sometimes referred to as higher-order effects, can be quantified through computational macroeconomic models. Such forecasts are subject to empirical validation, employing diverse economic indicators such as gross domestic product (GDP), trade patterns, and employment figures (Botzen et al., 2019).

Aggregate damage functions are defined to assess from a top-down perspective how changes in climate or weather can imply economic impacts. A *climate damage function* is, therefore, a simplified expression of economic damages (which theoretically can encompass both positive and negative effects) as a function of climate inputs, such as changes in temperature (Neuman et al., 2020).

1.3.4.3.1 Nordhaus; Weitzman; Dietz and Stern

Climate damage functions assess the economic risks posed by climate change, quantifying the impact on the economy. Economic climate damage is defined as the proportionate reduction in annual economic output at a specific degree of warming compared to output in the absence of warming. These functions illustrate the decline in output across various warming scenarios, with all indicating greater output loss as temperatures rise. However, consensus is lacking among estimated climate damage functions regarding the progression of damages with incremental warming. We present here the three most influential damage functions of the literature, their specifications, and their implications in terms of losses.

Nordhaus (2018) includes a damage function in his Integrated Assessment Model, DICE (see more details in Chapter 2), which has the following specifications:

$$\Omega(t) = \frac{1}{\left[1 + 0.0028 T_{AT}(t)^2\right]}. \tag{1.1}$$

With $\Omega(t)$ representing one minus the fraction of aggregate output (in trillion USD) lost due to climate change.

In the above equations, t is time (decades in DICE) and T_{AT} is the global mean surface temperature. For a zero temperature change $\Omega(t) = 1$ (no damage) and for very large temperature changes it approaches 0 (maximum damage). The DICE damage function is calibrated to damages in the range of 2°C–4°C.

Other economists have proposed more convex functions, notably Weitzman (2010) and Dietz and Stern (2015).

Weitzman (2010) proposes an alternative damage function, namely,

$$\Omega(t) = \frac{1}{\left[1 + \left(\dfrac{T_{AT}(t)}{20.46}\right)^2 + \left(\dfrac{T_{AT}(t)}{6.081}\right)^{6.754}\right]}. \qquad (1.2)$$

This establishes a tipping point at which the damage function illustrates significant impacts once the temperature rises beyond 6°C. At this juncture, the specification indicates approximately a 50 percent damage threshold. Weitzman supports this by citing an expert panel study involving fifty-two experts, which suggests that at this temperature increase, three out of five critical tipping points for major climate change events or scenarios are anticipated to emerge.

Dietz and Stern (2015) modify the Weitzman-based function by different parameters:

$$\Omega(t) = \frac{1}{\left[1 + \left(\dfrac{T_{AT}(t)}{18.8}\right)^2 + \left(\dfrac{T_{AT}(t)}{4}\right)^{6.754}\right]}. \qquad (1.3)$$

In addition to a different functional specification for the damage function itself, Dietz and Stern (2015) also consider the effects of damages to capital and to TFP, instead of damages to output only.

Figure 1.7 illustrates the different behaviors of the functions in (1), (2), and (3). Although hardly visible, the Weitzman damage is slightly lower than Nordhaus damage for temperature increases from 0.5 up to a little above 2.5°C. However, with more warming, the damages increase dramatically. According to Weitzman (2012), an increase in warming by 6° would be exceptionally uncommon in Earth's climatic history and would vastly surpass human experience. Hence, suggesting a 50 percent economic damage escalation at this warming level is not unjustified. At 4°, Weitzman-based damages amount to 9 percent, exceeding Nordhaus-based damages for the same warming level by more than double. The possibility of significant economic upheaval at 4°C, potentially heightened by social unrest and substantial population movements, provides the impetus for the Dietz-Stern damage function, as depicted in Figure 1.7. Dietz-Stern-based damages

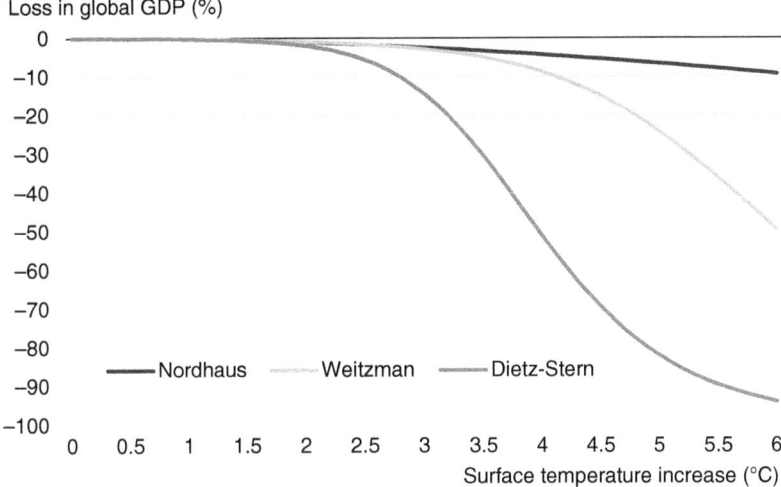

FIGURE 1.7 Damage functions

adjust Weitzman-based damages, resulting in economic losses escalating to 50 percent by the time warming reaches 4°C.

Aggregate climate damage functions have been criticized, especially by climate scientists, as too simplistic and underestimating the actual damages due to climate change. The Nordhaus version has, in particular, been criticized as it assumes that damages are a quadratic function of temperature change and does not include sharp thresholds or tipping points, while the existence of tipping points in the Earth's climate is now an established part of the scientific literature on climate change (Keen et al., 2021).

Developing a comprehensive climate damage function poses a significant challenge, primarily due to the need to effectively combine numerous highly diverse effects and the available data for a global climate damage analysis are insufficiently comprehensive (Bretschger and Pattakou, 2019). Although bottom-up studies may offer insights for crafting a general formula, their inherent limitations constrain their applicability. Consequently, determining the appropriate functional form for the damage function remains uncertain (Moore and Diaz, 2015), raising questions about capturing all aspects through a simple function (Farmer et al., 2015). Criticisms have also been directed toward integrated assessment models, particularly regarding the inadequate addressing of risks, heterogeneity, and technical change (Farmer et al., 2015). Model specifications greatly influence the outcomes and associated policy recommendations in these domains (see Revesz et al., 2014).

1.3.4.3.2 **Empirical Assessments** The number of estimates of the total economic impact of climate change has risen rapidly in recent years. Richard Tol has conducted several meta-analyses to account for the wide range and seemingly incommensurate estimates, distinguishing studies that assess the effects of climate change from those focusing on weather shocks.

Research on the economic consequences of climate change employs various methodologies, including enumeration, elicitation, computable general equilibrium, and econometrics, each carrying its advantages and drawbacks. Investigations into the economic ramifications of weather exclusively utilize econometric approaches, employing two distinct specifications: one where temperature influences economic growth and another where temperature change impacts growth. As indicated below, the former contradicts findings in the climate literature, while the latter is theoretically congruent, contingent upon a specific scenario and model.

Drawing from data provided by thirty-three studies, Tol (2022) demonstrates that comparing economies under recent conditions with and without anticipated future climate change reveals significant implications. Specifically, a global warming scenario of 2.5°C would result in the average individual experiencing a perceived income loss of 1.7 percent, nearly doubling to around 3.4 percent at 4.5°C. While the central estimate consistently indicates a negative impact of global warming, the wide confidence interval undermines the certainty of these findings.

Certain scholars have assessed the effects of weather on various economic sectors. Economically speaking, weather is considered stochastic, thus enabling accurate identification of its impact. However, it is crucial to note that the repercussions of a weather-related shock differ from those of climate change (Dell et al., 2014). Specifically, studies on weather examine the short-term economic reactions, whereas the focus lies on understanding the long-term response, encompassing adaptations in capital, behavior, and technology. There is, again, a large variety of results. The most pessimistic is the one by Kalkhul and Wenz (2020). Utilizing annual panel models, long-difference regressions, and cross-sectional regressions, they examine the impacts on both productivity levels and productivity growth. Their findings suggest no lasting effects on growth rates, yet compelling evidence indicates a significant impact of temperature on productivity levels. Specifically, a projected rise in global mean surface temperature of approximately 3.5°C by the century's end is forecasted to yield a reduction in global output ranging from 7 percent to 14 percent by 2100, with particularly heightened damages anticipated in tropical and economically poor regions.

Kalkhul and Wenz estimates have been included in the quantitative assessment of physical risks in the NGFS scenarios. These scenarios also distinguish acute from chronic risk-related impacts. Figure 1.8 shows how GDP would be impacted across scenarios. Short and long-term, acute physical risk emerges as the predominant risk factor. Given its resistance to short term mitigation efforts, acute physical risk remains consistent across scenarios until 2040, experiencing a significant increase in losses under Current Policies thereafter. Over time, chronic physical risk progressively gains significance, exerting the most substantial adverse impact on GDP within the Current Policies scenario. By 2050, economic losses associated with chronic physical risk will nearly double compared to those projected under the Net Zero 2050 scenario.

The climate economic impacts literature typically uses macro-level data (Tol, 2009 or Burke et al., 2015; Dell et al., 2012). A *New Weather Economics* literature has recently emerged which assesses the impacts of climate/weather drawing on the aggregation

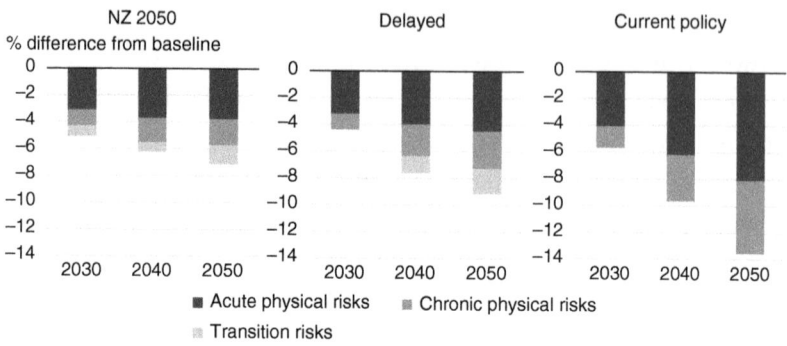

FIGURE 1.8 Global GDP impact by climate risk source
Source: NGFS (2023)

of microeconomic data (e.g., Burke et al., 2015 or Kolstad and Moore, 2019). The microeconomic nature of the data refers both to the sector of activity and to their location, reminding the importance of accounting for the heterogeneity of impacts at industrial and geographical levels when studying the effects of climate change on the economy.

Finally, given the fragmentation of production processes, the impact assessment of climate and weather-related shocks needs to account for their effects along the supply chain. For instance, Forslid and Sanctuary (2023) investigate the impact of the severe 2011 Thailand flood on Swedish businesses that relied on imports from Thailand. Results show that output from affected firms decreased by 8 percent in 2012. In total, this led to a reduction of 1.08 billion SEK in imports from Thailand for these firms, resulting in a loss of sales exceeding 29.7 billion SEK. The notable amplification effect underscores the significant repercussions. Despite the relatively swift recovery in Thai production, the effects of the flood persisted, indicating substantial fixed costs associated with establishing supply network connections.

1.4 CONCLUSION

The exploration of climate change and its economic impacts reveals a multifaceted challenge that demands both immediate attention and long-term strategic thinking. The interconnectedness of environmental, economic, and social systems demonstrates how shifts in climate can profoundly influence economic stability and growth. One key lesson is the critical importance of understanding the scientific underpinnings of climate change, including the roles of the greenhouse effect and human activities, as these are foundational to crafting effective policy responses.

Another significant insight is the potential for irreversible changes and tipping points, which highlights the urgency of timely action. The economic implications of climate change extend far beyond immediate physical risks, impacting everything from asset valuations to national economies. The rising frequency and costs associated with climate-related disasters underscore the importance of preparedness and resilience.

The use of scenario analysis has emerged as a vital tool in climate economics and finance, helping stakeholders anticipate a range of possible futures and the associated economic impacts. This approach facilitates better decision-making and planning by providing a clearer understanding of potential risks and uncertainties.

Overall, the intersection of climate change and economic activity presents both a challenge and an opportunity. The lessons learned emphasize the necessity of integrating climate considerations into economic and financial systems, fostering resilience, and promoting sustainable development.

2 The Economics of Climate Change Mitigation

2.1 INTRODUCTION

For years, scientists have cautioned about the dire environmental repercussions if the global temperature continues to ascend at its present rate. As per a 2021 evaluation by the IPCC, the Earth's average temperature has surged by around 1.1°C above preindustrial levels. Drafted by over two hundred scientists from sixty-plus nations, the report forecasts that even with nations taking drastic emission reduction measures, the world is on track to surpass 1.5°C of warming within the next two decades.

Urgent action is therefore required to limit global warming and safeguard the well-being of present and future generations. Awareness of the potential impacts of greenhouse gas (GHG) began to increase in the late twentieth century and led to establishing the Intergovernmental Panel on Climate Change (IPCC) in 1988. The United Nations Framework Convention on Climate Change (UNFCCC) in 1992 laid the groundwork for international cooperation to address climate change (see Table 2.1 for a brief history of UN Climate talks). The Kyoto Protocol, adopted in 1997, marked the first significant international agreement to reduce GHG emissions, setting binding targets for developed countries. However, its effectiveness was limited by the lack of participation from major emitters such as the United States and China.

In the early twenty-first century, momentum for climate action continued to build, culminating in the Paris Agreement, established in December 2015 under the UNFCCC. The Paris Agreement aims at limit global warming well below 2°C above preindustrial levels, with an aspiration to limit it to 1.5°C. Central to the agreement is the commitment of participating countries

Table 2.1 *Timeline of UN climate talks since 1992*

Year	Event	Main takeaway
1992	Rio Earth Summit (Rio de Janeiro)	Initial international agreements on climate change; establishment of the UNFCCC.
1995	COP1 in Berlin	Formation of COP1 and the Berlin Mandate, laying the groundwork for the Kyoto Protocol.
1997	Kyoto Protocol Adoption (COP3)	Adoption of the Kyoto Protocol, setting emissions reduction targets for developed countries and establishing emissions trading.
2001	Negotiations Breakthrough in Bonn	Agreement on rules for meeting Kyoto targets, despite US withdrawal from the protocol (COP7 in Bonn).
2005	Kyoto Protocol Entry into Force	Entry into force of the Kyoto Protocol, with notable emissions reduction commitments from several developed countries.
2007	Negotiations Begin for Kyoto 2.0 (COP13 in Bali)	Initial discussions for a successor to the Kyoto Protocol, with focus on including developing countries in emission reduction efforts.
2009	Copenhagen Summit (COP15)	Failure to reach a binding agreement at COP15 in Copenhagen, highlighting challenges in global climate negotiations.
2010	Cancun Agreements (COP16)	Commitment to limit global temperature increase to below 2°C, along with establishment of the Green Climate Fund.
2011	Durban Climate Conference (COP17)	Agreement in Durban to work toward a new climate treaty applicable to both developed and developing countries.
2012	Doha Negotiations (COP18)	Extension of the Kyoto Protocol but failure to secure commitments from major emitters, leading to criticism from environmental groups.

(continued)

Table 2.1 *(cont.)*

Year	Event	Main takeaway
2013	Warsaw Climate Conference (COP19)	Stalemate over funding mechanisms for loss and damage due to climate change, highlighting divisions between developed and developing nations.
2015	Paris Agreement Adoption (COP21)	Adoption of the Paris Agreement, with nearly all countries committing to emissions reduction goals but lacking enforcement mechanisms.
2018	Katowice Climate Conference (COP24)	Agreement on implementation rules for the Paris Agreement, but postponement of discussions on carbon trading regulations.
2019	UN Climate Action Summit (New York)	Call for increased emissions reduction targets ahead of COP26, highlighting the urgency of climate action.
2019	Madrid Climate Conference (COP25)	Failure to make significant progress at COP25, leading to criticism from environmental activists and disappointment among delegates.
2020	COP26 Postponement (Glasgow)	Postponement of COP26 due to the COVID-19 pandemic, with temporary reductions in global emissions but concerns over long-term sustainability.
2021	COP26 in Glasgow	Submission of updated emissions reduction targets by several countries, with mixed levels of ambition, ahead of COP26.
2021	Glasgow Climate Pact Adoption	Adoption of the Glasgow Climate Pact, including commitments to reduce coal use and fossil fuel subsidies, but criticism over insufficient action to limit temperature rise.
2022	COP27 in Egypt	Establishment of a fund for loss and damage compensation, but lack of commitments to phase out fossil fuels and peak emissions by 2025.

Table 2.1 (cont.)

Year	Event	Main takeaway
2023	Global Stocktake Findings Release	Assessment of progress toward the Paris Agreement goals, indicating insufficient action to limit temperature rise but some improvement in emission reduction efforts.
2023	Fossil Fuels Transition Agreement (COP28 in Dubai)	Agreement to accelerate transition from fossil fuels, with focus on renewable energy and methane emissions reduction, despite criticism over lack of explicit phase-out language.

Source: Adapted from Timeline: UN Climate Talks (cfr.org)

to submit nationally determined contributions (NDCs) outlining their efforts to reduce GHG emissions and adapt to the impacts of climate change (Figure 2.1). The agreement emphasizes transparency, accountability, and international cooperation in addressing climate challenges. Since its adoption, the Paris Agreement has become a cornerstone of global climate action, symbolizing a collective commitment to safeguarding the planet for future generations. Despite challenges and setbacks, it continues to serve as a framework for ongoing dialogue, cooperation, and ambitious climate action at a global scale.

Climate action requires profound changes within our economic systems, moving away from fossil fuel reliance toward renewable energy sources and sustainable practices. This shift involves reconsidering production and consumption patterns to emphasize resource efficiency, circularity, and emission reduction. Moreover, it demands investments in green technologies, infrastructure, and innovation to promote decarbonization across all sectors. Additionally, resilience-building and adaptation measures are crucial to mitigate the impacts of climate change on economies and communities. Overall, addressing climate change necessitates comprehensive systemic changes in economic structures, policies, and behaviors.

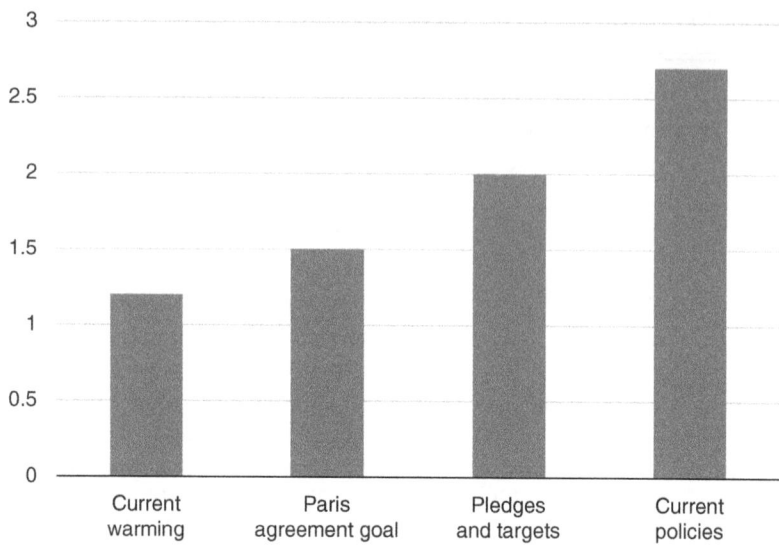

FIGURE 2.1 Implication in terms of global temperature rise of various policies and targets (°C above preindustrial average)
Source: Climate Action Tracker
Note: Current policies and pledges and targets are projections. In each scenario, the temperature shown is the most likely of a range of possible outcomes. Pledges and targets include submitted and binding commitments for 2030 and beyond.

Transitioning to a low-carbon economy may initially entail costs related to investments in renewable energy infrastructure, technology development, and adaptation measures. However, there are potential long-term cost savings, including reduced environmental damage, health benefits, and improved energy efficiency. This trade-off forms the basis of the economics of climate mitigation.

2.2 THE ECONOMICS OF CLIMATE MITIGATION

Maintaining the global climate balance is a shared global responsibility that necessitates policy action at various levels, including local, national, continental, and global scales. Firstly, emitting greenhouse gases (GHGs) essentially depletes this global resource, resulting in negative consequences for all economic entities, including households, businesses, and public institutions. This negative impact extends globally, affecting the entire planet regardless of the emission's geographical origin. Consequently, addressing climate change encounters the *tragedy of the commons* dilemma, wherein individual self-interest leads to the overuse of shared resources. Secondly, the quality of the climate hinges on the cumulative concentration of GHGs in the atmosphere, emphasizing the significance of past and future emissions accumulation over current emission rates. Thus, given that future generations will bear the brunt of today's emissions, often in uncertain degrees, a *tragedy of horizons* emerges alongside the tragedy of the commons. Addressing this dual challenge requires sustained international cooperation and long-term regulatory efforts aimed at safeguarding the well-being of future generations.

Stabilization of global warming at any level requires bringing CO_2 emissions to zero. To keep warming below 1.5° or 2°C, CO_2 emissions need to decline immediately and reach zero around 2050. In parallel, there is also a need to dramatically reduce non-CO_2 emissions like methane (see Chapter 1). The relationship between GHG emissions and temperature is not strictly linear; instead, it is complex and can be influenced by various factors, including feedback loops, natural variability, and nonlinear responses within Earth's climate system. However, over longer timescales, there is a general correlation between increasing GHG emissions and rising global temperatures. This correlation forms the basis of climate science and underpins the urgency of reducing GHG emissions to mitigate the impacts of climate change. Therefore, every tonne of CO_2 causes about the same amount of warming, no matter when and where it is emitted. More specifically, every time the CO_2 concentrations rise by 10 ppm (parts per million), the mean global temperature increases by 0.1°C (factsonclimate.org).

2.2.1 *The Concept of* Carbon Budget

A powerful tool to express a temperature target as the maximum amount of CO_2 that can still be emitted relies on the concept of *carbon budget*. Carbon budgets represent the finite amount of carbon dioxide emissions that can be released into the atmosphere while still adhering to specific climate targets, typically expressed as a temperature limit, such as the goals outlined in the Paris Agreement (Figure 2.2). These budgets are crucial in guiding efforts to mitigate climate change, as they provide a tangible framework for understanding the remaining capacity for emissions within a given timeframe. Carbon budgets consider factors such as historical emissions, projected future emissions trajectories, and the need to limit global warming to avoid catastrophic climate impacts. As such, they serve as a yardstick for policymakers, businesses, and individuals to gauge progress toward decarbonization goals and inform decision-making regarding the transition to a low-carbon economy. Adhering to carbon budgets requires concerted efforts across sectors to reduce emissions through renewable energy adoption, energy efficiency improvements, and sustainable land use practices. Additionally, robust monitoring

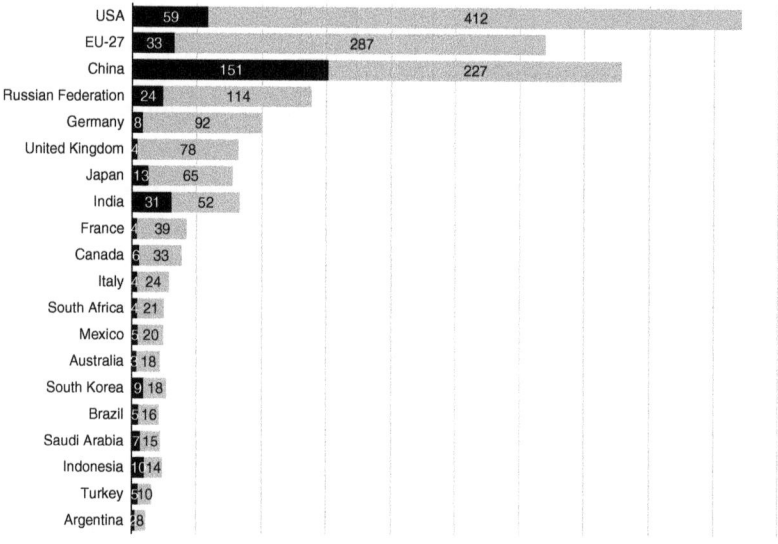

FIGURE 2.2 Carbon emissions to date and carbon budget remaining by G20 nations in Gt of CO_2
Source: Institute for Sustainable Futures at the University of Technology Sydney (UTS)

and accountability mechanisms are essential to ensure that emissions remain within budgetary constraints and that global warming targets are met. The budget is not annual but rather cumulative, meaning once it has been spent, net emissions must be held to zero to avoid exceeding the temperature target. The remaining carbon budget to limit global warming to 1.5°C and 1.7°C is equivalent to nine and sixteen years from 2022, respectively.

In line with the past emissions and the carbon budget, the remaining budget to meet a specific temperature target is calculated. The IPCC 1.5°C scenario report shows how emissions should decline to reach the 1.5°C–2°C target. This requires emissions to become net zero by mid century, which means every tonne of CO_2 emitted should be totally removed from the atmosphere via negative emissions. Overshoot scenarios are optimistic scenarios where temperatures go beyond 1.5°C and get back lower and beyond the target, thanks to negative emissions. Most scenarios that keep global warming below 1.5°C today are overshoot scenarios where temperatures exceed the target and reduce dramatically thereafter. These *techno-optimistic* scenarios generally do not account for tipping points, irreversibility, and inertia related to warming surface temperatures.

Global GHGs must be cut by 25 percent to 50 percent from 2019 levels by 2030 to limit global warming to 1.5°C–2°C – the central goal of the Paris Agreement. Most attention has so far focused on carbon dioxide produced by burning fossil fuels, but it is also critical to cut methane emissions – not least because methane has a more powerful near-term warming effect than CO_2, and cutting methane emissions would have a more immediate impact on the climate. Most low-cost opportunities for cutting methane emissions are found in the extractive industries and in producing more food from plants and less from livestock. In agriculture, emissions could be reduced by transitioning to more productive cattle herds. Additionally, methane released from landfills can be captured and used as a source of energy. Methane fees could become a promising and practical instrument to lower emissions, especially if they build on existing business taxes that are common in the extractive sector and, in some cases, agriculture (Black et al., 2022).

Adherence to the Paris Agreement requires the establishment of ambitious national targets and universal compliance, particularly among major emitters. While the issue is global in scope, the primary tools for driving mitigation policies lie within national jurisdictions, relying on traditional economic policy instruments such as regulation, taxation, and public investments. International collaboration, particularly in research, can bolster these mitigation efforts. Nevertheless, effective international coordination is imperative to equitably distribute the global carbon budget, considering both the historical emissions responsibilities of developed nations and each country's unique circumstances.

2.2.2 Assessing the Cost of Climate Policy

There is a large literature assessing the cost of policy inaction to measure the trade-off between the mitigation costs and the negative impacts that insufficient policies could have regarding climate-related impacts. Alestra et al. (2022) estimated that without action, the permanent loss of global gross domestic product (GDP) due to climate change would be around 13 percent by 2100. Stern (2007) estimated that inaction would have an intergenerational welfare effect equivalent to a permanent consumption loss ranging between 5 percent and 20 percent, similar in magnitude to the effects of a permanent COVID-19 crisis (see Chapter 1 for assessment methodologies). Confidence in these estimates is constrained by the significant nonlinearity of the climate system and the damage function that links temperature change to its environmental, health, and social impacts (further details on the economic consequences of climate change are in Chapter 1).

Determining the optimal path for emission reduction involves three key factors: defining climate objectives, identifying decarbonization technologies, and establishing a framework for distributing efforts over time to achieve optimal technology implementation. Establishing emission targets entails identifying the most effective level of emissions by a specific horizon, typically set at 2050. This process typically relies on either a cost-benefit analysis or a cost-effectiveness approach.

The *cost-benefit approach* stands out as the most economically intuitive method, as it determines the optimal emissions target internally by weighing the costs of emissions-induced damages against the costs of mitigation measures to prevent them (Figure 2.3a). This requires precisely defining the damage function through a comprehensive and updated assessment of the short-, medium-, and long-term impacts of emitting one tonne of CO_2, a task fraught with practical challenges. Notably, significant uncertainty exists regarding the monetary valuation of climate damages, encompassing both market costs (such as productivity loss and

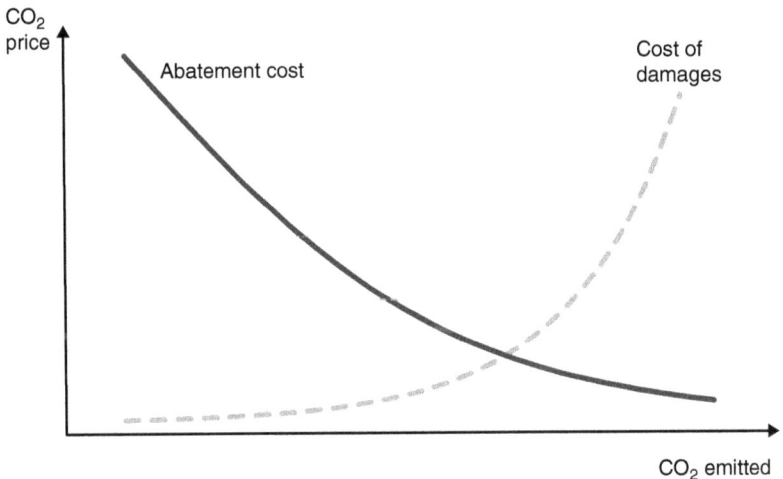

FIGURE 2.3 Cost-benefit approach vs. cost-effectiveness approach: (a) cost-benefit approach; (b) cost-effectiveness approach
Note: Figure 2.3a shows the curves of the marginal costs of damages (increasing with CO_2 emitted) and abatement costs (decreasing with CO_2 emitted), based on the idea that the decarbonation is becoming more costly during the transition. In Figure 2.3b, the damage costs become infinite from a certain emission threshold corresponding to the exhaustion of the carbon budget.

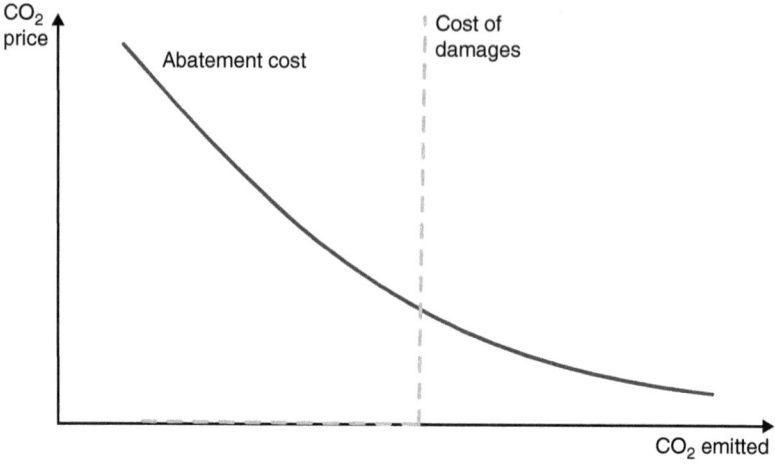

FIGURE 2.3 (cont.)

agricultural yield decline) and nonmarket costs (like biodiversity loss and ecosystem destruction), the latter being particularly challenging to quantify accurately. Additionally, damages unfold over time, and beyond marginal impacts, there exists a risk of severe and irreversible consequences not factored into this approach. Consequently, damages are often underestimated, leading to climate targets that diverge significantly from the prevailing scientific consensus (see Chapter 1). For instance, according to the damage function of the DICE model (Nordhaus, 1992), the climate's optimal state would theoretically occur at a temperature increase of around +4°C compared to pre-industrial levels, a notably optimistic scenario given recent findings from the IPCC.

In contrast, the *cost-effectiveness approach* appears more aligned with the global community's aspirations outlined in the Paris Agreement, which aims to cap GHG emissions within a specified timeframe to limit temperature rise. This method establishes an ex-ante external emissions reduction target based on existing climate commitments. Consequently, the damage function is implicitly determined by the objective, where damages are assumed to escalate infinitely or transcend quantification if the target is exceeded (Figure 2.3b).

2.2.3 Carbon Pricing

Each of the previous approaches generates a distinct definition of the carbon price, reflecting the underlying economic logic. In the cost-benefit approach, the corresponding price is called the social cost of carbon; in the cost-efficient approach, the price is called the shadow carbon price (or the value for climate action).

The *social cost of carbon* (SCC) is a metric used to quantify the economic damages associated with emitting one additional tonne of carbon dioxide (CO_2) or its equivalent GHGs into the atmosphere. It represents the present value of the future economic costs, such as those related to climate change impacts on agriculture, health, infrastructure, and ecosystems, resulting from the emission of an additional unit of CO_2. The SCC is utilized in cost-benefit analyses of climate policies and projects to assess the net societal benefits of reducing GHG emissions and to inform decision-making regarding mitigation and adaptation strategies. The SCC is usually estimated using Integrated Assessment Models (IAMs), which integrate principles from both climate science and economics into a unified modeling framework (see Box 2.1). For instance, the SCC utilized for evaluating climate policies by US federal agencies has been calculated using three standard IAMs: DICE (Dynamic Integrated Climate-Economy), FUND (Climate Framework for Uncertainty, Negotiation, and Distribution), and PAGE (Policy Analysis of the Greenhouse Effect).

IAMs operate on the fundamental assumption that the monetary value of climate change damages can be weighed against the costs of GHG mitigation actions to determine the most *optimal* climate policy level. These models employ a damage function to translate climate conditions, typically represented by temperature, into the collective economic consequences of those conditions, enabling the calculation of the SCC. However, uncertainty remains very high, particularly for temperature increases beyond +2°C. Moreover, economists do not agree on the discount rate to discount these damages, many of which materialize in the distant future. All in all, to estimate the SCC, a discount rate of 2 percent or 3 percent seems justified. Nordhaus (2018), based on a discount rate of 4.5 percent, recommends a carbon price of around 35 euros/tCO$_2$ in 2020 and 100 euros/tCO$_2$ in 2050. In contrast, Stern (2007), based on a much lower discount rate of around 1.4 percent, obtained much higher estimates of the SCC. For the intermediate range of discount rates that we recommend, from 2 percent to 3 percent, the SCC and the dual value of carbon for 2020 are both in the same range, between 50 and 100 euros/tCO$_2$. Carleton and Greenstone (2021) suggest a discount rate of 2 percent and an SCC of 100 euros/tCO$_2$.

The *carbon shadow price* refers to the implicit or explicit monetary value of carbon emissions in economic analyses, policies, or financial decisions. It represents the price of carbon (or its equivalent GHGs) that would ensure the achievement of the objective of limiting the global temperature rise and reducing global GHG emissions. This price is often used to internalize the external costs of carbon emissions, such as environmental damage and climate change impacts, into decision-making processes. The carbon shadow price can vary depending on factors such as regional regulations, market mechanisms, and the SCC, and it serves as a tool to guide investment, pricing, and policy decisions to reduce GHG emissions. Unlike other carbon pricing policies, such as carbon taxes, this approach does not involve direct expenditures. Instead, the shadow carbon price operates internally within financial evaluations, effectively penalizing high-emission projects. Ideally, when properly calibrated, this internal pricing mechanism ensures that only investments aligned with a low-carbon transition are approved.

An increasing number of companies are implementing a carbon shadow price strategy to efficiently reduce their carbon footprint costs (Morris, 2015). Carbon shadow pricing involves integrating a hypothetical premium into market prices for goods or services with significant carbon emissions throughout their supply chain. For instance, when assessing the acquisition of new energy-consuming equipment, a company would factor in anticipated energy expenses along with an additional charge linked to the carbon dioxide emissions resulting from fuel combustion. This shadow pricing approach can be applied across various analyses, including investment evaluations, procurement processes, and strategic decision-making, to favor options that are more emissions-efficient, all else being equal. By making such decisions, companies can gradually decrease their emissions up to the incremental cost reflected in the applied carbon price.

Over time, conventional methods for carbon shadow pricing are beginning to surface, yet the methodologies for shadow pricing are not as advanced as those for GHG emissions inventories. The cost per metric tonne of carbon dioxide emissions utilized by firms typically falls within the range of USD 6–USD 60, and their approaches differ based on factors such as the year, scope of application, and pricing strategy. Companies interested in implementing shadow pricing have limited public models to guide their efforts.

Multilateral Development Banks (MDBs) also use shadow carbon prices to assess the financing of investments. The High-Level Commission on Carbon Prices (HLCCP), a World Bank initiative, recommends carbon prices of USD 40–USD 80 per tonne of CO_2 by 2020 and USD 50–USD 100 per tonne by 2030 to keep global warming below 2°C. Similarly, governments could implement shadow pricing for their own emissions, tailored to the needs of public entities. This approach involves considering the carbon intensity of energy sources when analyzing efficiency upgrades for public facilities. Implementing this approach would help mitigate fiscal risks for the government as a major energy consumer, align abatement incentives across agencies, and streamline federal investments amidst competing priorities. Furthermore, the government can use this initiative to spark broader public discussion, demonstrating the effectiveness of carbon pricing and potentially influencing firms with large public contracts.

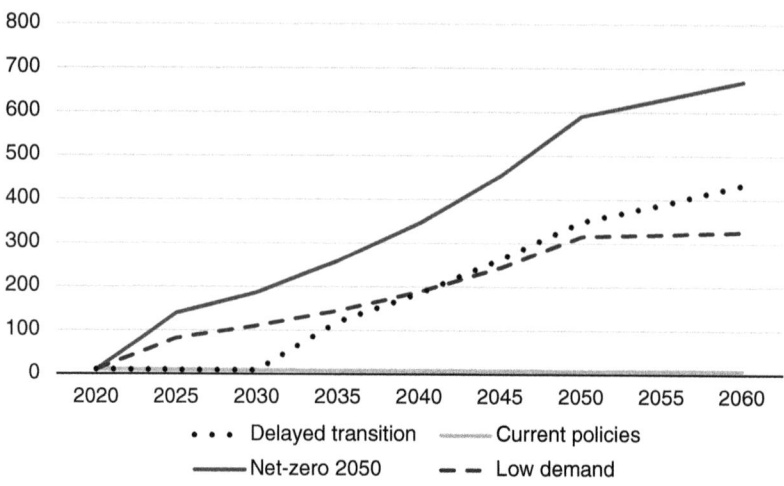

FIGURE 2.4 Carbon price in NGFS scenarios (in USD per tonne of CO_2)
Source: NGFS (2023)

Within the IAMs utilized to generate the NGFS scenarios, an elevated emissions price indicates more rigorous policy implementation. According to models, achieving a transition toward net zero by 2050 would necessitate a carbon price of approximately USD 160 per tonne by the decade's end (as illustrated in Figure 2.4). Emissions' prices are defined as the marginal abatement cost of an incremental tonne of GHG emissions. Prices are influenced by the stringency of policy as well as how technology costs will evolve. Prices tend to be lower in emerging economies, which reduces efficiency but reflects equity considerations.

The NGFS shadow emissions prices are influenced by several factors as follows:

- The degree of commitment to mitigating climate change, with heightened ambition correlating to increased emissions prices.
- The timing of policy enactment, wherein delayed action necessitates higher emissions prices in the medium to long term.
- The allocation of policy measures across different sectors and regions.
- Assumptions regarding technology, including the availability and feasibility of carbon dioxide removal methods.

2.2.4 Abatement Costs

Irrespective of the approach chosen, one important concept to correctly assess the price of carbon is the marginal abatement cost. The concept of the socioeconomic abatement cost of a decarbonization action refers to a unit cost, from society's perspective, of reducing GHG emissions. For example, an individual who replaces a gas boiler with a heat pump reduces their GHG emissions. However, they must pay for the installation of the heat pump, cover the electricity needed to operate it, and save money by no longer purchasing gas. The marginal abatement cost is calculated by relating the net implementation cost of the action to the total volume of emissions avoided, and is typically expressed in EUR/tCO_2 equivalent. This cost can be positive, but also negative, depending on the case (which is likely the case for the heat pump, thanks to greater energy efficiency).

To select priority actions for the climate, assessing the abatement cost is a logical starting point. Negative abatement costs correspond to opportunities to reduce emissions with a net economic gain and the lowest abatement costs indicate opportunities to avoid emissions at low cost.

This is how marginal abatement cost curves were created. There are three main approaches to compute them (Criqui, 2023). According to the economic theory of investment, the calculation of the net present value (NPV) of a project determines whether its implementation adds net value compared to a baseline scenario. The calculation involves comparing the total discounted benefits over its lifespan with the discounted costs of implementation.

Approach #1: Carbon budget abatement cost
Economic literature typically adopts a mathematical formulation of the socioeconomic abatement cost, which is directly derived from the definition provided above. This formulation places the discounted socioeconomic incremental cost associated with the project over its entire lifespan in the numerator and the total volume of emissions it helps avoid in the denominator. This approach assumes

that the value of a tonne of avoided CO_2 is independent of the timing of its avoidance: A tonne avoided tomorrow or the day after has the same value as a tonne avoided today.

$$AC_i^1 = -\frac{\sum_{t=0}^{N-1} \frac{\Delta C_{i,t}}{(1+r)^t}}{\sum_{t=0}^{N-1} \Delta E_{i,t}},$$

where AC_i^1 is the abatement cost of project i (approach #1), $\Delta C_{i,t}$ is the additional cost of a project i compared to the reference option at date t, r is the discount rate, and $\Delta E_{i,t}$ is the change in the project's GHG emissions compared with the reference option. N is the lifetime of project i.

This generic formula is useful for comparing two technologies and for international comparisons of abatement costs. Since it does not involve a carbon price, the abatement costs obtained are not contingent upon it.

Approach #2: Carbon price-adjusted abatement cost
The second approach for calculating abatement costs depends on the trajectory of the carbon price over the investment period.

$$AC_i^2 = -\frac{\sum_{t=0}^{N-1} \frac{\Delta C_{i,t}}{(1+r)^t}}{\sum_{t=0}^{N-1} \frac{CP_t}{CP_0 (1+r)^t} \Delta E_{i,t}}$$

where AC_i^2 is the abatement cost of project i (approach #2), CP_0 and CP_t are the carbon price at the beginning of project i and at time t, respectively.

The abatement cost obtained in this way has the advantage of being directly comparable to the carbon price at the time of investment to assess the socioeconomic profitability of the project. This formula would be equivalent to the carbon budget abatement cost (approach #1) if the carbon price increased at the same rate as the discount rate.

This formula can pose interpretation difficulties, particularly because two investments with identical cost and emission reduction characteristics but carried out at different dates will not have the same abatement cost: More precisely, the *carbon price-adjusted abatement cost* is lower the earlier the implementation, whereas the *carbon budget* abatement cost is independent of the implementation date (all else being equal regarding costs and emissions avoided).

Approach #3: Private abatement cost

In a private economic calculation, abatement costs are computed using a third method, in which emissions in the denominator are discounted. This formula gives more weight to short-term emission reductions, as it reduces the value of emission reductions in the medium and long term.

$$AC_i^3 = -\frac{\sum_{t=0}^{N-1} \frac{\Delta C_{i,t}}{(1+r)^t}}{\sum_{t=0}^{N-1} \frac{\Delta E_{i,t}}{(1+r)^t}}$$

The method, without anticipating any increase in the price of carbon, leads to a lower value of future reductions, solely due to discounting. The abatement costs evaluated in this case can be interpreted as constant carbon price signals (or anticipated as such) that would trigger actions considered by economic agents, with their own discount rate. This third approach to computing abatement cost, not anticipating an increase in the initial carbon price over the lifespan of the investment, results in a higher abatement cost than the *carbon budget* abatement cost and, therefore even higher than the *carbon price-adjusted abatement cost*.

In practice, marginal abatement costs are helpful in choosing among projects that are the most cost-efficient. Hence, various options to reduce emissions, each with their cost and potential, can be ranked from the least expensive to the most expensive. It would then be rational to start with the least expensive options and proceed to more expensive ones until financial capacity is reached or until a reduction target is achieved. Decarbonisation projects can be classified based on their marginal abatement costs. Some actions, such as optimizing public transport systems or promoting urban densification, can yield net mitigation benefits, as their costs are significantly lower than the expected gains. In contrast, interventions like reforestation or wildfire management are generally associated with positive net costs.

There are, however, limits to the use of marginal abatement costs. First, the current approach to emission reduction is marginal and inadequate for achieving carbon neutrality. While this strategy may suffice for minor emission reductions, it falls short when aiming for near-zero emissions. Cost considerations may lead to inefficient choices, favoring marginal improvements over transformative measures needed for deep decarbonization. For instance, while it is cheaper to marginally improve gasoline cars, true decarbonization requires radical shifts like investing in public transport and electric vehicles. These transformative strategies may involve higher upfront costs but deliver larger emission reductions, aligning more effectively with the goal of carbon neutrality (Hallegatte, 2023). Second, the transition to carbon neutrality requires integrated strategies considering the interplay between various measures and the pacing of the transition. Isolated investments are no longer viable as emissions reductions from technologies such as heat pumps depend on the carbon intensity of electricity – an intensity that, in turn, is influenced by factors like demand and system flexibility, both of which are influenced by the adoption of heat pumps. Thus, decisions on investments in one sector affect the outcomes in another, calling for an integrated approach. Third, the timing of transitions plays a critical role. Delaying the adoption of electric vehicles until full decarbonization is achieved is impractical; greater efficiency is achieved by initiating action early in harder-to-decarbonize sectors, even when upfront costs are elevated (Vogt-Schilb, Meunier, and Hallegatte, 2018). In the building sector, while postponing renovations may seem economical on a per-building basis, this strategy is incompatible with the urgency of reaching carbon neutrality. The key lies

2 THE ECONOMICS OF CLIMATE CHANGE MITIGATION

in finding the most cost-effective sequencing strategy, considering the collective costs across all sectors, balancing the pace of transition to capture economies of scale while avoiding resource constraints and inefficiencies. Comparing costs per tonne between sectors may then be ineffective when the task involves comprehensive action across all sectors. Finally, the evolving nature of technology is a key factor in determining costs during transitions. For instance, solar and wind energy have become cheaper over time as a result of sustained investment and marginal abatement costs must also take these trends into account. Similar support is now needed for emerging technologies like carbon-free cement and hydrogen-based fertilizers (Hallegatte, 2015).

BOX 2.1: Integrated Assessment Models

Assessing the global costs and benefits of climate change policy has been a primary interest for climate economists. Nordhaus introduced the pioneering DICE model, which integrated climate science and damage modules into the standard economic growth model (Ramsey model). This work has evolved over time and was recognized with the Nobel Prize. DICE has paved the way for the development of IAMs. IAMs are methodologies that connect key aspects of society and the economy with the biosphere and atmosphere within a unified modeling structure. Typically, they integrate a macroeconomic model with a climate risk model to simulate the economic consequences of climate change. Policymakers use IAMs to assess both the economic consequences of climate change and the impacts of climate policy measures.

The proliferation of IAMs has accelerated, particularly in recent years, as scientists increasingly recognize the importance of integrating climate change into economic models. As early as the late 1990s, Kelly and Kolstad (1999) identified 21 major IAMs. Today, modern IAMs can be highly intricate, encompassing social factors (such as inequality, education, health, and food security), industrial considerations (including sectors, infrastructure, and rare earth elements), biodiversity aspects (such as species, ecosystems, and food systems), and more. This box provides a brief introduction to the DICE model, one of the simplest yet most well-known integrated assessment models, followed by a rapid overview of more recent IAMs, particularly those used to develop scenarios for climate stress testing in financial institutions.

B2.1.1 THE DICE MODEL

DICE utilizes the Ramsey-Cass-Koopmans model, a standard neoclassical framework for economic growth. This model extends the Solow model by considering the saving rate as endogenous rather than constant. The social planner aims to maximize the welfare utility function and determine the optimal trajectory of saving rates to enhance future global consumption.

$$\max_{c(t)} W = \max_{c(t)} \left[\int_0^\infty U[c(t)] e^{-\rho t} dt \right] \quad (2.1)$$

subject to

$$c(t) = M\big[z(t); x(t); \alpha; \varepsilon(t)\big], \quad (2.2)$$

where W is the welfare; U is the utility function, which depends positively on $c(t)$, which is consumption; $z(t)$ are other endogenous variables (such as global temperature); $x(t)$ are exogenous variables (such as population); α are parameters (such as climate sensitivity); ρ is the pure rate of time preference; and $\varepsilon(t)$ are random variables in the stochastic versions. This highly simplified representation shows an optimization of the path of consumption in (2.1) subject to a complex constraint in (2.2).

Nordhaus incorporates the adverse effects of climate change as a negative externality impacting the economy and output. To mitigate the costs associated with climate-related physical risks, the social planner can adjust climate investments using a control variable for climate transition risks. Consequently, the overall equilibrium hinges on two key decision variables: the saving rate and the climate control variable. Traditional economic models do not make the distinction between the production $Y(t)$ and the net output Q(t), so that Y(t) = Q(t). In DICE, net output takes into account negative externalities due to climate change (both physical and transition risks).

$$Q(t) = \Omega_c(t)Y(t) \leq Y(t),$$

where $\Omega_c(t)$ is the loss of production due to climate-related externalities. It combines both costs due to natural disasters (through a damage function, $D(t)$) and transition costs (through abatement cost function, $A(t)$):

$$\Omega_c(t) = \frac{1}{1+D(t)}(1-A(t)) \qquad (2.3)$$

$$D(t) = \varphi_1 T(t) + \varphi_2 T(t)^2 \qquad (2.4)$$

$$A(t) = \theta_1 m(t)^{\theta_2} \qquad (2.5)$$

Damages are a quadratic function of temperatures, $T(t)$, and abatement costs depending of the abatement effort, $m(t)$, and θ_1 and θ_2, the parameters of the convex cost function (the more a technology abates CO_2, the more it costs).

Consumption $C(t)$ is then equal to

$$C(t) = (1-s(t))Q(t) = (1-s(t))\Omega_c(t)Y(t). \qquad (2.6)$$

The GHG emissions $E(t)$ is related to the production $Y(t)$ and the land-use emissions $E_{Land}(t)$:

$$E(t) = (1-m(t))\sigma(t)Y(t) + E_{Land}(t), \qquad (2.7)$$

where $\sigma(t)$ is the impact of the production on GHG emissions. Then, in order to relate the carbon emissions $E(t)$ and the temperature $T(t)$, the DICE model uses a reduced form of a general circulation model describing the evolution of GHG concentrations in three carbon-sink reservoirs: the atmosphere, the upper ocean, and the deep (or lower) ocean. The next step consists of linking accumulated carbon emissions in the atmosphere and global warming at the Earth's surface through increases in radiative forcing (Figure B2.1.1).

To achieve carbon emissions reduction, the transition can take three different avenues (eq. (2.7)):

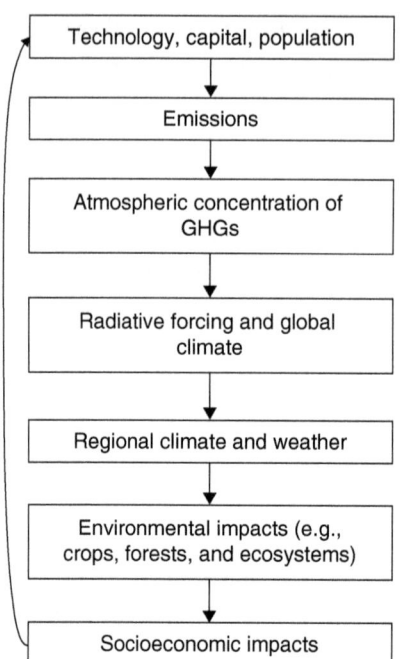

FIGURE B2.1.1 Climate Change in IAMs: Linking Emissions, Climate Response, and Impacts

1. Reducing the production $Y(t)$;
2. Reducing the carbon intensity $\sigma(t)$ of industrial activities;
3. Increase the mitigation effort $m(t)$ and accelerate the transition to a low-carbon economy.

The final objective of the DICE model is not to estimate the optimal pathway of $m(t)$, which is a conceptual measure of the mitigation effort. The main goal is to compute the SCC, which is the central pillar in the cost-benefit analysis of climate change policies (Nordhaus, 2017).

$$\mathrm{SCC}(t) = \frac{\frac{\partial W(t)}{\partial E(t)}}{\frac{\partial W(t)}{\partial C(t)}} = \frac{\partial C(t)}{\partial E(t)}.$$

It is expressed in USD/tCO_2. The DICE model can be applied to different scenarios. For instance, we can consider the baseline scenario ($m(t) = m(t0)$), the optimal scenario (social welfare maximization),

Table B2.1.1 *Global SCC under different scenario assumptions (in USD/tCO$_2$)*

Scenario	2015	2020	2025	2030	2050
Baseline	31.2	37.3	44.0	51.6	102.5
Optimal	30.7	36.7	43.5	51.2	103.6
2.5°C-max	184.4	229.1	284.1	351.0	1006.2
2.5°C-max for 100y	106.7	133.1	165.1	203.7	543.3

Source: Nordhaus (2017)

or a scenario that limits the maximum temperature T. Table B2.1.1 gives the corresponding carbon prices of the various scenarios.

B2.1.2 CRITIQUES OF THE DICE MODEL

In 2007, Nicholas Stern released a report titled "The Economics of Climate Change: The Stern Review," commissioned by the British government (Stern, 2007). The review advocated for urgent action to stabilize GHGs, asserting that "the benefits of strong, early action on climate change outweigh the costs." Weitzman (2007) identifies two primary arguments supporting this conclusion. The first revolves around the significant discount rate employed by IAMs and the DICE model. The second argument is more ethical and pertains to the considerable uncertainty surrounding the world's future. Consequently, the Stern Review suggests using a discount rate of $\rho = 0.10$ percent. Table B2.1.2 shows the implication of choosing

Table B2.1.2 *Global SCC under different discount rate assumptions*

Discount rate	2015	2020	2025	2030	2050
Stern	197.4	266.5	324.6	376.2	629.2
Nordhaus	30.7	36.7	43.5	51.2	103.6
2.5%	128.5	140.0	152.0	164.6	235.7
3%	79.1	87.3	95.9	104.9	156.6
4%	36.3	40.9	45.8	51.1	81.7
5%	19.7	22.6	25.7	29.1	49.2

Source: Nordhaus (2017)

different values for ρ. The value suggested by Stern leads to much higher carbon prices than those advocated by Nordhaus.

B2.1.3 AN OVERVIEW OF THE MAIN IAMS

During the 1990s, three groundbreaking models emerged: DICE (Nordhaus, 1992), PAGE (Hope et al., 1993), and FUND (Tol, 1997), all aiming to quantify the most effective reactions to climate change. These three cost-benefit IAMs have been used by the US government Inter-Agency Working Group to compute the SCC.

Grubb et al. (2021) count twenty-eight major climate economic models and distinguish between stylized simple IAMs and complex IAMs. While the first category is focused on the optimal path of the economy based on policy optimization, the second category generally aims to evaluate the impact of a climate scenario or a given policy on the economy.

Stylized simple models typically assume a fixed and predetermined abatement cost curve, treating costs as independent of time. However, empirical evidence highlights the inertia and path dependence inherent in the global energy system, underscoring the need for more dynamic modeling approaches. Recent conceptual advances recognize that abatement costs are not isolated factors but rather reflect the differential between high- and low-carbon investment trajectories, with faster learning in the latter potentially driving systemic shifts. Moreover, inertia fundamentally alters optimal abatement dynamics. More complex IAMs now capture these complexities. Although they are still used primarily for climate mitigation, they are versatile enough to be applied to address air pollution, water use, and sustainable development strategies. Beyond the cost-benefit IAMs, as the DICE model, process-based IAMs have also been developed to delve into the complexities of transformation processes, considering various activities that produce emissions and their broader environmental impacts. While these models do not directly simulate the economic effects of climate change they explore emission scenarios and mitigation strategies, shedding light on policy implications and trade-offs. Finally, global IAMs project emissions scenarios on a global scale, while regional IAMs provide more detailed insights into specific geographies. These regional models offer higher sectoral and policy resolution, taking into account boundary conditions set by global markets and international policies.

Table B2.1.3 lists the main IAMs used today. Three of them (GCAM, Message, and Remind) have been used by the NGFS to

Table B2.1.3 *Main integrated assessment models*

Model	Reference	Name
Stylised simple models		
DICE	Nordhaus and Sztorc (2013)	Dynamic Integrated Climate-Economy
FUND	Anthoff and Tol (2013)	Climate Framework for Uncertainty, Negotiation and Distribution
PAGE	Hope (2011)	Policy Analysis of the Greenhouse Effect
Complex models		
AIM/CGE	Fujimori et al. (2017)	Asia-Pacific Integrated Model/Computable General Equilibrium
GCAM	Calvin et al. (2019)	Global Change Assessment Model
GLOBIOM	Havlik et al. (2014)	Global Biosphere Management Model
IMACLIM-R	Crassous et al. (2006)	Integrated Model to Assess Climate Change
IMAGE	Stehfest et al. (2014)	Integrated Model to Assess the Greenhouse Effect
MAGICC	Meinshausen et al. (2011)	Model for the Assessment of Greenhouse Gas-Induced Climate Change
MAgPIE	Dietrich et al. (2019)	Model of Agricultural Production and its Impact on the Environment

(continued)

Table B2.1.3 (cont.)

Model	Reference	Name
MESSAGEix	Huppmann et al. (2019)	Model for the Energy Supply Strategy Alternatives and their General Environmental Impact
REMIND	Aboumahboub et al. (2020)	Regional Model of Investments and Development
WITCH	Bosetti et al. (2006)	World Induced Technical Change Hybrid

Source: Adapted from Grubb et al. (2021)

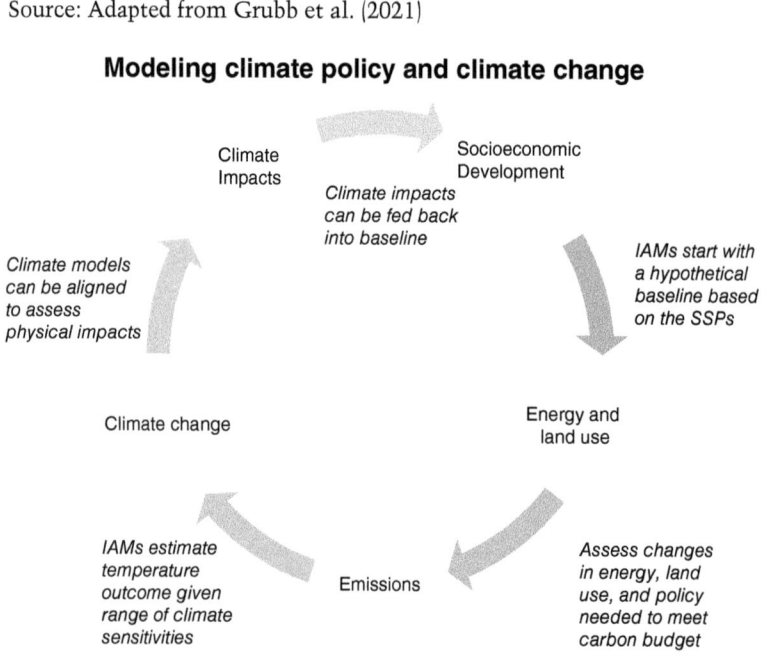

FIGURE B2.1.2 Modeling climate policy and climate change

construct scenarios for financial stability assessment. These IAMs have the capability to evaluate alterations in energy, land use, and climate-related policy instruments required to achieve a specific temperature target or carbon budget (as depicted in Figure B2.1.2).

> These models suggest that a carbon price of around USD 160/tonne would be needed by the end of the decade to incentivize a transition toward net zero by 2050. However, this price may diverge from the socially optimal level, which depends on evaluating the benefits of avoided damages and accounting for the distribution of impacts over present and future generations.

2.3 POLICY OPTIONS TO REDUCE GHG EMISSIONS AND MITIGATION STRATEGIES

There is a wide array of policy tools available to help nations reduce GHG emissions, many of which can be strengthened or redesigned to enhance their effectiveness. Table 2.2 offers a comprehensive overview of the diverse policy instruments available in the toolkit for achieving net-zero emissions. These encompass not only climate policy instruments explicitly designed to mitigate GHG emissions but also nonclimate policy instruments, which, while not primarily focused on climate objectives, are nonetheless highly relevant for shaping climate-related outcomes (e.g., household subsidies). These instruments, whether climate-specific or not, can be categorized as either price-based, directly altering the costs of activities or assets and allowing the market to respond to price signals (e.g., carbon taxes or emissions trading systems (ETS)), or nonprice-based. Nonprice-based instruments, such as emission intensity standards and energy efficiency regulations, impose restrictions on producers and consumers, compelling them to engage only in activities or investments that meet regulatory criteria. Unlike price-based instruments, nonprice-based ones offer less flexibility to market participants in reducing emissions. The instruments are applied across a wide range of sectors, including energy, transport, buildings, industry, land use and human settlements, and infrastructure. This overview highlights the diversity of climate actions, not only in terms of policy instruments but also in their areas of application.

In what follows, we will distinguish four major categories of policy options (or instruments) to reduce GHG emissions: (i) market-based policies (rows 1 and 2 of Table 2.2), (ii) command-and-control

Table 2.2 Overview of policy instruments to mitigate climate change

Policy instruments	Energy	Transport	Buildings	Industry	AFOLU	Human settlements and infrastructure
1. Economic instruments – Taxes	Carbon tax	Fuel taxes, congestion charges, registration fees, road tolls Vehicle taxes	Carbon and/or energy taxes	Carbon tax or energy tax, waste disposal taxes or charges	Fertilizer or nitrogen to reduce nitrous oxide	Sprawl taxes, impact fees, exactions, split-rate property taxes, tax increment finance, congestion charges
2. Economic instruments – Tradable allowances	Emissions trading, emission credits, Tradable Green Certificates	Fuel and vehicle standards	Tradable certificates for energy efficiency improvements	Emissions trading, emission credit, Tradable Green Certificates	Emission credits, compliance schemes, Voluntary Carbon Markets	Urban-scale Cap and Trade

3. Economic instruments – subsidies	Fossil fuel subsidy removal, Feed-in-tariffs, capital subsidies	Biofuel subsidies, vehicle purchase subsidies, feebates	Subsidies or tax exemptions for investment in efficient buildings, retrofits and products, subsidized loans	Subsidies, fiscal incentives	Credit lines for sustainable agriculture and forestry	Special improvement and redevelopment districts
4. Regulatory approaches	Efficiency or environmental performance standards	Energy performance standards, regulatory restrictions	Building codes and standards, equipment and appliance standards	Energy efficiency standards, energy management systems, voluntary agreements, labeling and public procurement regulations	National laws and policies, land-use planning and governance	Development restrictions, building and infrastructure codes, design standards
5. Information programs		Fuel labeling vehicle efficiency labeling	Energy audits, labeling programs, energy advice programs	Energy audits, benchmarking, brokerage for industrial cooperation	Certification schemes, information policies	

(continued)

Table 2.2 (cont.)

Policy instruments	Energy	Transport	Buildings	Industry	AFOLU	Human settlements and infrastructure
6. Government provision of public goods and services	Research and development, infrastructure expansion	Investment in transport infrastructure	Public procurement of efficient buildings and appliances	Training and education	Protection of forests, investment in innovative agriculture and forestry	Provision of utility infrastructure, park and trail improvements
7. Voluntary actions			Labeling programs for efficient buildings, product eco-labeling	Voluntary agreements on energy targets or resource efficiency	Promotion of sustainability by developing standards and educational campaigns	

Source: Adapted from IPCC (2014)
Note: AFOLU stands for Agriculture, Forestry and Other Land Use.

instruments (row 3), (iii) public support, either indirect (transfers or subsidies; including tax expenditures) (row 4) or direct (public investment) (row 6), and (iv) voluntary instruments (rows 5 and 7). After reviewing each type of instrument, we will assess their effectiveness based on a set of criteria, before examining how they have been implemented globally to date.

2.3.1 Review of the Main Policy Instruments

We present here the main policy instruments designed to encourage economic agents to shift away from carbon-intensive activities and adopt low-emission technologies. These instruments may influence relative costs – such as through market-based mechanisms – or impose quantity limits via regulations or outright bans. Governments can provide incentives either directly or indirectly to support such choices and the necessary investments in clean technologies and infrastructure. Finally, some actions are voluntary, reflecting social preferences or emerging norms, such as environmental labels.

2.3.1.1 Market-Based Policies

Market-based policies encompass a range of mechanisms aimed at reducing carbon emissions by adjusting price signals, thereby creating direct financial incentives for polluters to lower their emissions. The main market-based mechanisms for managing GHGs are taxes and tradable permits.

With an *emissions tax*, a fee is applied for each unit of pollutant released, or alternatively, the carbon content of fossil fuels can be taxed. This tax, levied based on the carbon content of each fuel, covers potential CO_2 (or other gases) releases from subsequent combustion. As this tax is passed down the supply chain, it results in higher end-user prices for fossil fuels and electricity, thereby incentivizing emission reduction measures across various sectors. In contrast, *emissions trading (or cap-and-trade) systems* allocate permits to polluters, allowing them to buy and sell these permits among themselves. By assigning a value to emissions allowances, these systems drive emissions reductions by influencing fuel and electricity prices.

These market-based approaches encourage firms to reduce emissions in a cost-effective way by choosing abatement levels where their marginal abatement costs are equal to those of other firms – thereby minimizing the total cost of pollution reduction across the economy. Ultimately, market-based mechanisms have the potential to be cost-effective by optimizing pollution reduction efforts.

Market-based policies are often applied with partial coverage, focusing on emissions from large emitters (power and industrial plants, transportation,...). For instance, the European Union Emissions Trading System (EU-ETS), while covering a significant portion of energy-related CO_2 emissions, falls short of addressing all emission sources.

Other *energy taxes*, such as excise taxes on electricity use or vehicle ownership, can also affect GHG emissions. Taxes on specific fuels, like coal, can be effective in reducing carbon-intensive practices. However, they remain narrowly focused on particular sources of emissions and may not sufficiently incentivize broader shifts toward more sustainable alternatives.

Carbon taxation is generally considered as a Pigouvian tax. Named after the economist Arthur Pigou, a Pigouvian tax is a corrective tax imposed on any market activity that generates negative externalities, which are costs borne by third parties not involved in the transaction. The tax is set equal to the external cost created by the activity, with the intention of internalizing these costs and aligning private incentives with social welfare goals. In the context of environmental economics, a Pigouvian tax can be applied to activities that cause pollution or environmental degradation, such as emissions from factories or vehicles. By imposing a tax on these harmful activities, policymakers aim to encourage individuals and firms to reduce their pollution levels or invest in cleaner technologies.

2.3.1.2 Command-and-Control Instruments

Traditional *regulatory standards*, known as *command-and-control* regulations, come in two main forms: technology-based and performance-based (Stavins, 1997). Technology-based standards require firms to use specific equipment or processes, while performance-based standards set emission or activity-level targets but give firms flexibility in achieving them. While technology-based and performance-based standards can both contribute to environmental goals, these regulatory approaches often lead to high compliance costs and may discourage innovation. In particular, technology-based standards restrict technological choices, while performance-based standards often fail to provide ongoing incentives for adopting cleaner technologies.

The main command-and-control instruments include (Parry, 2012):

- *Energy efficiency standards* mandate minimum fuel economy requirements for vehicles sold by different manufacturers or set a maximum CO_2 emission rate per kilometer. Credits trading can allow some producers to offset deficiencies by purchasing credits from others exceeding the standard. These standards also extend to improving energy efficiency in new buildings, household appliances, and other electricity-consuming durable goods.
- *Emissions standards* cap the maximum allowable CO_2 emissions per kilowatt hour generated by power plants, with flexibility provided through credit trading. Some generators that fall short of the standard can buy credits from those that surpass it.

In practice, governments often adopt a combination of regulatory measures, using multiple independent instruments to target emission reductions in a way that can resemble the effects of comprehensive carbon pricing. For example, emissions standards for power plants are frequently paired with energy efficiency standards for vehicles and electricity-consuming goods.

2.3.1.3 Public Support

Public support includes *transfers* to households and *subsidies* to businesses to incentivize emission reduction and energy intensity, as well as *public expenditures* for environmental protection or promoting cleaner technologies. This category also encompasses *fiscal expenditures*, such as tax credits or targeted tax reductions. This indirect support is supplemented by *direct intervention* by public authorities involving public investment (including fundamental research) or green public procurement.

Incentives are often targeted at specific technologies or sources, such as renewable fuels. These include a variety of policies aimed at supporting renewable energy production, including generation subsidies and feed-in tariffs that guarantee fixed prices for electricity from renewable sources.

Feed-in tariffs (FITs) are renewable energy support mechanisms that provide guaranteed payments to renewable energy producers for the electricity they generate and feed into the grid. Under a feed-in tariff scheme, renewable energy producers, such as homeowners with solar panels or wind farm operators, are compensated at a predetermined rate for each kilowatt-hour of electricity they produce, typically over a fixed contract period, regardless of the market price for electricity. Feed-in tariffs are designed to incentivize investment in renewable energy generation by offering producers a stable and predictable income stream, thus reducing the financial risks associated with renewable energy projects. FITs aim to accelerate the adoption of renewable energy technologies, stimulate renewable energy production, and contribute to the transition toward a low-carbon energy system.

Feebates are another policy tool commonly used, particularly in the automotive and power sectors. In the context of vehicle sales, feebates involve imposing fees on new vehicles with CO_2 emissions above a predetermined pivot point, while offering rebates or subsidies for vehicles with emissions below that threshold. Similarly, in the power sector, feebates charge generators per kilowatt-hour based on their CO_2 emissions per kWh relative to the pivot point, with rebates granted to generators falling below this benchmark. Feebate schemes can be designed to either generate revenue or remain revenue-neutral, depending on whether the pivot point is set above or below the industry's average emission rate.

Finally, shifting toward *environmentally friendly (or green) public investment* will help reduce GHG emissions. Encouraging green public investment requires policymakers to clearly define what qualifies as *green* investment and to ensure that this definition guides the evaluation of spending proposals. This understanding should be embedded in both government budget planning and long-term economic strategies. According to Bowen (2021) "public investment is green if and only if it augments production of green industries, supports green occupations or skills, or promotes consumption of goods and services deemed to be green." In addition, substantial public investment will be essential for developing infrastructure that strengthens economies' resilience to climate change and related natural disasters.

Direct public interventions primarily take the form of support for green R&D, investment in large-scale infrastructure, and efforts to improve the energy efficiency of both public and private buildings. The public sector's role in the transition is justified by the fact that environmental issues largely arise from market failures – such as those linked to human-induced climate change, unpriced externalities like local pollution, and network effects observed in systems like power grids. For example, environmental R&D is often underfunded by the private sector. Although knowledge related to natural capital and environmental technologies is non-rivalrous, intellectual property rights create a degree of exclusivity that incentivizes innovation. However, perfect exclusivity is rare, meaning that private actors typically cannot capture the full social value of new ideas, resulting in suboptimal levels of investment in R&D (Bowen, 2021).

2.3.1.4 *Voluntary Instruments*

In addition to mandatory policy measures, voluntary instruments can also play a significant role in strategies to reduce GHG emissions. In some cases, the prospect of future regulatory requirements is enough to motivate firms to enter into voluntary agreements. Companies may proactively reduce emissions to avoid the risk of more stringent, binding regulations. This dynamic helps explain the growing appeal of voluntary measures in climate policy frameworks (see Chapter 7).

Large companies seeking to achieve carbon neutrality increasingly rely on *Voluntary Carbon Markets* (VCMs) to offset their emissions. These markets enable entities to purchase carbon credits that represent verified reductions in greenhouse gas (GHG) emissions. By doing so, companies can invest in projects such as reforestation, renewable energy, or methane capture to compensate for their residual emissions. As of 2022, the VCM had grown into a USD 2 billion market, underscoring its expanding role in global climate action.

Voluntary actions can also take place at the household level supported by initiatives such as labeling programs for energy-efficient buildings, vehicles, and appliances. More broadly, households can contribute by switching to energy-efficient lighting, purchasing low-consumption equipment, reducing unnecessary packaging or opting for recyclable and sustainable packaging materials, and adopting more climate-friendly diets.

2.3.2 Assessment of Policy Instruments

Carbon pricing mechanisms, such as carbon taxes and emissions trading systems (ETS), are widely recognized as effective tools for reducing GHG emissions, primarily because they offer a cost-efficient means of abatement from both economic and social perspectives. Their effectiveness lies in the market-based nature of the instrument: by sending an explicit carbon price signal, they encourage shifts in behavior and production choices while minimizing adjustment costs. In contrast to prescriptive regulations or standards that typically focus on specific sectors or activities, carbon pricing promotes efficiency by equalizing marginal abatement costs across all emitters, allowing for more flexible and economically optimal emission reductions.

However, the effectiveness of carbon pricing depends heavily on its design. Well-crafted policies that generate public revenue and allocate it toward socially beneficial uses are particularly impactful. For example, ETS require robust credit markets and mechanisms to stabilize prices in order to function effectively. Despite their advantages, carbon pricing mechanisms can be politically and socially difficult to implement, as they may impose disproportionate burdens on households and trade-exposed industries – often more so than other policy tools.

In the absence of carbon pricing, alternative instruments such as regulations and public investments can provide viable alternatives, though generally with lower overall efficiency. Regulatory measures must be carefully crafted to harness mitigation potential across all sectors and should ideally be complemented by broad credit trading systems to minimize costs. Public investments play a critical role in delivering public goods that markets tend to underprovide, such as foundational research and breakthrough technologies like carbon capture. By contrast, subsidies and fiscal expenditures are often considered less effective, as they risk distorting markets by favoring specific technologies over potentially more cost-effective alternatives.

Regarding acceptability, carbon pricing often encounters greater resistance than alternative instruments like regulations and public investments. Regulatory measures, public spending, and subsidies tend to enjoy broader public support, largely because carbon taxes raise concerns about potentially regressive distributional impacts. Emission quota systems (such as cap-and-trade) may be marginally more acceptable to consumers, as their price effects are less direct and typically absorbed first by producers before being passed on to end-users.

Overall, while carbon pricing remains the preferred instrument for its effectiveness and efficiency in reducing GHG emissions, alternative instruments such as regulations and public investments can complement efforts, especially in addressing acceptability concerns and achieving broader societal consensus. However, a careful balance must be struck between effectiveness, efficiency, and acceptability when selecting and implementing policy instruments to tackle climate change effectively.

In practice, countries have implemented multifaceted mitigation strategies that combine a range of policy instruments, including carbon pricing, investment tax credits, subsidies, infrastructure investments, regulations, and R&D support for low-carbon technologies. These strategies vary across countries, shaped by their distinct political, institutional, and cultural contexts. Box 2.2

> **BOX 2.2: Diverging Policy Packages across Countries: The European Union's *Fit-for-55* and the US Inflation Reduction Act**
>
> The EU-ETS, initiated in 2005, is a cornerstone of the EU's efforts to combat climate change, covering around 40 percent of GHG emissions in Europe. However, the system has faced challenges, particularly an oversupply of emission allowances leading to low prices that fail to drive significant emissions reductions. In response, the European Commission introduced the *Fit for 55 package* in July 2021, proposing reforms to the EU-ETS. This includes punctually lowering the emission cap upon the package's enactment and then instituting a more aggressive annual reduction rate of 4.2 percent, compared to the current 2.2 percent.
>
> To address concerns about carbon leakage and ensure competitiveness, the *Fit for 55* package introduces a Carbon Border Adjustment Mechanism (CBAM). This mechanism aims to prevent a widening gap between EU carbon pricing and that of third countries, thereby reducing the risk of increased emissions in non-EU countries due to stricter EU climate policies. Notably, the CBAM recognizes the EU's efforts in reducing territorial carbon emissions over recent decades while acknowledging its status as a major global importer of GHGs. The CBAM will be phased in gradually from 2023 to 2026 and will apply to imported products, particularly those from sectors deemed to have a high risk of carbon leakage. Projections indicate that the CBAM could lead to additional costs for European industries, impacting their price competitiveness. However, the effect on consumer prices is expected to be moderate, primarily due to substitution effects between intermediate consumption. Nonetheless, there may be limitations in representing certain substitution scenarios due to data aggregation (Bellora and Fontagné, 2023).
>
> The *Inflation Reduction Act* (IRA), which was passed in August 2022, is one of the most significant federal efforts to combat climate change in US history. This nearly USD 400 billion funding is channeled through a combination of tax incentives, grants, and loan guarantees focused on clean energy, over the next ten years. The IRA is expected to catalyze reductions in US GHG

by about 40 percent by 2030, relative to 2005 levels. IRA's wide-ranging provisions are designed to spur innovation and investment in renewable energy, energy efficiency, and the transition to a cleaner economy. The Act includes incentives for the adoption of electric vehicles, investments in renewable energy sources such as solar and wind power, and funding for the development of carbon capture and storage technologies. It also promotes the production and use of clean hydrogen and supports the modernization of the electric grid to enhance its reliability and capacity to integrate renewable energies.

Additionally, the IRA contains significant provisions for tax credits and rebates directly aimed at both businesses and consumers to encourage the shift toward more sustainable practices and technologies. For households, this includes incentives for energy-efficient home improvements, the installation of solar panels, and the purchase of electric vehicles, making clean technologies more accessible and affordable. For industries, it offers tax credits for renewable energy projects and green manufacturing, fostering a more sustainable industrial base.

illustrates two different transition strategies between Europe and the United States. Table 2.3 gives a detailed assessment of the type of instrument used.

Scholars studying sustainability transitions have extensively analyzed the effectiveness of these policy tools, emphasizing the importance of policy mixes tailored to different transition phases. Such analyses highlight the need to align policies with the specific transition stage, combining instruments that support emerging low-carbon solutions with those that actively phase out carbon-intensive practices (Meadowcroft and Rosenbloom, 2023). Managing policy feedback processes is also crucial for accelerating change. Transition phases – emergence, acceleration, and stabilization – require different policy approaches, ranging from supporting R&D and fostering innovation to scaling up solutions and stabilizing new institutional contexts (Figure 2.5). Government procurement policies and adoption

Table 2.3 Assessment of policy instruments

Instrument	Criteria	Environmental effectiveness	Cost-effectiveness	Meets distributional considerations	Institutional feasibility
Regulations and standards	Emissions level set directly, though subject to exceptions.	Depends on deferrals and compliance.	Depends on design; uniform application often leads to higher overall compliance costs.	Depends on level playing field. Small/new actors may be disadvantaged.	Depends on technical capacity; popular with regulators in countries with weakly functioning markets.
Taxes and charges	Depends on ability to set tax at a level that induces behavioral change.	Better with broad application; higher administrative costs where institutions are weak.	Regressive; can be ameliorated with revenue recycling.	Often politically unpopular; may be difficult to enforce with underdeveloped institutions.	
Tradable permits	Depends on emissions cap, participation and compliance.	Decreases with limited participation and fewer sectors.	Depends on initial permit allocation.	May pose difficulties for small emitters.	Requires well-functioning markets and complementary institutions.

Voluntary agreements	Depends on program design, including clear targets, a baseline scenario, third-party involvement in design and review, and monitoring provisions.	Depends on flexibility and extent of government incentives, rewards and penalties.	Benefits accrue only to participants.	Often politically popular; requires significant number of administrative staff.
Subsidies and incentives	Depends on program design; less certain than regulations/standards.	Depends on level and program design; can be market-distorting.	Benefits selected participants, possibly some that do not need it.	Popular with recipients; potential resistance from vested interests. Can be difficult to phase out.
Research and development	Depends on consistent funding, when technologies are developed and policies for diffusion. May have high benefits in the long term.	Depends on program design and the degree of risk.	Benefits initially selected participants; potentially easy for funds to be misallocated.	Requires many separate decisions. Depends on research capacity and long-term funding.

(continued)

Table 2.3 (cont.)

Instrument	Criteria	Environmental effectiveness	Cost-effectiveness	Meets distributional considerations	Institutional feasibility
Information policies	Depends on how consumers use the information; most effective in combination with other policies.	Potentially low cost, but depends on program design.	May be less effective for groups (e.g., low-income) that lack access to information.	Depends on cooperation from special interest groups.	

Source: IPCC (2018)

Note: Evaluations are predicated on assumptions that instruments are representative of best practice rather than theoretically perfect. This assessment is based primarily on experiences and published reports from developed countries, as the number of peer-reviewed articles on the effectiveness of instruments in other countries is limited. Applicability in specific countries, sectors, and circumstances – particularly developing countries and economies in transition – may differ greatly. Environmental and cost-effectiveness may be enhanced when instruments are strategically combined and adapted to local circumstances.

2 THE ECONOMICS OF CLIMATE CHANGE MITIGATION

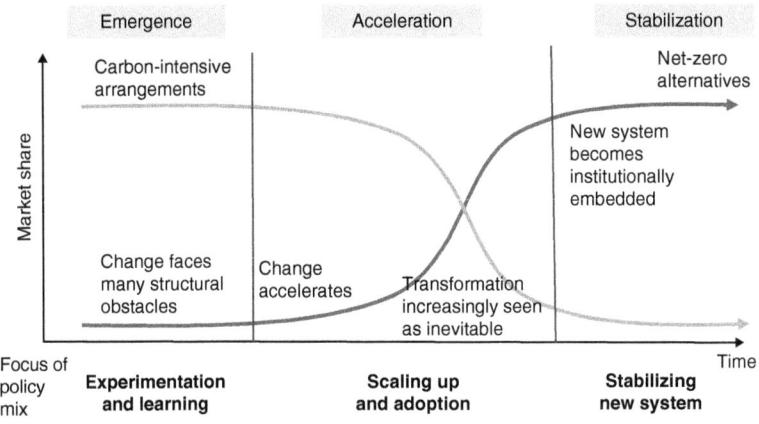

FIGURE 2.5 Transition phases
Source: Meadowcroft and Rosenbloom (2023)

incentives are effective in the early transition stages, while mandates for renewable energy and electric vehicles are vital during later phases. Carbon pricing and regulatory measures often extend across multiple phases of the transition, requiring adjustments as transitions progress. These insights underscore the dynamic and iterative nature of policy formulation and implementation in driving long-term sustainable transformation.

2.3.3 Developments and General Trends in Mitigation Policies

The OECD has been actively involved in documenting climate policies across countries. One significant contribution is the Climate Actions and Policies Measurement Framework (CAPMF), which is the most comprehensive internationally harmonized climate mitigation policy database available. It tracks 130 policy variables, which are aggregated into 56 key climate actions and policies from 1990 to 2022 for OECD countries and OECD partner countries (49 countries). CAPMF assesses policy stringency, which measures how strongly policies encourage emissions reductions. It also offers average stringency values and the number of adopted policies for different sectors or policy areas, such as electricity and GHG emissions targets, as

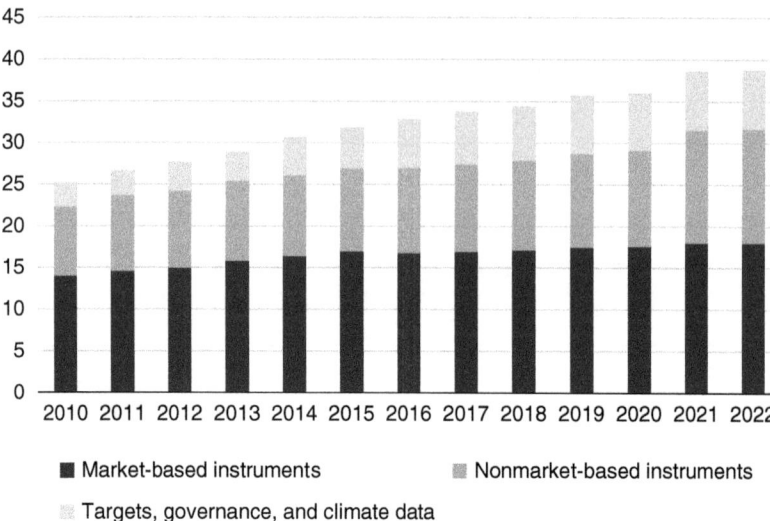

FIGURE 2.6 Evolution of policy adoption – number of adopted policies, 2010–2022, OECD average
Source: OECD

well as for policy types, including sectoral, cross-sectoral, and international policies. The framework's structure is detailed in Nachtigall, et al. (2022). The number of policies adopted has increased over 2010–2022 at the OECD average level, in particular for nonmarket-based instruments (Figure 2.6). It reached close to forty measures in 2022, out of fifty-six. When accounting for non-OECD countries, the average reached thirty-one policies in place in 2020, indicating that there are still additional policy options countries may consider. In 2020, the number of policies in place varies considerably across countries, ranging from thirteen in Peru to forty-five in France.

The OECD's Effective Carbon Rates (ECRs) report also offers a comprehensive assessment of ETS, carbon taxes, and fuel excise taxes, while also detailing how these policies are applied across different sectors and fuels. According to the latest update of the OECD Effective Carbon Rates database, covering G20 countries except for Saudi Arabia, it was found that 49 percent of CO_2 emissions from energy use were priced in 2021, up from 37 percent in 2018. This notable increase was primarily driven by changes in ETS, including significant developments in Canada, China, and Germany.

During the period from 2018 to 2021, explicit carbon prices resulting from carbon taxes or ETS witnessed a substantial increase, leading to higher effective carbon rates across various fossil fuels, particularly coal and natural gas. Presently, thirteen G20 countries have implemented explicit carbon pricing instruments at either the national or subnational level or have participated in the EU-ETS. However, there remains a significant disparity in coverage and rates across countries and sectors, with average explicit carbon prices remaining relatively low when considering all emissions and countries (OECD, 2022).

According to the IMF, the latest G20 average explicit carbon price is estimated at USD 8. Carbon prices show increasing divergence among countries, raising concerns about competitiveness and potential leakage (see Chapter 3). While countries with the highest effective carbon rates in 2018 experienced further price increases, those with low rates saw little change. Moreover, substantial variation persists in effective carbon rates across sectors, with major emitting sectors still facing very low average effective carbon rates.

2.4 CONCLUSION

The exploration of the economics of climate change mitigation underscores the complex interplay between economic growth, environmental sustainability, and policy intervention. A significant takeaway is the central role of economic mechanisms, such as carbon pricing, in driving effective climate action. Carbon pricing, whether through taxes or cap-and-trade systems, provides a market-based approach to internalizing the external costs of emissions. This mechanism aligns economic incentives with environmental goals, promoting cost-effective emissions reductions. However, the implementation and scaling of such mechanisms remain challenging, often requiring careful consideration of socioeconomic impacts, equity concerns, and political feasibility. Policy instruments for reducing GHG emissions are diverse, from regulatory approaches to market-based solutions. Each instrument comes with its own set of strengths and trade-offs, emphasizing the need for a comprehensive and flexible policy mix. This approach is critical for addressing the multifaceted nature of climate change, which impacts different sectors and regions in varying ways. However, while the global trend is moving toward more stringent and sophisticated mitigation policies, the pace and effectiveness of these measures vary significantly across countries. This variation underscores the importance of international cooperation and the sharing of best practices to enhance global mitigation efforts.

3 The Macroeconomic Effects of Mitigation Policies

3.1 INTRODUCTION

The transition to a low-carbon economy requires a major transformation, on a scale comparable to past industrial revolutions. This transformation is based on three main changes that concern all economic agents. First, on the corporate side, the challenge is to redirect technical progress toward green technologies, which requires new investment expenditures, with a possible impact on productivity and, therefore, on growth. Second, capital must move from the carbon-intensive sector to the green sector, implying a massive reallocation of financing flows on capital markets, with possible assets becoming *stranded* or unproductive due to changes in regulations. Third, on the household side, behaviors must adapt to the transition with the need to consume differently, but also less – what we usually call *sobriety* – with a potential impact on well being and aggregate demand. All these changes will have macroeconomic impacts both in the short and the long run.

Given the still limited level of international coordination on mitigation policies, a key macroeconomic aspect of the transition lies in competitiveness challenges that emerge from differences in national approaches. These divergences, along with the policy responses they prompt, can generate significant shifts in trade flows and broader impacts on economic stability.

The overall effect of the transition on growth and welfare is far from conclusive. In the long term, the reorientation of technical progress may lead to green growth that is stronger than the growth based on fossil fuel was or would have been. The falling cost of renewable energies is a sign that new growth is possible. However, during the transition, financing the necessary investments, which do not increase growth potential, is likely to incur an economic and social cost. While the extra investment will have a positive effect on growth via demand, it will be channeled toward reducing fossil fuel use rather than enhancing efficiency or expanding productive capacity. As a result, the transition may temporarily dampen productivity and carry a well-being cost that conventional indicators such as GDP do not fully capture.

3.2 MITIGATION POLICIES AND ECONOMIC GROWTH

Mitigation policies are generally perceived as a burden on economic activity, at least during the transition phase. In the short term, these policies, whether in the form of carbon pricing or environmental regulation, increase production costs and limit the range of available technologies. Hence, mitigation policies are commonly perceived as having negative impacts on productivity and, therefore, on economic growth. In the longer term, however, well-designed mitigation policies, by promoting innovation, could lead to increased profitability and productivity, compensating possibly the cost of the policies. This is the hypothesis proposed by Michael Porter in the early 1990s.

3.2.1 *Green Innovation and Productivity*

The relationship between green innovation and productivity has given rise to an abundant literature, both on the theoretical and empirical sides. Overall, while the effects of the energy transition on the corporate sector are far from clear-cut, it is key to understand the various mechanisms at play to fully capture the growth impact of climate mitigation policies.

3.2.1.1 *Direct and Indirect Transmission Channels of Mitigation Policies in the Corporate Sector*

Climate mitigation policies, whether environmental regulations or carbon taxes, require firms to use some of their resources to reduce pollution or limit production. Environmental taxes, tradable emission permits, or fees impose additional costs on consumers and increase production costs for firms. Hence, at least in the short and medium term, traditional conceptions of environmental policy tend to view it as a cost or burden on economic activity. Environmental regulations and mitigation policies (carbon taxes, tradable emission permits, waste treatment costs, or performance standards) often require corporations to allocate resources to pollution prevention and abatement, which are not typically considered value-added activities because they add cost to something that would otherwise be free. Alternatively, companies may reduce production to comply with these regulations, which may constrain operational scale and hinder growth. The effects of these regulations can be both direct, such as increased business costs due to pollution reduction, and indirect, such as higher input prices in industries affected by regulation (Koźluk and Zipperer, 2014). Indirect effects may take the form of effects on firm survival rates, and if environmental protection forces less efficient firms out of the market, overall productivity is likely to increase. However, additional (entry) costs or age-differentiated regulations may discourage entry and exit, reduce market competition, and protect potentially inefficient incumbents and obsolete capital stock, leading to lower productivity levels and growth. On the other hand, environmental policies can also encourage the creation of industries or activities that would not otherwise exist or that would benefit from economies of scale.

Encouraging innovation through policies can boost productivity growth. In the 1990s, Michael Porter suggested that effectively crafted environmental regulations (strict but flexible) might spur innovation in firms (develop new, less costly production processes and high-value-added products), leading to increased productivity and profitability. Such regulations, serving as lasting incentives for innovation, could positively impact both the level and growth rate of productivity by influencing input composition or altering the production process through the development and adoption of new technologies. These innovations may even offset the increased costs of reducing emissions. Porter's hypothesis has been met with much skepticism. Critics generally focus on the argument that if productive opportunities existed, they would already be exploited by firms. Porter's hypothesis would be valid because of market imperfections that prevent firms from taking profitable actions. Moreover, still, according to Porter, countries that adopt stringent environmental standards first (*first movers*) also enjoy a competitive advantage over their competitors (Gray and Shadbegian, 1993, 1995).

Jaffe and Palmer (1997) introduced two versions to facilitate empirical tests and result interpretation. The *weak* version of the Porter Hypothesis suggests that environmental regulation drives innovation without specifying its economic effects. In this scenario, firms innovate to reduce compliance costs, representing the initial causal link in Figure 3.1. Importantly, the *weak* version does not assess whether this innovation positively or negatively impacts a firm's economic performance. On the other hand, the *strong* version contends that regulation compels firms to discover new products or processes, increasing profits while adhering to regulations (the second causal link in Figure 3.1). In this view, the benefits of regulation outweigh the associated costs.

Firms within the supply chain, both upstream and downstream of regulated entities, may also be indirectly impacted by regulations and respond through innovation (Dechezleprêtre and Kruse, 2022). Greaker (2006) and Heyes and Kapur (2011) theoretically outline these mechanisms in a model where the downstream-regulated firm prompts innovation in its specialized technology supplier (upstream), seeking a temporary monopoly through a patent for pollution

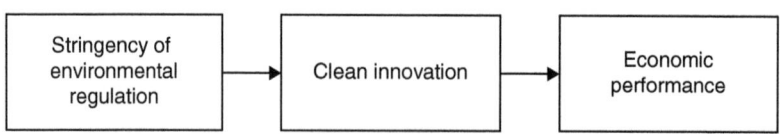

FIGURE 3.1 Causal links involved in the Porter Hypothesis
Source: Dechezleprêtre and Kruse (2022)

abatement technology supply. Their model suggests that neglecting these indirect effects significantly underestimates the innovation response by firms.

3.2.1.2 Empirical Evidence of Mitigation Policy Effects on Productivity

Studies on the impact of climate policy on productivity have produced mixed results, as the relationship between productivity gains and mitigation policies is complex. Pollution-control technologies, as a result of environmental regulation or carbon taxation, can have a negative, positive, or zero effect on the production process itself.

3.2.1.2.1 Negative Effects Negative effects can occur in both short and long term, and have a variety of origins. A few empirical studies (Christiansen and Haveman, 1981) consider that the fall in factor productivity between the early 1960s and the late 1970s in the United States can be partly attributed to environmental regulation, although there is no consensus on this thesis. The main explanation lies in the reallocation of productive resources: shifting inputs from production to pollution control is estimated to have accounted for 8 to 12 percent of the slowdown in productivity growth in the US manufacturing sector during the 1965–1979 period. There may also be crowding-out effects, as resources are diverted away from primary production and other productive activities, including R&D, toward the development and implementation of pollution abatement technologies (Sims and Smith, 1985). An efficiency problem can be observed insofar as the activity of pollution control and abatement, and the adjustments it involves in the firm, can interfere with the existing production process and reduce the efficiency of inputs that have not been diverted to the abatement activity (Gray and Shadbegian, 1995, and Everett, 2010). Barbera and McConnell (1986) show that the costs generated by environmental regulations have partially dampened labor productivity in several US industries. Negative effects via investment may also drive lower productivity: Environmental regulations can drive up the price of capital by increasing the cost of capital goods required for pollution control. Uncertainty about the evolution of regulations can also slow down investment or R&D, as the company will have to adjust to an unforeseen polluting and costly investment by reducing production or making new investments (Viscusi, 1983).

3.2.1.2.2 Positive Effects Climate mitigation policies can have positive effects on productivity by contributing to capital renewal (Barbera and McConnell, 1990), for example, by shortening the economic life of polluting production technologies (Meyers and Nakamura, 1980). However, Barbera and McConnell (1990) point out that the overall effect is uncertain, as there may be offsetting effects between the costs of different factors of production. In addition, distortions arising due to the asymmetric design of mitigation policies, such as targeted taxes instead of a uniform carbon tax, may dampen the positive effects of these measures. Stricter regulations applied to new installations compared to older ones can hinder capital renewal (Jaffe et al., 1995; Ambec et al., 2013). Everett et al. (2010) highlight the disincentive effect firms face when they anticipate overly stringent environmental regulations. Their argument suggests that, in response to tighter rules, firms may develop innovative compliance strategies that succeed in lowering GHG emissions – but often at the expense of production. In such cases, environmental innovations become technological trade-offs, balancing regulatory compliance with goals related to productivity and competitiveness.

3.2.1.3 Impact of Mitigation Policies on Innovation and R&D
Numerous empirical studies have also explored Porter's hypothesis, examining the interplay between environmental regulation, innovation, and economic performance. Early research concentrated on the *strong* form of the hypothesis but produced mixed and inconclusive results. On the other hand, empirical tests currently focus on the *weak* version of the hypothesis. These tests also contribute to endogenous growth models, specifically addressing directed technical

progress, wherein the central focus is on how regulation influences innovation.

An influential article by Popp (2002) first highlighted, based on US data, the effect of energy prices on innovative activity (patent productivity) over the period 1970–1994. The author finds that a 10% rise in energy prices leads in the long term to a 4% increase in patents filed in the energy sector. Beyond the US case, Verdolini and Galeotti (2011) estimate Popp's model on Italian data and obtain similar results. Koleda and Pillu (2011) estimate the same model for Germany, France, Japan, and the United States on patent stocks over a period from 1978 to 2003. They show that a 10% rise in energy prices indeed induces an increase of around 10% in patent filings toward renewable and efficient energy technologies.

These positive effects are more marked in certain sectors. For example, Aghion et al. (2016) examine innovation activity in the automotive industry and show that companies tend to innovate more in low-carbon technologies (electric or hybrid cars) and less in high-carbon technologies when faced with higher fuel prices. The authors show that a 10% higher fuel price is associated with around 10% more low-carbon patents and 7% fewer high-carbon patents.

Studies that seek to characterize the main determinants of green innovation show that regulation is the factor that has significant effects, whether direct (e.g., taxes) or indirect (e.g., via the impact on energy prices) on innovation efforts, alongside other factors such as corporate organizational strategies, technology and market forces (Horbach et al., 2013). Studies also show that the innovation response can be rapid following a rise in energy prices.

Popp (2006) also confirms the importance of national legislation on corporate environmental innovation decisions in the US, Japan, and Germany. The author finds an almost immediate response (between three and five years) from innovation to low-carbon regulations in these three countries. Similarly, Calel and Dechezleprêtre (2014) show that in the European Union, innovation activity (measured by invention patent filings) in low-carbon technologies by companies participating in the EU Emissions Trading System (EU-ETS) has increased, bearing in mind that, prior to the introduction of the EU-ETS, innovation activity by companies participating in the scheme and those not participating were similar.

More recently, Dechezleprêtre and Kruse (2022) empirically evaluate the impact of climate policy stringency on innovation and economic performance, both directly in regulated sectors and indirectly through supply chain connections. Utilizing global firm-level and sector-level data, their results indicate that climate policies effectively drive innovation in low-carbon technologies within directly regulated sectors. However, there is no significant evidence of climate policies inducing innovation along the supply chain. Additionally, the study finds that climate policies, facilitated by clean innovation, do not adversely affect or improve the economic performance of directly regulated firms. This suggests that past climate policies have not substantially burdened firms' performance, and clean innovation may help offset the potential costs of new climate policies.

Studies also highlight the crucial role of environmental policy implementation (market reaction, guaranteeing the value of investments). For a whole stream of literature (including Acemoglu et al. (2006), or Frondel et al. (2007)), the rigorous implementation of environmental policy is a key factor in encouraging innovation, more so than the choice of environmental policy instruments.

Finally, Jorgenson and Wilcoxen (1990) found that investment to increase capital in response to a more restrictive environmental policy in the US would have reduced economic growth by 0.2 percent per annum between 1974 and 1985, but that these effects could have been much smaller if more effective environmental policy choices had been made.

Overall, the empirical literature enables us to identify the optimal combination of policies likely to achieve the required emissions reduction at the lowest cost. It also shows that a low-carbon economy, oriented toward a more efficient use of its energy resources, will require investment in innovation and new technologies, including investment to renew the capital stock, to replace ageing infrastructure, and thus reduce future risks linked to environmental change. Moreover, undertaking these structural changes early can significantly reduce the overall cost of shifting to a more sustainable growth path. For Everett et al. (2010), economic growth thus makes it possible to allocate these changes without necessarily reducing investment in other areas that concern the well-being of individuals and societies. Acemoglu et al. (2012) point out that "public intervention should start as soon as possible, especially with regard to subsidies for research and the dissemination of green technologies."

3.2.2 Investment Needs

Additional investment is another key aspect of how the green transition affects the corporate sector, as firms must upgrade production processes to reduce carbon intensity. Green investments span several categories, including renewable energies, energy efficiency and conservation, sustainable agriculture and forestry, sustainable transport, and waste management and recycling. Meeting the intermediate CO_2 reduction targets by 2030 and achieving net-zero emissions by 2050 necessitates significant investment in infrastructure, particularly in energy and transport networks. According to the OECD, a modest 10 percent annual increase in investment (from USD 6.3 trillion to USD 6.9 trillion by 2030) could align infrastructure development with the Paris Agreement goals. However, the shift toward a zero-carbon economy demands more than incremental improvements; it calls for a systemic transformation of existing infrastructures. Given that many electricity and transport infrastructures are due for replacement, decarbonization could serve as a catalyst to expedite their substitution and enhance overall quality. The electricity and transport sectors, contributing over 50 percent of total GHG emissions in OECD countries, warrant special attention.

Achieving net-zero emissions necessitates the phasing out of high-carbon energy systems and substantial investment in new clean energy infrastructure. The electricity network, in particular, assumes a crucial role in the future, aligning with countries' decarbonization strategies that prioritize *electrifying everything* with an increased share of renewable energy sources. Success depends on upgrading electricity networks to accommodate both intermittent energy sources and increased grid demand. Coordinated progress in both areas is essential. Recent trends in global energy investment reflect a strong shift: since 2021, investment in clean energy has outpaced fossil fuel investment by nearly a factor of three, led primarily by advances in clean electrification. Should this growth trajectory persist, projected expenditures in 2030 on low-emission power, grids, storage, and end-use electrification would surpass the levels required to meet worldwide climate commitments.

Despite notable progress in clean energy technologies and rising global investment, significant disparities in the energy transition remain. Grid expansion and modernization investments lag in several countries, undermining the integration of renewable energy sources. While solar and wind technologies receive growing support, they require complementary investments in infrastructure that enhances system flexibility and reliability. Supply chain constraints, workforce skill gaps, and uneven geographic distribution of clean energy financing further complicate the transition. In many emerging economies, the pace of clean energy investment remains sluggish, and large segments of the population still lack access to modern, reliable energy services.

Beyond clean electrification, progress across other areas of the energy transition remains less encouraging. Although energy efficiency investments are rising, they fall short of meeting ambitious climate goals. Low-emission fuels are attracting more capital, driven largely by supportive policy measures, but growth is occurring from a low base.

According to the International Energy Agency (IEA)'s Net Zero Emissions (NZE) scenario, clean energy investment is expected to outpace fossil fuel investment by a ratio of about 10 to 1 in 2030,

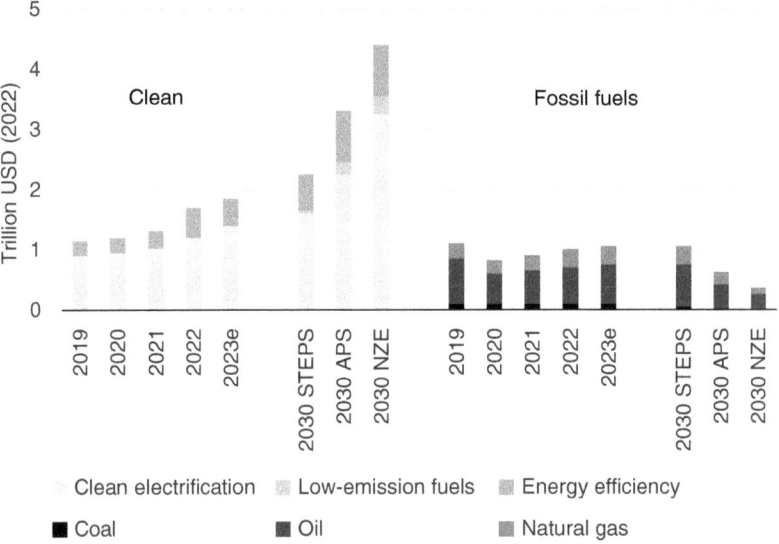

FIGURE 3.2 Historical investment in energy benchmarked against needs in the IEA scenario in 2030
Source: IEA, World Energy Investment (2023)
Notes: STEPS: Stated Policies Scenario; APS: Announced Pledges Scenario; NZE: Net Zero Emissions by 2050 Scenario. 2023e: estimated values for 2023.

rising from a factor of approximately 1.8 to 1 in 2023. Achieving this scenario hinges on a substantial and sustained uptick in clean energy investment, emphasizing that the pace of such investments directly influences the speed of the transition away from fossil fuels (Figure 3.2).

A primary clean energy transition challenge in transport networks is ensuring an adequate number of recharging stations to meet the rising demand for electric vehicles. Furthermore, emerging technologies like hydrogen and energy storage may require substantial investments in production, storage, and pipeline infrastructures to support their integration into the broader energy landscape.

In addition to energy and transportation, a major share of the required clean investment must go toward building renovation to improve energy efficiency. In residential buildings, the transition requires investment to replace heating vectors (oil and gas) and thermal insulation. In the tertiary sector, the total investment required to renovate areas subject to country-specific regulation could also be important. Investment required in industrial and agricultural sectors is generally smaller but varies across countries depending on their production structure. In advanced economies, such as the EU member states, building energy efficiency may account for between one-third and one-half of total green spending (Tagliapietra et al., 2022).

Green investments contribute not only to environmental sustainability but also to broader macroeconomic gains. By reducing energy consumption, greater efficiency lowers energy costs and creates positive spillovers across the economy. These effects can boost output, support job creation, and ease pressure on energy prices, thereby strengthening the overall competitiveness of economies.

The IEA identifies two primary drivers of these positive macroeconomic impacts, as depicted in Figure 3.3 (IEA, 2014). First, investments in sectors that produce green goods and services directly boosts production and employment. Second, energy efficiency improvements reduce energy demand and generate cost savings. These savings raise household disposable income, which can in turn stimulate greater consumption of other goods and services (spending effect).

Furthermore, the cost savings from energy efficiency measures can raise profits for firms and producers. These gains may

FIGURE 3.3 Energy demand reduction effects
Source: IEA (2014)

be reinvested (the reinvestment effect) or passed on to consumers through lower prices (the price effect) (IEA, 2014). Together, these channels illustrate the multifaceted macroeconomic benefits of green investments, reinforcing the link between environmental responsibility and economic prosperity.

A final key question related to the macroeconomic impact of green investment expenditures is the extent to which new capital may crowd out other forms of investment. Firm-level studies provide evidence of such effects: Popp and Newell (2012) show that alternative energy R&D displaced other R&D in the United States between 1971 and 2002, while Hottenrott and Rexhäuser (2013) find that regulation-induced green technologies crowded out other R&D investment in Germany between 2006 and 2008. Beyond innovation-specific investments, broader analyses of environmental protection spending also point to crowding-out risks. Using Germany – where environmental regulation is particularly stringent – as a test case, Weche (2019) identifies crowding-out effects of environmental protection investment on other business investment, both overall and within subcategories such as add-on measures and investments in renewable energy.

Crowding-out effects could also arise from government expenditures in support of green investment that would take place at the expense of other investments from the private sector. Battini et al. (2021) empirically show that, independently of the sector, spending on measures targeting good environmental outcomes, like investing in clean energy and ecosystem conservation, can produce more growth than environmentally detrimental measures. By contrast, spending on non-eco-friendly energy generation is found to crowd out other forms of domestic spending to a larger extent.

3.3 IMPACT ON CAPITAL MARKETS – THE ISSUE OF ASSET STRANDING

The second type of macroeconomic impact of mitigation policies comes from capital markets. The primary risk facing the capital market is the potential for stranded capital, a concept encompassing significant and potentially irreversible losses across physical, intangible, and human capital, as well as productive and residential assets. The transition to a low-carbon economy can cause capital and assets to become *stranded* as demand and revenues shift. Such unexpected devaluations or write-downs may in turn affect the financial wealth of households, companies, banks, other financial institutions, and public administrations.

Two main types of stranded assets can be distinguished: *stranded capital* and *stranded value*. Stranded capital refers to losses incurred due to transition risks associated with capital spending on a project, such as an amount invested in oil exploration and development (e.g., drilling rigs/seismic vessels), production and processing facilities (e.g., processing terminals), or distribution infrastructure (e.g., pipelines, tankers). This risk is driven by the higher cost of equipment, labor, or other inputs needed for the project. Stranded value, on the other hand, represents the losses incurred due to transition risks associated with the market valuation of a firm or project, such as the forward-looking impact on future expected profits from the projects or a firm.

Assuming a late and abrupt transition, IEA (2017) estimated stranded assets – understood here as *stranded capital* – at around USD 2.2 trillion. More recently, Semeniuk et al. (2022) calculated that global stranded assets as the present value of future lost profits in the upstream oil and gas sectors reached USD 1.4 trillion (Figure 3.4). After determining the stranded assets, the study outlines a four-stage ownership chain to trace how losses are transmitted and who ultimately bears them. At stage 1, asset stranding is attributed to the country where the sites are located (loss at oil/gas field). Stage 2 aggregates the ownership of stranded assets by fossil-fuel companies (loss at headquarters). Stage 3 allows for further tracing of financial losses through the directed graph of ownership using a network model (corporate owner loss). Finally, at stage 4, all losses are tracked to their ultimate owners, including governments and individuals, as shareholders or outright owners of companies or

3   THE MACROECONOMIC EFFECTS OF MITIGATION POLICIES   107

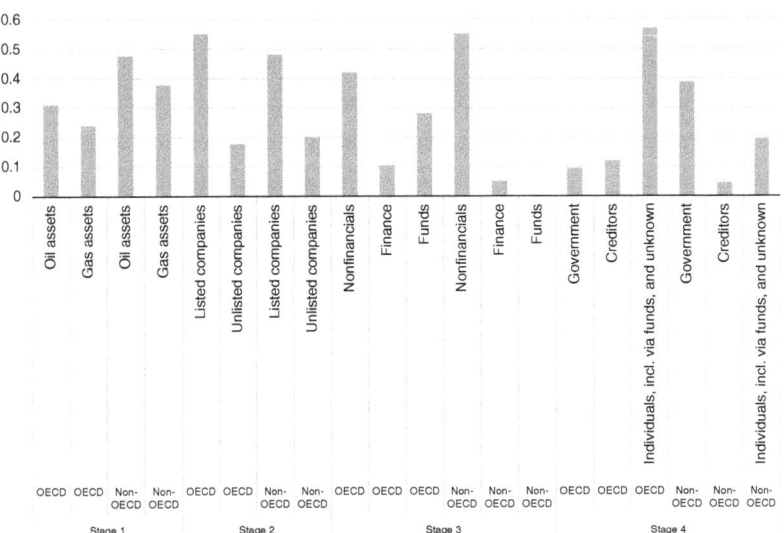

FIGURE 3.4 Ownership chain of stranded assets by OECD/non-OECD geography and major institutional categories (USD trillion)
Source: Semieniuk et al. (2022)
Note: The sum of the bars for each stage represents USD 1.4 trillion in losses from medium expectations realignment at successive ownership stages, divided into OECD and non-OECD losses, and within each geography into major institutional categories.

investors in funds, including pension funds (ultimate owner loss). They find that the majority of the market risk is borne by private investors, primarily in OECD countries, with significant exposure through pension funds and financial markets. The distribution of ownership reveals that more than 15 percent of the global stranded asset risk is transferred to OECD-based investors. Crucially, as long-standing backers of the fossil-fuel economy and potentially exposed owners of stranded assets, stakeholders in advanced economies have a major interest in how the transition in oil and gas production is managed.

When sectors beyond energy are included in the calculation of stranded value, the estimates rise sharply. IRENA (2017) estimates a potential for stranded assets of USD 18 trillion. IRENA's asset-stranding calculations for oil and gas companies now include the potential priced-in market value of explored reserves, which is higher than the cost of exploration. Additionally, IRENA has found more than USD 9 trillion of stranded value in other sectors, particularly in the building sector, which was neglected in previous estimates. This large amount is related to the significant retrofitting of the existing building stock that is needed to reduce the carbon footprint of buildings. These required investments, in turn, reduce the value of the buildings compared to a scenario without transition.

In macroeconomic terms, accelerated obsolescence of the capital stock can raise the cost of capital and trigger a surge in investment to offset lost assets, with the risk of crowding out consumption and other forms of investment (see Section 3.2). Ex-ante assessments, which typically model this shock as a higher depreciation rate or lower capital utilization, point to negative effects on activity and employment. The IRENA estimates the annual flow of devalued productive capital worldwide to amount to 0.5 points of GDP in 2019 in the case of an orderly transition, and 1 point of GDP in the case of a transition delayed until 2030. The impact would fall primarily on construction and fossil fuel extraction, and to a lesser extent on industry and fossil fuel power generation.

3.4 CONSUMPTION BEHAVIORS, SOBRIETY, AND WELL-BEING

While climate change policies primarily target high-emitting activities, especially the energy and industrial sectors, the demand side is equally important for decarbonizing the economy. Households play a central role by adapting their consumption patterns to climate challenges.

3.4.1 Potential Emission Reductions from Final Consumption through a Change in Behaviors

The sixth report from Group III of the Intergovernmental Panel on Climate Change (IPCC) examines strategies for curbing greenhouse gas (GHG) emissions by managing demand. This mitigation approach works through multiple channels, including changes in behavior, urban planning, and infrastructure policies designed to reduce energy use (refer to Section 3.2.1). Broadly framed as demand restraint – not limited to households cutting direct energy consumption – this perspective suggests that GHG emissions from end-use sectors could be reduced by about 30 percent relative to a business-as-usual scenario. The largest potential reductions are in the food sector (15%), buildings (5%), and land mobility (5%) (Figure 3.5).

According to the IEA, alterations in behavior are projected to contribute to approximately 8 percent of the overall emissions decline by 2050, compared to present levels, within their *Net Zero Emissions* scenario. A large share of this reduction would come from improvements in material efficiency in the industrial sector, such as greater recycling and reuse. These gains are partly driven by evolving societal preferences – for instance, moving away from standardized packaging – and supported by regulatory changes and technological advances. The reduction follows strategies grouped under the Avoid, Shift, Improve (ASI) principles:

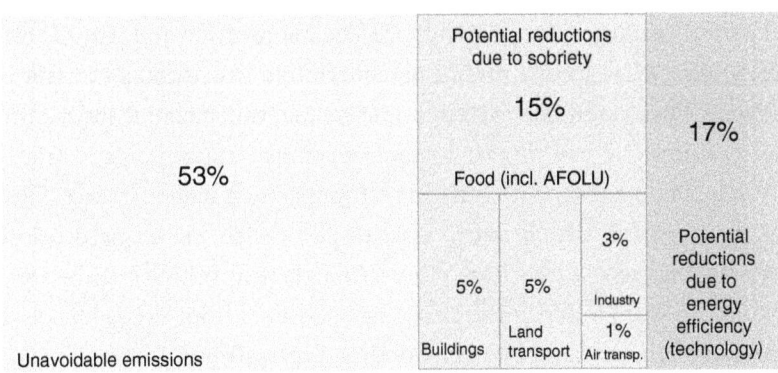

FIGURE 3.5 Reduction potential in global GHG emissions of final consumption sectors in 2050 through demand
Source: IPCC (2022)
Note: AFOLU stands for Agriculture, Forestry and Other Land Use.

- *Avoid* unnecessary consumption by implementing *no-regrets* actions in all sectors, like soft mobility, *eco-actions* in the home, and incentives to extend the lifespan of products or to favor low-carbon materials in the industry. In addition to the cultural and behavioral changes that this implies, it requires a joint adaptation of institutions, production sectors, technologies, and infrastructures.
- *Shifting* to low-carbon goods and services. This also involves adapting behavior and social norms (cultural change not necessarily linked solely to climate change considerations) to new infrastructures/modes of transport, diet, and other aspects. These strategies include urban planning policies (e.g., *compact cities*), the sizing and sharing of spaces, or the development of processes for reusing materials in industry.
- *Improving* energy efficiency, which involves more technology (innovation) than behavior and preferences.

If fully implemented, these strategies could reduce direct and indirect emissions by 2050 by 44 percent in the food sector, 59 percent in transport, 66 percent in buildings, and 29 percent in industry worldwide. Behavioral changes alone would account for about 17 percent of the potential cumulative reduction across these four sectors, compared with 8 percent from infrastructure changes. Their role is especially pronounced in food and aviation, where shifts in behavior could deliver nearly 90 percent and 75 percent, respectively, of the effort required for demand-side decarbonization (refer to Table 3.1). These changes manifest as a reduction in waste and a transition toward a healthier, less carbon-intensive diet on one hand and a shift away from long-haul flights toward rail transportation on the other. At the same time, they influence emissions linked to rising electricity demand, which is expected to grow with the electrification of applications such as heat pumps and electric vehicles. However, the estimated 60 percent increase in emissions from this additional demand can be offset by behavioral and infrastructure strategies in the sectors reliant on this electricity.

The IEA estimates that these behavioral shifts could reduce energy-related activities by about 10–15 percent, contributing roughly

Table 3.1 *Distribution of decarbonization effort by demand through sufficiency and energy efficiency, and median share of emissions avoided in the sector by 2050*

Sector	Channel	Sobriety		Energy efficiency
	Strategy	Sociocultural factors/behavioral changes (%)	Infrastructure usage (%)	Technology adoption (%)
Food (including LULUCF)	Share of sector emissions	40	4	
	Share of total emissions (*)	14	1	
	Effort distribution in sector	**90**	**10**	
Building	Share of sector emissions	15	17	34
	Share of total emissions (*)	3	3	6
	Effort distribution in sector	23	**26**	**52**
Ground Transport	Share of sector emissions	5	28	33
	Share of total emissions (*)	1	4	5
	Effort distribution in sector	7	**43**	**50**
Aviation	Share of sector emissions	40	-	14
	Share of total emissions (*)	1	-	0.5
	Effort distribution in sector	**74**	-	**26**
Maritime Transport	Share of sector emissions	-	-	29
	Share of total emissions (*)	-	-	1
	Effort distribution in sector	-	-	100

(continued)

Table 3.1 (cont.)

Sector	Channel	Sobriety		Energy efficiency
		Sociocultural factors/behavioral changes (%)	Infrastructure usage (%)	Technology adoption (%)
	Strategy			
Industry	Share of sector emissions	5	5	19
	Share of total emissions (*)	1	1	5
	Effort distribution in sector	17	17	66
Potential reduction in total emissions of sectors using final energy in 2050		**20**	**10**	**17**

(*) Emissions from sectors consuming final energy.

In bold, distribution of the effort (in %) in each sector between sociocultural factors/behavioral changes, Infrastructure usage and Technology adoption.

Source: France Stratégie, based on IPCC (2022)

Reading note: By 2050, 90% of the decarbonization effort in the food sector will depend on sociocultural factors (changes in eating habits, reduction of waste, etc.). This effort represents nearly 40% of the sector's emissions and 14% of total emissions from final consumers.

Note: LULUCF stands for Land Use, Land Use Change and Forestry.

8 percent of total emissions reductions by 2050 compared with 2020. This impact occurs through three primary channels:

- Decreasing excessive or wasteful energy usage in housing (e.g., lowering heating temperatures) or transportation (e.g., reducing traffic speeds).
- Altering transportation modes (e.g., shifting from private cars to sustainable modes of mobility or from airplanes to trains).
- Achieving *material* efficiency improvements, such as increasing recycling rates, phasing out single-use packaging, or enhancing the design and construction of buildings and vehicles.

The first two channels are closely aligned with the Avoid and Shift strategies mentioned earlier, while the third is more associated with supply-side changes in behavior, particularly within the industrial sector.

3.4.2 The Role of Mitigation Policy in Changing Consumption Patterns

By encouraging a shift from high- to low-carbon goods, climate mitigation policies shape consumer preferences through changes in relative prices. High-emission products become more expensive, while low-emission alternatives, supported by advances in green technology, become increasingly affordable. While these adjustments ideally only shift consumption patterns within household spending, climate policies can, at least in the short to medium term, affect overall consumption levels by raising the cost of the consumption basket, particularly its energy component. Additionally, policies can directly encourage more restrained consumption habits through mechanisms such as consumer information (e.g., the increasing use of labels to raise awareness of the carbon footprint of products) or nonmonetary incentives (like *nudges*).

The overall effects of mitigation policies are generally assessed as adverse. Känzig (2023) shows that carbon pricing raises energy prices, lowers emissions, and stimulates green innovation, but also leads to a temporary decline in economic activity and a persistent increase in consumer prices. Labor market impacts are pronounced, with higher unemployment and lower wages reducing real disposable income. As a result, while carbon pricing effectively cuts emissions by raising the cost of polluting, it also generates economic repercussions, particularly for consumption. These burdens are unevenly distributed: low-income households reduce consumption substantially and persistently, while wealthier households are less affected. Lower-income groups are disproportionately impacted because they devote a larger share of income to energy expenses and are more likely to work in sectors vulnerable to the policy. Känzig estimates that indirect income effects could account for up to two-thirds of the total impact on consumption.

Given these unequal outcomes of mitigation policies, redistribution strategies are essential in policy design. Targeted fiscal measures, especially alongside carbon pricing, can help ease the economic burden of mitigation. Moreover, since energy demand tends to be inelastic – especially among low-income households – this does not necessarily undermine the effectiveness of emission reduction efforts. Känzig (2023) illustrates that reallocating carbon revenues to the most affected households can alleviate the aggregate consumption impact and reduce inequality without compromising emission reductions. This aligns with preliminary evidence from the British Columbia carbon tax in Canada, where Konradt and Weder di Mauro (2023) find that the progressive redistribution scheme accompanying the tax has effectively mitigated its adverse economic effects.

Finally, it is important to assess how climate policies influence consumer preferences. Mattauch et al. (2022) investigate whether carbon taxes and regulations encourage or discourage voluntary initiatives. They find that certain policies clearly shift preferences toward more sustainable choices: investments in urban transport infrastructure foster greater use of public transit and cycling, while public health policies steer diets toward healthier and more environmentally friendly products.

3.4.3 Implications of Emission Mitigation for Well-Being

Traditional national accounting measures such as GDP or aggregate consumption are inadequate for assessing social progress, particularly in a context of growing environmental concerns (Stiglitz et al., 2009). These metrics were never designed for that purpose, and even economists do not treat GDP as a universal objective to be maximized at all costs. By contrast, the concept of well-being has long been used as a broader gauge of progress, taking into account not only gains but also the negative side effects of growth. To quantitatively assess whether the pursuit of climate neutrality through mitigation policies can go hand in hand with improvements in well-being, it becomes necessary to assign value to the non-monetary benefits of the transition.

The central question is how to incorporate the direct co-benefits of the transition, such as improvements in health, leisure, and quality of life, which may offset its financial cost. Conversely, there are nonmonetary aspects that could exacerbate rather than mitigate the costs of the transition. Although the objective is to reduce the negative externality of global warming and its associated impacts, important structural changes can trigger major labor market disruptions, with job losses that carry adverse effects on well-being. Likewise, the push for moderation or new urban policies may result in denser housing arrangements, running counter to recent trends and potentially diminishing individual well-being.

Climate change mitigation policies can generate a wide range of secondary benefits that extend beyond the direct gains of avoiding climate impacts. Depending on the context, measures promoting clean energy technologies or energy efficiency often bring immediate improvements in local and indoor air quality, reducing health risks and enhancing living environments. These additional advantages are commonly referred to as *co-benefits* of mitigation policies. Bollen et al. (2009) review the literature on co-benefits, much of which examines the links between climate change mitigation and local air pollution policies, particularly their impacts on human health. A smaller but growing body of work also explores how local air pollution affects crops and interacts with climate policies. The main conclusion drawn from this review of available estimates is that co-benefits are expected to offset a significant portion of the costs of climate change mitigation. Extending this effort, de Serre and Murtin (2014) propose a simple index of economic progress that incorporates both the monetary costs of mitigation policies and the health benefits from reduced local air pollution. Their valuation of pollution's impact, based on its effect on life expectancy, shows that accounting for health gains significantly reduces the net cost of mitigation in countries such as China and India, as well as in fossil fuel–intensive economies like Australia, Canada, and the United States.

As shown in Figure 3.6, emission cuts would lower average GDP growth by about 0.15 percentage points in non-EU Eastern countries, China, and oil-exporting countries (OPEC + Mexico), compared with less than 0.05 percentage points in most other regions. In all regions, part of the GDP slowdown is offset by gains in life expectancy. Not surprisingly, the offset is largest in countries where the gains in life expectancy are strongest (i.e., China, India, and the United States), and remains substantial in commodities-rich, energy-producing countries such as Australia and Canada. In the United States, welfare is found to increase following the emission cuts, reflecting the combination of a relatively low cost in terms of foregone GDP growth combined with large gains in life expectancy.

Health-related benefits alone only partly offset the costs of mitigation in this simplified analysis, which makes it important to also consider the broader advantages of avoiding climate-related damages (see Chapter 1 for an assessment of reduced GDP loss from damage avoidance in transition scenarios). Even within the health domain, further externalities matter, including the impact of climate change

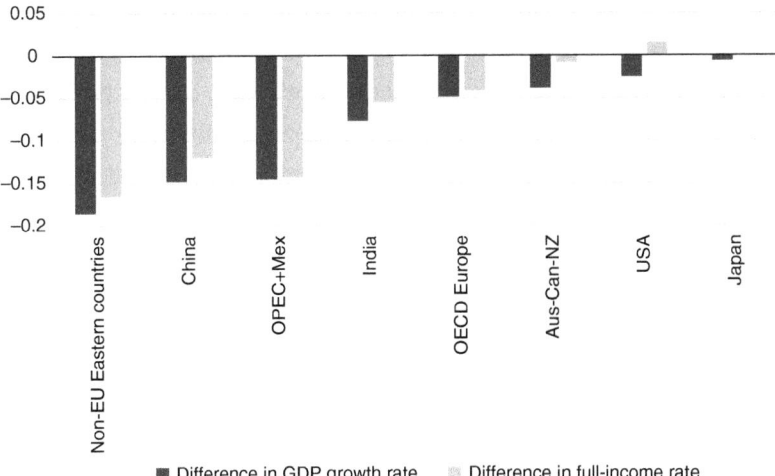

FIGURE 3.6 Variations in annualized growth rates in GDP and welfare (full-income) due to climate change mitigation (annualized difference in growth rate between GHG 50 percent reduction and BAU, in percentage points)
Source: de Serre and Murtin (2014) based on Bollen et al. (2009)
Note: OECD Europe includes all European countries that are members of the OECD, and non-EU eastern countries regroup countries that were members of the former Soviet Union.

on water quality and scarcity, ozone depletion, and the spread of infectious diseases, all of which could pose serious future health hazards. Furthermore, while de Serre and Murtin (2014) primarily focused on mortality risks, the adverse effects on morbidity also deserve attention potentially resulting in greater welfare gains from mitigation efforts (Hunt, 2011).

3.5 MITIGATION POLICIES IN AN INTERNATIONAL CONTEXT AND COMPETITIVENESS ISSUES

Chapter 2 shows that, despite shared characteristics, national climate policies exhibit considerable diversity, both in terms of their ambition – that is, the extent of their commitments to decarbonization – and the specific policies (such as pricing mechanisms, regulations, and subsidies) they employ. Given the inherent challenges of comparing decarbonization efforts across countries, reducing this diversity to a single standardized metric, such as an equivalent carbon price that reflects regulatory or incentive measures, is unrealistic. As a result, significant disparities in international carbon pricing persist, creating distortions in global competition.

Whatever instruments are used, the heterogeneity in climate mitigation industries to regions with lower emissions. As highlighted by Stiglitz (2006), countries with lower or no carbon taxes effectively subsidize their high-emission industries. Consequently, emissions may merely be shifted from more ambitious countries to those with less ambitious targets, resulting in what is commonly termed *carbon leakage*. However, while distortions in competition due to subsidies fall within the realm of trade defense measures provided by multilateral regulations, efforts by countries to decarbonize, akin to subsidies, are essentially beyond challenge within the framework of multilateral trade rules. Therefore, it becomes necessary to employ instruments to mitigate leakage, leveraging potential environmental exceptions within international trade regulations.

While traditional trade defense mechanisms address distortions caused by explicit subsidies, climate mitigation efforts – though similarly distortionary – remain largely outside the scope of multilateral trade disciplines. As such, to contain the risk of leakage, it becomes essential to deploy tailored instruments that operate within the environmental exceptions permitted under international trade law.

3.5.1 *Coordinated or Uncoordinated Actions?*

The Paris Agreement lays out a framework characterized by uncoordinated and nonbinding commitments, which poses a fundamental challenge to effective climate action (Nordhaus, 2020). This absence of strategic coordination – no global planner tasked with distributing emissions reductions across countries – makes it harder to collectively meet shared climate goals.

Following the adoption of the United Nations Framework Convention on Climate Change in 1992, the international community engaged in over two decades of negotiations to establish legally binding regulations to curb GHG emissions. In 1997, the Kyoto Protocol introduced an initial framework for these regulations, albeit with relatively modest targets. Industrialized countries listed in Annex I were required to reduce their GHG emissions between 2008 and 2012 by an average of 5 percent below 1990 levels while exempting developing countries (referred to as non-Annex I countries). The protocol was expected to evolve, and the Copenhagen Conference 2009 aimed to produce a new agreement involving non-Annex I countries, some of which, like China, had witnessed significant increases in emissions in the intervening period. Although Annex I countries collectively adhered to the treaty's provisions, it had little impact on the global trend of increasing GHG emissions. Consequently, the second commitment period aimed to elevate reduction ambitions globally. However, the focus on legally binding commitments and the rigid dichotomy between Annex I and developing countries, which perceived emission limitations as constraints on their economic development, ultimately led to the failure of COP 15 in Copenhagen.

Nevertheless, the Copenhagen Conference 2009 was not just a setback; it laid the groundwork for resolving the longstanding deadlock over mitigation responsibilities. This effort culminated in the Paris Agreement in 2015, at COP 21, whereby signatory countries established their individual levels of ambition for climate change mitigation by submitting Nationally Determined Contributions (NDCs) to the dedicated UN secretariat, which are updated every five years. Despite the bottom-up nature of NDCs, the Paris Agreement includes certain obligations. Article 4.2 mandates that "Each Party shall establish, communicate and update its intended successive nationally determined contributions. The Parties shall take domestic mitigation measures to achieve the objectives of the said contributions." This bottom-up approach to NDCs is complemented by a top-down mechanism that evaluates their content, implementation, and progress over time based on an accusatory but nonpunitive principle.

This is reflected in Articles 4.3 ("The next [NDC] of each Party shall represent progress in relation to the previous [NDC]") and 14 ("The Conference of the Parties serving as the meeting of the Parties to this Agreement shall periodically review the implementation of this Agreement to assess the collective progress achieved (...). The Conference of the Parties serving as the meeting of the Parties to this Agreement shall conduct its (...) global review (...) every five years"). In practical terms, this review is conducted through a report published by the UNFCCC secretariat known as the NDC Synthesis Report. However, since NDCs are submitted voluntarily, there is no standardized framework for expressing or calculating them, and these commitments do not cover emissions from aviation and shipping.

Beyond marking a significant shift in approach – despite its recognized limitations – COP21 also served as a catalyst for a broad range of initiatives aimed at enhancing coordination across climate action efforts. This includes collaboration between states seeking to bolster their commitments to decarbonization, as well as efforts among various stakeholders to exchange best practices. Furthermore, an increasing number of countries have pledged to achieve net-zero emissions targets. By early 2023, seventeen countries and the European Union had enshrined such targets into legislation, with over a hundred countries expressing their intent to reach a net-zero goal. In most instances, these targets are set for 2050 (notably for the EU and its member states, as well as the United States), or even as far out as 2060 (for Russia) or 2070 (for India). Lastly, Article 2.1(c) of the Paris Agreement mandates signatories to ensure that "financial flows are in line with a pathway towards low greenhouse gas emissions and climate-resilient development." International climate policy relies on various financial architecture elements, including the Special Climate Change Fund, the Climate Change Adaptation Fund, and the Green Climate Fund (refer to Chapter 4 for more details).

These broad international commitments are further broken down across multiple levels – national, regional, and industry-specific – often tailored to particular industrial sub-sectors. Efforts to develop a metric for comparing mitigation began at the 2014 Lima talks, driven by concerns over *free riding* on environmental targets. Multiple approaches have been developed to compare mitigation efforts across countries and regions worldwide.

- The narrowest definition involves *explicit carbon prices*, encompassing only the marginal incentives provided by a carbon tax or a tradable permit system (Dolphin et al., 2020). However, this definition overlooks the full spectrum of emission reduction policies, prompting the exploration of alternative metrics.
- The OECD has expanded the definition to include *implicit carbon prices* (OECD, 2013; Marcantonini and Ellerman, 2013), incorporating all policies supporting low-carbon energy development. This scope differs from that subsequently adopted by the organization.
- The IMF has proposed a distinct methodology based on modeling to derive an economy-wide carbon price equivalent (ECPE), representing the price required to achieve the same emissions reductions as the policies under consideration (Black et al., 2022). This method can also be applied at the sectoral level (sectoral carbon price equivalent – SCPE).

Despite these advancements, methodologies and models seeking to measure mitigation efforts remain tentative and lack broad consensus. Some approaches, such as those used to estimate the global carbon price (Carhart et al., 2022), apply a much stricter threshold for policy inclusion than the options outlined above (Figure 3.7). They consider any policy that offers a marginal incentive to reduce emissions and includes a price component – either through a direct price or a tradable tradable market instrument linked to a price. The key economic policy takeaway, consistent with the subsidiarity principle of the Paris Agreement, is that different policy mixes can yield the same overall carbon price, implying that countries can pursue distinct decarbonization pathways to achieve identical targets.

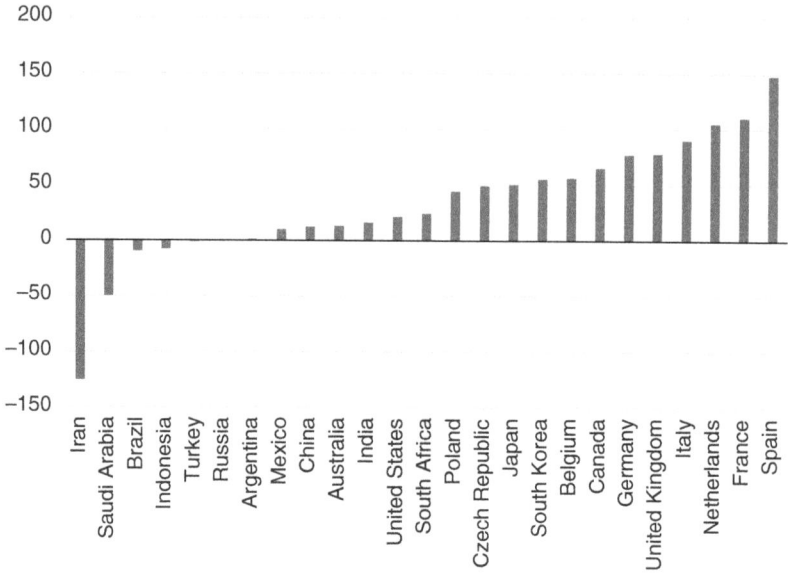

FIGURE 3.7 Country-level comprehensive carbon price by country (2019 USD per tonne of CO_2 emissions)
Source: Mark Carhart, Bob Litterman, Clayton Munnings and Olivia Vitali (2022)

3.5.2 Carbon Leakages and CBAM

In the presence of international disparities in carbon prices (explicit price) or nontariff climate policies (implicit price), part of the production from high-emission industries in more ambitious countries is redirected to countries with less stringent climate policies. Given the wide variation in climate policies and effective carbon prices across countries, a unilateral carbon tax can prompt the relocation of economic activity to regions with weaker climate commitments – undermining its effectiveness in reducing global emissions. This phenomenon, known as emission leakage (or carbon leakage), partially offsets emissions reductions in ambitious countries, as emissions rise in less regulated jurisdictions.

In addition to this carbon leakage, unilateral carbon pricing is likely to impact output and employment in energy-intensive and trade-exposed (EITE) sectors by diminishing their global competitiveness. The use of more carbon-intensive production techniques in less regulated countries further exacerbate this competitiveness leakage.

Therefore, the decarbonization efforts of ambitious countries are partially or fully offset by so-called *direct* leakages or *competitiveness channel* leakages. Additionally, *indirect* leakage can also occur through energy markets: lower fossil fuel demand in ambitious countries depresses global prices, encouraging increased consumption elsewhere. Taken together, these leakages undermine the effectiveness of ambitious climate policies and lead to an uneven distribution of global mitigation efforts.

The literature proposes various options to address potential carbon leakage and ease concerns of domestic EITE industries. Each comes with significant trade-offs, design challenges, and questions regarding consistency with current World Trade Organization (WTO) law. For instance, policymakers could consider partially or fully exempting EITE sectors from the carbon tax or providing rebates to EITE firms based on their output levels. A carbon border adjustment mechanism (CBAM) constitutes a promising approach to mitigate leakage risks. The mechanism imposes a levy on the carbon content of imported non-fossil fuel goods, complementing domestic carbon taxes applied to fossil fuels. Essentially, a CBAM would target goods imported from countries that do not price carbon at a level equivalent to or higher than the carbon price in the implementing country.

In principle, this approach seeks to level the playing field by preventing domestic emission-intensive goods from being disadvantaged relative to imports from countries with weaker climate policies. A CBAM can be designed to apply selectively to imports, varying by country and product based on average carbon intensity. For example, if the domestic carbon tax is USD 100 per metric tonne of CO_2 and steel production in Country X emits five metric tonnes of CO_2 per unit, the CBAM would charge USD 500 for each unit of steel imported from Country X into the domestic country. The objective is to mitigate unfair competition for domestic steelmakers due to lower environmental standards abroad, with the potential to incentivize emission reductions in exporting countries.

Alternatively, an export CBAM would refund the carbon tax paid by domestic producers on goods destined for export, helping maintain the competitiveness of emissions-intensive products in markets without comparable climate policies. Most analysts agree that an import CBAM could qualify for an environmental exception under WTO law, provided the adjustment does not exceed the domestic carbon tax. However, justifying an export CBAM under WTO law is more challenging, as it is grounded in trade competitiveness rather than environmental protection.

Several studies have examined carbon leakage, competitiveness, concerns, and policy options to address them. Böhringer et al. (2012) estimated aggregate leakage rates to range from 5 percent to 20 percent. In contrast, McKibbin et al. (2012a) found no evidence of energy-related emissions leakage. The magnitude of these effects varies across industries, with EITE sectors bearing a disproportionate impact (Fischer and Fox, 2012). Aldy and Pizer (2009) estimated that for EITE industries with energy costs exceeding 10% of shipment value, the maximum anticipated shift in production abroad would be around 1%. A substantial body of literature also shows that carbon taxes can simultaneously reduce emissions and generate significant fiscal revenues (McKibbin et al., 2012b; Rausch and Reilly, 2015).

Böhringer, Schneider & Asane-Otoo (2022) evaluated the effects of carbon tariffs and observed a notable increase in emissions embodied in imports from developing to OECD countries. While this outcome highlights the effectiveness of border carbon taxation (reducing leakage by 64% to 80% depending on the scenario) it also shifts the burden of adjustment onto developing countries.

In the European context, Bellora and Fontagné (2023) showed that under the European Green Deal (see Chapter 1), the CBAM helps curb carbon leakage and redistributes the climate policy burden among sectors covered by the Emissions Trading System (ETS) – notably between electricity generation and other emission-intensive industries. Over 2021–2040, the cumulative leakage associated with the Paris Agreement is reduced by an amount equivalent to two years of EU emissions. However, this comes at a cost: higher ETS allowance prices and rising input costs for downstream industries that rely on ETS-covered products. The study underscores a key tension in CBAM design – between a conservative approach that minimizes trade retaliation risks but achieves limited environmental impact, and a more ambitious model that more effectively reduces leakage and shields EU exporters, but applies greater differentiation among trading partners.

3.5.3 Coordination Efforts: Climate Clubs or Carbon Price Floors

To meet the 2°C target, projections indicate that the global carbon price should range between USD 50–USD 100 per tonne by 2030 (IMF, 2022a). Yet more than three-quarters of global emissions remain unpriced, and the IMF estimates the average carbon price at just USD 3 per tonne. This has spurred ongoing discussions in forums such as the G7 and G20 to broaden the geographical and sectoral coverage of carbon pricing. Still, the chances of agreeing on a uniform global carbon tax are slim, largely because of the principle of common but differentiated responsibilities (CBDR) enshrined in international environmental law. This principle recognizes that while all states share responsibility for addressing climate change, the burden falls more heavily on advanced economies.

Nevertheless, stronger international coordination of mitigation policies is essential to reduce the risks of policy fragmentation and carbon leakage. While a globally harmonized carbon price remains the ideal solution, it faces major political hurdles. As a more feasible alternative, several secondary approaches have emerged. Multilateral institutions advocate for a common effort metric and, as proposed by the IMF (Parry et al., 2012), an International Carbon Price Floor (ICPF) – a minimum price level that countries can voluntarily exceed. The proposal recognizes that some countries may use alternative policies to carbon pricing – regulations, for example – but these alternatives should achieve at least the same emissions reductions as the carbon price floor. These carbon price floors are differentiated by countries' development levels ranging from USD 25 to USD 75 per tonne of CO_2 equivalent for low-income, middle-income, and advanced countries, respectively. This tiered structure reflects the CBDR principle and aims to secure broader participation from emerging economies. Collective action is vital, as efforts by advanced countries alone cannot align global emissions with the Paris Agreement trajectory. Moreover, countries opting out of carbon pricing would not gain economically from inaction, as they would face indirect costs, such as reduced exports to countries applying carbon border adjustments.

However, this mechanism of tiered carbon price floors presents three difficulties (Fontagné et al., 2023):

- The bulk of the financial burden would fall on emerging countries such as China, India, Russia, Saudi Arabia, South Africa, and Turkey, as their NDCs currently imply an implicit carbon price significantly lower than the proposed floor price. Conversely, the USD 75 floor price is lower than the carbon price implied by the NDCs of most advanced countries.
- Disparities in carbon pricing among countries at varying levels of development could result in carbon leakage, disadvantaging the most ambitious nations.
- Considering that decarbonization can be achieved through a combination of carbon pricing, regulations, and/or subsidies, the question arises regarding how to account for the implicit price of nonprice measures.

Another pathway to international collaboration is the concept of a *Climate Club*. This idea originates in the social sciences, specifically Buchanan's (1965) theory of clubs, which highlights the need for collective mechanisms to curb free-riding in international agreements. In environmental policy, Nobel laureate William Nordhaus expanded this idea, proposing climate clubs that pair target carbon prices with trade sanctions.

The notion of a *Climate Club* inspired by Nordhaus's proposal has gained traction, albeit in a modified form, under the German presidency of the G7 in 2022. This version functions as an inclusive forum with flexible entry criteria, centered on sharing best practices, particularly for industrial decarbonization, and strengthening the assessment of mitigation policies through common metrics. Launched at COP28 in November 2023, the Climate Club currently consists of thirty-seven members and continues to grow. It serves as a key intergovernmental platform to advance climate action and industrial decarbonization, with a focus on supporting the Paris Agreement through openness, cooperation, and inclusivity.

The Climate Club operates on three main pillars:

- Advancing climate change mitigation policies: Members collaborate to expedite the transition to green economies by developing comparable methodologies for measuring, estimating, and reporting emissions data. They also seek synergies in their green growth policies and national systems to prevent carbon leakage in industrial sectors.
- Transforming industries: The club supports initiatives such as the G7 industrial decarbonization agenda, the hydrogen action pact, and the breakthrough agenda to drive industrial decarbonization and expand the production of green industrial products.
- Boosting international climate cooperation and partnerships: On a voluntary basis, the Climate Club aims to enhance collaboration between countries, address gaps in cooperation, and explore funding mechanisms to support climate initiatives.

Amid rising geopolitical tensions and growing policy uncertainty, the outlook for international cooperation appears increasingly bleak as nations drift into opposing camps. Yet the urgency of climate change compels collective action. Initiatives that foster cooperation on mitigation policies not only mark an essential step forward but also carry immense potential in the shared effort to limit global warming to below 2° Celsius.

3.6 CONCLUSION

Mitigation policies, while essential for addressing climate change, have far-reaching implications for economic growth, capital markets, and consumption behaviors. When well-designed, these policies can foster economic growth through green innovation and increased productivity. Investments in sustainable technologies and infrastructure not only reduce emissions but also stimulate economic activity, potentially setting economies on a green growth trajectory. While there are substantial upfront costs associated with transitioning to greener technologies and infrastructures, these investments often result in long-term economic benefits and resilience. However, the need for significant capital outlays also raises concerns about asset stranding, where investments in fossil fuel-related assets risk losing value in the shift to cleaner energy sources. This underscores the importance of financial planning and risk management in capital markets to avoid economic disruptions.

The socio-economic dimensions of mitigation policies, particularly how they influence consumption behaviors and overall well-being, show how policy measures can drive substantial emissions reductions by encouraging shifts in consumer behavior toward more sustainable practices. These changes, while often beneficial for the environment, must be carefully managed to ensure they do not negatively impact well-being, particularly for vulnerable populations. Striking a balance between promoting sustainability and maintaining quality of life is therefore critical in policy design.

In the international context, carbon leakage, where stringent policies in one region lead to increased emissions elsewhere, remains a pressing concern. Mechanisms like CBAMs can mitigate such risks, ensuring a level playing field and preventing carbon-intensive industries from relocating to regions with lax regulations. Ultimately, stronger international cooperation, through climate clubs or agreements on carbon price floors, offers the most effective path to enhance the effectiveness of global mitigation efforts and reduce competitiveness issues.

4 Climate Finance and Main Instruments

Climate finance has been expanding dramatically, growing more than threefold over the last decade, but it remains insufficient to cover the required investments needed to meet the Paris Agreement's temperature reduction goals. In 2024, investments in green-energy transitions reached a record USD 2.1 trillion, up 11 percent from the previous year (Cheung et al., 2025). This growth, although slower than the previous years, still set a new record. In 2024, China allocated around USD 650 billion to clean energy, thereby surpassing the joint investment of the United States, European Union, and United Kingdom. In the energy sector, achieving net-zero emissions by 2050 demands an annual investment of around USD 5 trillion, yet current investments are under USD 2 trillion. Taking a broader view, annual investment needs are estimated to range from USD 3.5 trillion (NGFS in a 1.5°C scenario) to more than USD 9 trillion between now and 2050. This range varies based on assumptions about redirecting current investments in dirty sectors toward the clean sector.

Despite significant progress in financing the transition, the annual investment gap remains large. Table 4.1 shows that, in the energy sector, investment in renewable energy is gradually increasing but remains lower than investment in fossil fuel, which remains broadly stable at around USD 1 trillion per year. This number would increase to USD 3.7 trillion if we include investment currently directed to dirty infrastructure – such as high-polluting oil and gas extraction, refining, combustion, and cement and steel production. While financing the transition could be addressed by redirecting the current investment in dirty sectors, the net remaining investment gap would still be substantial, estimated between 2 percent and 3 percent of the annual global GDP.

Table 4.1 *Estimated climate financing needs for EMDEs to meet the GHG emission reduction targets*

Average annual investment to 2050 (USD trillion)	Source	Scenario, scope, or estimation method
3.5	Network for Greening the Financial System	Total investment in 1.5°C scenario
4.1	Boston Consulting Group	Total investment, drawn from a range of estimates
4.4	International Renewable Energy Agency	Energy investment
3.5–5.1	BloombergNEF	Range of investment depending on technology path
4.5	International Energy Agency	Energy-related investments
9.2	McKinsey	Broad view investments on the demand side

Source: Barclays Research, BNEF, IEA, IRENA, NGFS, BCG, McKinsey

Although the funding gap is large, there is enough liquidity in capital markets, with over USD 128 trillion in assets under management globally in 2024 (Boston Consulting Group, 2025), and funds could be redistributed or reallocated to uses consistent with global climate goals. As seen in Chapter 2, public money could also be directed to finance the green transition. However, the imperative to address climate change risks has been overshadowed in the past few years by health crises, economic fluctuations, and geopolitical tensions. Instead of being directed to climate mitigation and adaptation, significant financial resources have been spent to counter recent adverse developments. Emergency fiscal measures implemented globally in response to the COVID-19 pandemic in 2020 neared USD 12 trillion (IMF, 2020). Fossil fuel subsidies surged to a record USD 7 trillion in 2022 as governments supported consumers and businesses during the

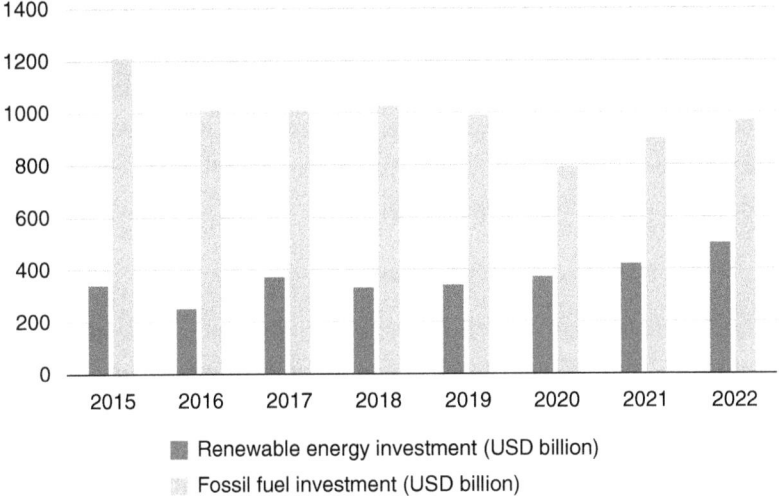

FIGURE 4.1 Global investment in renewable energy and fossil fuels (USD billion)
Source: IRENA and CPI (2023a)

global spike in energy prices caused by Russia's invasion of Ukraine and the economic recovery from the pandemic (Figure 4.1). Explicit subsidies (undercharging for supply costs) more than doubled to USD 1.3 trillion between 2021 and 2022, with an additional USD 5.7 trillion in implicit subsidies (IMF, 2023a). Implicit subsidies are projected to continue to grow in the coming years as developing countries are expected to increase their consumption of fossil fuels toward the levels of advanced economies.[1]

Emerging and low-income countries face a higher financial gap when tackling climate challenges. The majority of funding is concentrated in developed economies and China, focusing more on mitigation than adaptation. While the funding needs of EMDEs for meeting climate targets are significant, most governments typically have less fiscal space and restricted financing access than their developed economies counterparts. Private finance contributions are insufficient in EMDEs due to various barriers, and much of the climate

---

[1] www.imf.org/en/Blogs/Articles/2023/08/24/fossil-fuel-subsidies-surged-to-record-7-tn

finance is delivered as debt. Additionally, many EMDCs lack clear strategies and transition plans, particularly within the private sector, to effectively guide climate action. Addressing the investment needs in capital-scarce countries requires mobilizing resources from the private sector through innovative concessional finance solutions and de-risking strategies (see Chapter 7).

4.1 DEFINING CLIMATE FINANCE

Climate finance can be defined as "local, national or transnational financing – drawn from public, private and alternative sources of financing – that seeks to support mitigation and adaptation actions that will address climate change" (UNFCCC).[2] However, this definition entails various concepts that we need to clarify before providing a typology of climate finance.

4.1.1 *Unpacking Key Concepts in Climate Finance*

Climate finance encompasses financial flows to combat climate change, including efforts to mitigate effects, adapt to impacts, build resilience, address loss and damage,[3] and pursue environmental goals like biodiversity conservation and nature-based solutions (NbS). Terms such as *green*, *blue*,[4] *sustainable*, *clean energy*, *low-carbon*, and *biodiversity or nature* finance fall within the climate finance spectrum. These financial resources support various activities and sectors, from transforming energy systems and reducing methane emissions to advancing greenhouse gas (GHG) capture technologies. Whereas Environmental, Social, and Governance (ESG) finance encompasses a

---

[2] Introduction to Climate Finance | UNFCCC.
[3] Established at COP27 in 2022, the Loss and Damage Fund aims to provide financial assistance to developing nations disproportionately affected by climate change, encompassing extreme weather events and slow-onset disasters like sea-level rise. This initiative marks a significant step toward climate justice, recognizing the responsibility of industrialized nations to support vulnerable countries facing significant climate-related losses and damages.
[4] Blue finance covers projects and initiatives that mitigate the effects of climate change on marine environments, promote ocean conservation, and support sustainable maritime industries and infrastructure.

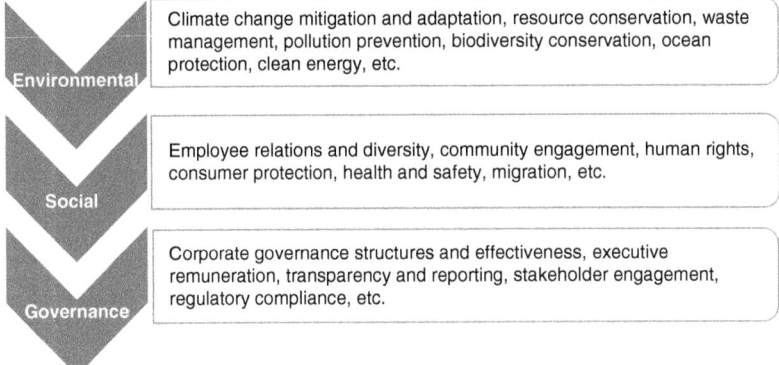

FIGURE 4.2 Sustainable/ESG finance subcomponents
Source: Authors

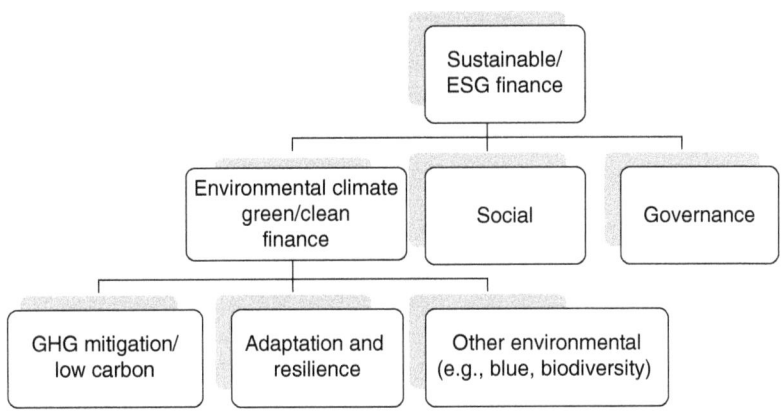

FIGURE 4.3 The scope of sustainable/ESG, low carbon, green, and climate finance
Source: Authors

broader range of investments considering environmental sustainability, social responsibility, and governance practices, climate finance focuses specifically on funding projects and initiatives to mitigate climate change and adapt to its impacts (Figure 4.2).

Sustainable finance, which is a much larger field than climate, considers ESG considerations when making investment decisions in the financial sector (Figure 4.3). Environmental considerations might include climate change mitigation and adaptation, as well as the environment more broadly, for instance, the preservation of biodiversity, pollution prevention, and the circular economy. Social considerations generally refer to inequality, inclusiveness, labor relations, investment in human capital and communities, and human rights issues. The governance sub-pillar relates to public and private institutions and includes management structures, employee relations, and executive remuneration. It also plays a fundamental role in ensuring the inclusion of social and environmental considerations in the decision-making process.

4.1.2 *A Typology of Climate Finance*

Climate finance comprises two main categories based on how funds are allocated and managed (Figure 4.4): activity-based and outcome-based. Activity-based finance dominates most of the climate finance landscape and covers the upfront costs of projects before they become operational. Outcome-based finance is small but has a great potential for expansion and disburses funds after achieving specific predefined results. Within the environmental sphere, mitigation finance refers to funds allocated to activities that reduce or avoid GHG emissions or enhance GHG sinks and reservoirs. Adaptation finance targets

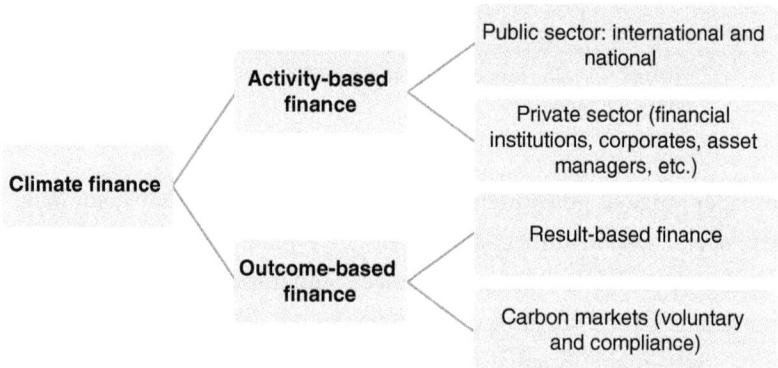

FIGURE 4.4 The typology of climate finance
Source: Authors

activities that decrease the vulnerability of human or natural systems to climate change impacts, enhancing their adaptive capacity and resilience. Dual benefits finance supports projects that simultaneously contribute to mitigation and adaptation, meeting the specific criteria for each category.

4.1.2.1 Activity-Based Finance

Activity-based finance accounts for around 95 percent of international *public and private climate finance*. It takes the form of loans, grants, equity, or guarantees to cover upfront costs before projects become operational. In most cases, these are debt-generating financial flows. Key sources of upfront climate finance include entities that offer concessional funds like Climate Investment Facilities such as the Global Environmental Facility (GEF) and the Green Climate Fund (GCF), multilateral development banks (MDBs), bilateral development banks, and direct aid flows.[5]

On the *national scale*, public climate finance includes domestic government expenditure aimed at climate objectives, such as enhancing public transportation's environmental sustainability or developing renewable energy infrastructure like hydroelectric plants. This funding is administered through public budgeting processes, state-owned enterprises (SOEs), public financial institutions, and national development finance institutions (DFIs).

Private climate finance targets climate projects with the expectation of financial returns. It is primarily driven by corporations, financial institutions, asset owners, and managers, focusing on investments that contribute to climate action and offer viable commercial returns. Examples include investments in green financial products and renewable energy projects to support climate goals through market-based solutions.

---

[5] Concessional finance offers more favorable terms than market loans, often involving lower interest rates, longer repayment periods, or grants, intended to stimulate development projects by reducing the cost of capital for beneficiary countries or entities.

4.1.2.2 *Outcome-Based Finance*

Outcome-based finance is an innovative approach in which funds are disbursed only after verifying specific climate-related outcomes. This segment of climate finance remains small, covering around 5 percent of the total finance, but it is rapidly expanding. This type of climate finance encourages innovation and efficiency by aligning financial incentives with climate action goals, such as emissions reductions, resilience milestones, or ecosystem service delivery. Funding projects only upon successful outcome verification motivates implementers to achieve or exceed targets, potentially leading to more impactful and cost-effective climate solutions without generating debt.

Results-based climate finance (RBCF) and carbon markets, two components of outcome-based finance, provide an additional source of funding that recognizes and rewards mitigation efforts. In RBCF, payments are made when predefined climate outcomes are met, often including interim milestones. RBCF creates incentives for climate action by boosting investments in climate change mitigation, such as planting trees on degraded land, expanding access to clean energy, or making industrial and manufacturing processes more energy efficient (World Bank).[6] The outcome-based finance category also encompasses voluntary and compliance carbon markets, including mechanisms like Article 6 and CORSIA, which support verifying and monetizing emission reductions through international carbon markets (see Chapter 7).

RBCF enhances traditional public climate finance by introducing an additional revenue stream and spurring private sector investment. Although carbon markets are currently small, they hold substantial potential as a revenue source for the green transition, rewarding verified emission reductions. These markets foster technological innovation and behavioral shifts by pricing carbon emissions. With 122 countries planning to use Article 6 to meet

---

[6] What is results-based climate finance and how is it different from most international public climate finance? www.worldbank.org/en/news/feature/2022/08/17/what-you-need-to-know-about-results-based-climate-finance.

their Nationally Determined Contributions (NDCs), fulfilling these pledges necessitates a broader mobilization of outcome-based finance.

Carbon credits are financial instruments for carbon pricing that assign a monetary value to reducing or removing carbon emissions. Demand for carbon credit comes from both carbon-regulated and nonregulated firms and organizations. In recent years, demand from nonregulated entities (and thus voluntary) has far outstripped regulated demand. This is driven by the net-zero commitments of firms that respond to pro-social preferences and expectations of customers, investors, or employees. Efforts to pre-empt future regulation are another key driver of carbon market expansion. While voluntary carbon markets allow for discretionary participation and are motivated by social responsibility or marketing benefits, compliance carbon markets are mandatory, regulated systems designed to reduce GHG emissions systematically through a market-driven approach. International carbon markets, particularly the voluntary segment, have to expand significantly shortly to enable countries to comply with their NDCs. To boost carbon markets, enhancing administrative capacities for wider participation while tailoring instruments, coverage, and pricing, which is vital to match each country's unique circumstances and goals, will be instrumental (see Chapter 2).

4.2 RECENT TRENDS AND DEVELOPMENTS IN CLIMATE FINANCE

The previously mentioned definition of climate finance encompasses the flow of funds to all activities, programs, or projects to address climate change. This includes both mitigation and adaptation efforts across all economic sectors worldwide. More specifically, it includes direct investments like bank loans to companies and equity investments in specific projects but excludes broader financial market activities to prevent the same funding from being counted more than once. Ensuring clarity in financial flows is crucial for avoiding double counting. For instance, a bank loan for a green hydrogen project and the subsequent investment in solar energy by the receiving company

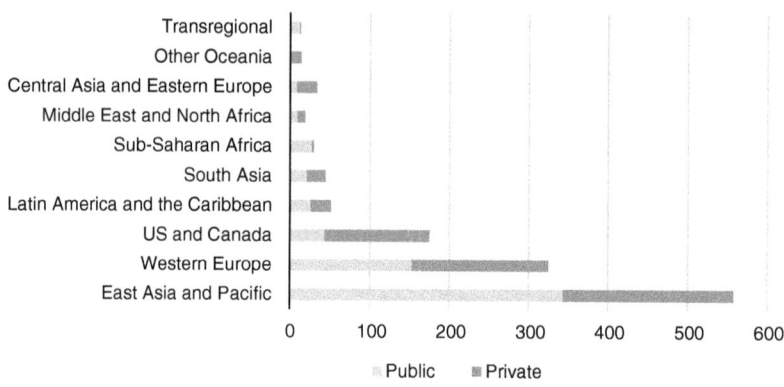

FIGURE 4.5 Public versus private climate finance by region (USD billion, 2021/2022 annual average)
Source: CPI

should not be counted as separate contributions. Instruments such as guarantees and insurance are not classified as climate finance since the funds are only utilized in the event of a borrower's payment default or an insurance claim. However, the growing use of these instruments could justify the creation of a separate tracking category in the future to better capture their role in climate-related financial activities.

Climate finance nearly doubled to USD 1.3 trillion on an annual average in 2021/2022 compared to USD 653 billion in 2019/2020 (CPI, 2023b). Yet its increase is uneven across sectors and regions (Figure 4.5), emphasizing the critical need to boost adaptation finance and private sector involvement. Private financing accounted for about half of climate finance flows, with developed countries far ahead of EMDEs in securing private investments.

In recent years, DFIs (national or multilateral) emerged as the primary sources of public climate finance (Table 4.2). SOEs and governments also contribute the most as sources of public climate finance. Public climate finance, from DFIs, has been the predominant source of climate finance in least developed countries (LDCs). Yet, their funds were mostly provided as market-rate debt, which has inadvertently increased the debt burden of some low-income

Table 4.2 *Breakdown of global climate finance by public and private sources (USD billion, biannual averages)*

Category	2017/18	2019/20	2021/22
Private	**273**	**318**	**625**
Commercial FIs	48	122	235
Corporations	156	125	192.5
Funds	8	5.5	6
Households/individuals	53	55	184.5
Institutional investors	8	4	6
Public	**299**	**334.5**	**639.5**
Bilateral DFIs	22	24	32.5
Export credit agencies	1	2	0
Governments	32.5	33.5	99.5
Multilateral climate funds	3	4	3
Multilateral DFIs	57	68.5	93
National DFIs	134	145	238.5
Public funds	2	2	0.2
SOEs	24.5	12.5	110.5
State-owned FIs	24	45	60.5
Total	**572**	**651.5**	**1264.5**

Source: CPI

countries already facing sustainability challenges. This underscores the critical need for a shift toward strategic public funding and concessional finance, which can attract private investment without worsening financial strains.

Private sector contributions are dominated by commercial financial institutions, with corporations and households also playing a notable role. The focus of investments has been predominantly on renewable energy and low-carbon transport, capturing the majority of corporate funding. Several barriers impede greater private sector involvement in financing climate action, including high commercial or perceived risks, unaffordable costs, a shortage of bankable projects, insufficient knowledge and institutional capacity, and misaligned policy incentives and regulations. While the private sector is crucial for scaling climate finance, its participation depends on active support from governments and international institutions to enhance project attractiveness, provide incentives, and mitigate risks. Moreover, establishing favorable investment conditions in developing countries is vital.

Most climate finance growth is concentrated in renewable energy and transport sectors within a handful of countries – China, the US, Europe, Brazil, Japan, and India, making up about 90 percent of the increase. In 2022, less than 3 percent (USD 30 billion) of global climate finance reached the LDCs, 15 percent went to EMDEs excluding China, and the ten most climate-affected countries received under 2 percent of the total, highlighting significant funding disparities. Yet, adaptation and resilience funding continued to lag during the same period. It represented only 0.3 percent of total private sources (1.6 percent if we include financing measures with dual benefits). Public sector sources remain predominant to finance adaptation expenditures (Figure 4.6), even though they also remain marginal (less than 10 percent of total public climate finance).

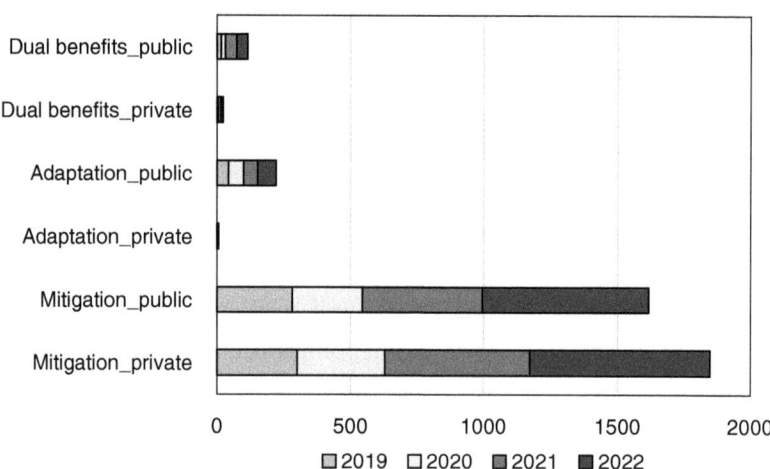

FIGURE 4.6 Breakdown of global finance for adaptation and mitigation (USD billion)
Source: CPI

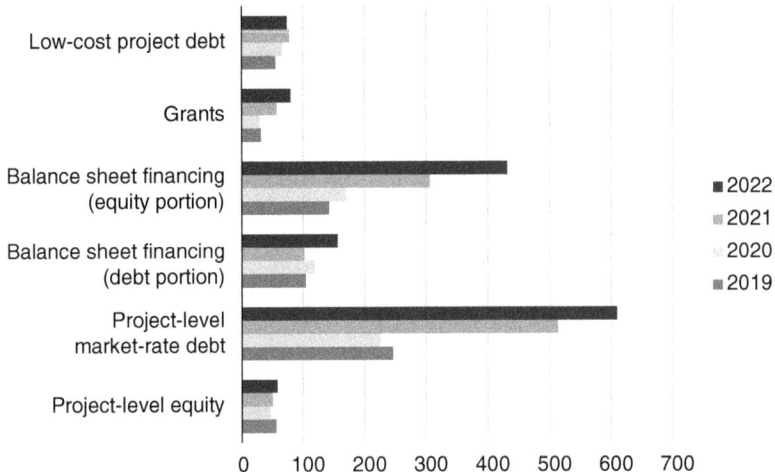

FIGURE 4.7 Breakdown of global climate finance by instruments (USD billion)
Source: CPI

Looking at direct climate financing instruments, debt appears to be the dominant instrument globally in 2021/2022, constituting 61 percent of the total, primarily at market rates, followed by equity at 33 percent and grants at 5 percent. Most market-rate debt supports energy, buildings, infrastructure, and transport sectors (Figure 4.7). Direct balance sheet debt accounted for 10 percent of climate finance, while concessional finance comprised 11 percent, highlighting its relatively minor role. Project-level debt, mostly from DFIs, represented a small fraction at 6 percent. Grants maintained a steady 5 percent share, growing from previous years, reflecting the broader range of financial instruments used for mitigation compared to adaptation due to the involvement of diverse actors with varying risk-return expectations.

Household spending was the largest private sector growth, which reached 31 percent of all private finance. Electric vehicle (EV) purchases comprised about one-third of all private climate finance, marking the highest share in a decade. Strong domestic policy initiatives encouraging the adoption of low-carbon technologies bolstered household EV purchases. Other key areas of household investment included residential solar photovoltaics, solar water heating, and energy-efficient home renovations. Institutional investors and funds contributed substantially to direct climate finance, focusing mainly on renewable energy projects and philanthropic efforts. While this section only covers direct investments in the real economy, Section 4.4 discusses institutional investors' indirect contributions through equity and bond markets.

4.3 GREEN CAPITAL MARKETS

Private investment is essential to meeting the financing needs for net-zero targets and strengthening resilience to intensifying extreme weather events, a priority underscored at international summits such as COP28. The market for GSS+ bonds (green, social, sustainable, and sustainability-linked) has expanded steadily over the past decade, with green debt issuances totaling over USD 2 billion. The Green, Social, and Sustainability + (GSS+) bond market now plays a pivotal role in channeling private capital, especially toward emerging markets where it is most needed. Maintaining this momentum in emerging markets is critical to scaling sustainable finance globally. Financial and capital markets are also critical for mobilizing additional funding from both private and public sources to support climate change mitigation and adaptation. They facilitate the mobilization of savings, direct capital to valuable investments, ensure market liquidity and effectively distribute risks and set prices. With global efforts to harmonize taxonomies and regulations, green capital markets are set to significantly enhance the mobilization and allocation of funds, supporting broad climate action initiatives.

4.3.1 *Regulation, Standards, and Taxonomies*

The sustainable and clean finance regulatory framework has significantly expanded in recent years, with many countries developing regulatory frameworks to support sustainable finance. New policy instruments such as taxonomies, standards for sustainable financial products, climate disclosure requirements, and carbon pricing mechanisms are being implemented to accelerate the shift toward a financial sector aligned with climate goals.

4.3.1.1 Disclosures

Capital market stakeholders are actively integrating climate strategies across investment processes, driving significant progress toward decarbonization. Mandatory and voluntary corporate ESG disclosures have been implemented across many countries for years, helping to align capital markets with sustainability goals. Since 2015, assets managed by investment funds with green or sustainable mandates have almost tripled reaching USD 0.84 billion in 2023, and their share rose to 13 percent of total bond issuance. Additionally, a growing number of stock exchanges now monitor the carbon footprints of their listed entities. Initiatives such as the Sustainable Stock Exchanges (SSE) Model Guidance on Climate Disclosure also support public markets, helping investors adapt to evolving regulatory demands and reporting frameworks.

Key regulatory developments have significantly facilitated the emergence of GSS+ bonds in the financial markets. One pivotal regulation that contributed to the introduction and growth of the market is the *EU Sustainable Finance Disclosure Regulation* (SFDR). To increase transparency in the finance sector, the SFDR requires fund managers and other financial market participants to disclose how they integrate ESG factors into their investment decisions.

Established by the Financial Stability Board in 2015, the *Task Force on Climate-related Financial Disclosures (TCFD)* guides over 1,000 firms worldwide with a combined market capitalization exceeding USD 12 trillion to disclose climate-related financial risks and opportunities. The Task Force seeks to establish consistent, voluntary disclosures on climate-related financial information to help investors, lenders, and insurers in accurately assessing and pricing risks, as insufficient information could result in capital misallocation. Disclosing actual and potential impacts of climate risks is crucial for pricing risks accurately. The TCFD framework focuses on governance, strategy, risk management, climate-related metrics, targets, and transition plans (see Box 4.1) to enhance transparency and help companies demonstrate how climate change affects their financial performance. This guidance supports investors, lenders, and underwriters in making informed decisions, promoting a sustainable financial system, and improving resilience to climate variability. The recommendations of the TCFD, initially voluntary, are becoming mandatory in several countries, including the UK and Japan, boosting the issuance of GSS+ bonds by integrating sustainability into financial reporting and investment processes, thereby strengthening investor confidence and market participation. Despite recommendations, disclosure of resilience strategies under different climate scenarios remains low. The TCFD has engaged in consultations to promote implementation, confirming the importance of financial impact information to users.

The most recent developments in climate regulation include mandatory corporate disclosure requirements on ESG and climate transition (Table 4.3). Furthermore, the International Sustainability Standards Board (ISSB) established a global voluntary baseline in mid-2023, which received significant backing from G7 and G20 nations and is anticipated to be adopted into national legislation. These ISSB standards require disclosures on entities' exposure to significant climate-related risks, opportunities, and transition plans (see Box 4.1), a move mirrored by proposed United States Securities and Exchange Commission regulations. More precisely, the International Financial Reporting Standards (IFRS) compels companies to disclose significant assumptions, particularly regarding climate-related risks, which could materially affect asset and liability values in the upcoming financial year. These disclosures help investors understand management's forward-looking decisions, encompassing the nature and sensitivity of these assumptions. Additionally, critical management judgments, such as those related to climate impacts on asset impairment testing, necessitate disclosure to clarify financial

Table 4.3 *TCFD recommendations*

Thematic area	Recommendations
Governance	Disclose the company's governance around climate-related risks and opportunities.
Strategy	Disclose the actual and potential impacts of climate-related risks and opportunities on the company's businesses, strategy, and financial planning where such information is material.
Risk management	Disclose how the company identifies, assesses, and manages climate-related risks.
Metrics and targets	Disclose the metrics and targets used to assess and manage relevant climate-related risks and opportunities where such information is material.

Source: TCFD (2021)[7]

statement amounts. Moreover, a new International Accounting standard requires disclosing material information beyond IFRS standards, especially relevant for companies heavily influenced by climate matters. Furthermore, the standard mandates management to assess the company's ability to continue as a going concern, including evaluating climate-related uncertainties, with any doubts requiring disclosure and significant judgments made in this assessment.[8]

Other recent regulatory developments have further refined the expectations and methodologies underlying climate-related financial disclosures and commitments. For instance, enhanced transparency requirements and integrating science-based targets into corporate strategies are becoming standard practice, driven by global agreements and localized regulatory advancements. These shifts aim to standardize climate-related financial products and ensure that they contribute substantively to the international efforts under the Paris Agreement, particularly in hard-to-abate sectors.

[7] 2021-Metrics_Targets_Guidance-1.pdf (bbhub.io)
[8] effects-of-climate-related-matters-on-financial-statements.pdf (ifrs.org)

> BOX 4.1: **Climate Transition Plans**

Climate transition plans are crucial for demonstrating a corporation's commitment to a 1.5-degree pathway and ensuring its business model remains viable in a net-zero carbon economy. These plans articulate how an organization will align its assets, operations, and overall strategy with the latest climate science recommendations and relevant policy goals. Specifically, they outline the steps to halve GHG emissions by 2030 and achieve net-zero emissions by 2050, thereby limiting global warming to 1.5°C.

B4.1.1 KEY ASPECTS OF CLIMATE TRANSITION PLANS

Strategic Alignment: Transition plans enable corporates to align with the latest and most ambitious climate science, ensuring their strategies are consistent with or ahead of policy goals.

Profitability and Relevance: By adopting a climate transition plan, corporations can demonstrate to investors and stakeholders that they have a viable strategy for remaining profitable in a net-zero economy.

Catalyst for Action: These plans are fundamental in driving the actions needed to achieve a sustainable economy, helping corporates navigate increased stakeholder interest, investor awareness, and an evolving regulatory landscape.

B4.1.2 BENEFITS OF REPORTING FOR FINANCING NEEDS

Reporting on transition plans and related metrics enhances investor confidence by providing forward-looking indicators of a firm's climate-related planning. This transparency ensures that investors understand how a corporation positions itself to remain relevant and profitable in a net-zero carbon economy.

Nonfinancial firms' transition plans also play a crucial role in informing financial institutions' climate-related risk management and facilitating transition finance. When consistently and comparably disclosed, these plans provide valuable insights for financial institutions to shape their decarbonization strategies, identify financing opportunities, and manage climate-related risks.

While currently used mainly to support decarbonization commitments, financial institutions also see these plans as potential tools for adapting business strategies and assessing investment opportunities (NGFS, 2024). However, the nascent nature of transition plans and varying experience levels among financial institutions pose challenges regarding data availability, comparability, and reliability.

To enhance the usefulness of these plans, financial institutions can engage more directly with nonfinancial firms, particularly to assess the resilience of business models to transition and physical risks. Such engagement can improve the quality and decision-usefulness of transition plans. Policymakers and standard setters can support this by developing clear national climate strategies and converging on international standards, providing nonfinancial firms with the necessary frameworks to plan their transitions effectively (NGFS, 2024).

In summary, climate transition plans are essential for firms to demonstrate commitment to ambitious climate goals, safeguard long-term profitability, and navigate growing stakeholder expectations and regulatory requirements.

4.3.1.2 Green Taxonomies

A *green taxonomy* classifies economic activities as environmentally sustainable if they significantly contribute to climate or environmental objectives without undermining social or environmental standards. This framework standardizes and harmonizes the identification of such activities that are essential for sustainable finance and environmental governance. The taxonomy provides reliable data on sustainability risks and opportunities, serving as a benchmark for regulators and product developers in tracking and reporting environmental and climate-related funds. By establishing a common language for stakeholders, green taxonomies help solidify regulatory and fiscal measures to enhance market integrity and prevent *greenwashing*.

The European Union (EU) taxonomy, introduced in 2020, provides a detailed framework for classifying sustainable economic activities and aims to set a global standard for harmonization. This classification system, developed by the Technical Expert Group on Sustainable Finance (TEG), outlines clear definitions to guide investors, policymakers, and companies in identifying sustainable activities. Central to the EU Green Deal and increasing green investments across the EU, the taxonomy defines activities that significantly contribute to six environmental objectives: climate change mitigation, climate change adaptation, sustainable use and protection of water and marine resources, transition to a circular economy, pollution prevention and control, and the protection and restoration of biodiversity and ecosystems. Additionally, to be considered sustainable under this framework, an activity must not significantly harm any of these objectives (Do No Significant Harm, or DNSH, principle) and adhere to minimum social safeguards.

Various countries and regions, including China, Malaysia, Singapore, the ASEAN, and India, are developing their green taxonomies to support environmental sustainability and green finance, tailoring approaches to local conditions and priorities. Malaysia utilizes a principle-based approach, primarily excluding certain *prohibited* activities, while Singapore adopts a structured methodology that aligns closely with the EU, focusing on precise sustainable investment definitions. China has implemented three green taxonomies since 2012, addressing green loans, bonds, and industries. The ASEAN Taxonomy for Sustainable Finance, effective from the first quarter of 2024, introduces the *Plus Standard* for technical screening of economic activities against environmental objectives. Building on its commitment to green financing, India launched its Sovereign Green Bond Framework in November 2022. It issued its debut sovereign green bond in early 2023, demonstrating an evolving and structured approach to financing environmental initiatives.

The proliferation of over 30 taxonomies and 200 sustainability reporting frameworks across 40 countries can sometimes complicate rather than clarify climate finance. Harmonization and improved interoperability of these frameworks are crucial for reducing reporting burdens and ensuring consistency among climate finance actors. The G7 and G20 play key roles in fostering cohesion in reporting and disclosure across major economies, supported by targeted national initiatives that offer practical solutions. Additionally, aligning new taxonomies with other jurisdictions is necessary to enhance comparability. The Common Ground Taxonomy (CGT) exemplifies this effort by comparing and contrasting the EU and China's green taxonomies, focusing on their approaches to climate change mitigation. However, it currently does not address other environmental objectives.

Furthermore, there is an urgent need for a standardized and centralized system for tracking climate finance data, building on existing efforts like the G20 Data Gaps Initiative to make data more accessible and streamline global efforts toward climate goals. Establishing a unified global methodology for green taxonomies is essential, as it would help policymakers formulate strategies to meet commitments such as NDCs and Sustainable Development Goals (SDGs), and encourage the development of innovative green financial products like bonds and ETFs.

Greenwashing refers to entities exaggerating their environmental benefits. It significantly jeopardizes the integrity and development of green capital markets by eroding investor confidence and obstructing the transition to a low-carbon economy. The risk of greenwashing is aggravated by the lack of unified standards and the proliferation of ESG rating agencies, contributing to market fragmentation and confusion. To combat greenwashing, it is crucial to enhance the transparency and credibility of environmental disclosures by publishing comprehensive, forward-looking environmental information and implementing uniform disclosure standards that enable effective comparison and auditing. Additionally, the differentiation between green and ESG products and the verification processes for green bonds tend to suffer from a lack of standardization. Sustainability-linked bonds (SLB) and loans link borrowing costs to sustainability performance and also require standardized and transparent assessments to effectively contribute to the low-carbon transition and counteract greenwashing risks. Progress in developing taxonomies and guidelines, enhancing market supervision, and the self-regulating impact of an increasingly sophisticated investor pool will also play crucial roles in curbing greenwashing.

4.3.1.3 Financial Instrument Standards

Financial instruments need certification to be labeled as *green instruments*. Several initiatives have been developed to create standards and certification. *Climate Bonds Initiative* is an international organization working to mobilize global capital for climate action by developing the Climate Bonds Standard and Certification Scheme, a labeling scheme for entities, assets, and debt instruments. Several scientific criteria are developed to ensure that certified investments in climate mitigation are consistent with the Paris Agreement targets. This scheme is used globally by bond issuers, governments, investors, and the financial markets to prioritize investments that genuinely contribute to addressing climate change.

Another crucial regulatory framework is the *Green Bond Principles* (GBP), endorsed by the *International Capital Market Association* (ICMA). These principles provide voluntary guidelines for issuing green bonds, including transparency, reporting, and disclosure recommendations. The GBP has been instrumental in standardizing practices and ensuring the integrity of green bonds as a credible tool for financing projects with environmental benefits. By setting clear criteria for what constitutes a green bond and how proceeds should be managed and reported, the GBP has supported a trusted market where investors can trust that their funds contribute to authentic environmental improvements.

In Europe, the *European Green Bond Standard*, effective from January 2025, aims to establish a clear benchmark for green bonds within the EU. This voluntary standard uses the detailed criteria of the EU taxonomy to define green economic activities, ensures transparency in line with market best practices, and establishes supervision for companies conducting pre-and post-issuance reviews at the European level. The European Securities and Markets Authority (ESMA) will oversee these external reviewers. The creation of this standard was recommended in the final report of the Commission's High-Level Expert Group on sustainable finance.

4.3.2 Green Financial Products GSS+

ESG funds and other green financial instruments like green, social, sustainable, and sustainability-linked (GSS+) bonds serve to promote sustainable investments, yet they vary in structure and focus (Figure 4.8). ESG funds are diversified investment vehicles that integrate ESG criteria into their investment strategies, encompassing various issues from carbon emissions to labor practices and corporate governance. These funds typically invest in a diverse portfolio of assets such as stocks, bonds, or other securities of companies that demonstrate strong ESG practices across multiple sectors.

Category	Description
Green	Blue, climate, green, biodiversity debt for nature, carbon neutrality, renewable energy, energy efficiency, solar, environmental, sustainable water and wastewater management, Property Assessed Clean Energy (PACE), sustainable management of natural resources and land use, climate change adaptation, clean transportation, pollution prevention and control, green buildings, circular economy
Transition	Blue transition, green transition, low-carbon transition
Sustainability	Green and social benefits combined into one instrument: ESG, positive impact, sustainability, sustainability awareness, Sustainable Development Goals (SDG), socially responsible investing (SRI), sustainable development, green innovation, employment generation, and gender equality.
Social	Affordable housing, food security and sustainable food systems, education, equality, gender, healthcare, SDG housing, town revitalization, youth, employment generation, socioeconomic advancement, and empowerment
Sustainability-linked	General purpose finance: sustainability-linked, ESG-linked, social impact-linked, and SDG-linked

FIGURE 4.8 Typology of GSS+ financial instruments
Source: Adapted from CBI

Table 4.4 *Sustainable fixed-income market 2023 – GSS+*

GSS+ market (2023)	Label	Market size	Number of currencies
Use of proceeds	Green	$2.8 trillion	53
	Social	$821 billion	46
	Sustainability	$768 billion	43
Performance-linked	Sustainability-linked	$48.6 billion	21
GSS+	Aligned GSS+ total	$4.4 trillion	64

Source: Authors, CBI

Conversely, GSS+ bonds are specific fixed-income instruments aimed at raising capital for projects that deliver clear environmental or social benefits. These bonds can attract significant private capital, particularly from institutional investors who might not usually invest in individual projects. Unlike ESG funds, which assess companies' overall sustainability performance, green bonds, for instance, are solely dedicated to financing projects that directly benefit the environment.

Use-of-proceeds bonds dominate the sustainable debt market (Table 4.4). The debt instruments exclusively finance eligible green or social projects, either in full or in part. UoP bonds include several subcategories, notably green bonds, blue bonds, biodiversity, transition bonds, social bonds, mixed sustainability bonds (instruments that raise funds for projects with environmental and social benefits).

4.3.2.1 Use of Proceeds Instruments

Green bonds are instruments dedicated to financing or refinancing, either partially or fully, new or existing eligible green projects in strict alignment with the GBP. The ICMA has established the four core components of GBP to maintain the integrity and transparency of the market. These principles refer to the use of proceeds, project evaluation and selection processes, management of proceeds, and reporting. Various nations and jurisdictions have formulated their

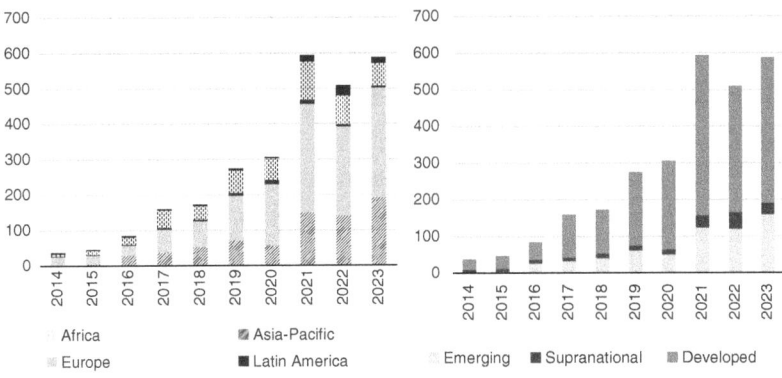

FIGURE 4.9 Breakdown of green bonds by region and issuer (USD billion)
Source: CBI (Market Data | Climate Bonds Initiative)

green bond guidelines, largely in alignment with these principles. The standards for green bonds vary, often referencing specific taxonomies or guidelines such as the Climate Bonds Taxonomy and Certification Scheme, the EU Green Bond Standard, China's Green Bond Guidelines, and ASEAN Green Bond Standards, which set regional or international criteria for environmental sustainability. National or sector-specific taxonomies of green activities further define which activities or assets qualify as green, while reducing the risk of greenwashing.

In 2023, green bond issuance grew by 10 percent to reach USD 575 billion, driven primarily by robust European issuance despite a continued contraction from North American issuers (Figure 4.9). Nonfinancial corporates remained the largest contributors to the market, closely followed by the financial services sector, which has seen significant growth over the past three years. Sovereign issuances were particularly strong, setting a new record with USD 160 billion, surpassing the previous high of USD 117 billion set in 2021. Notable issuers included France, Germany, Italy, and the UK, each exceeding USD 10 billion in sovereign green bonds.

Regionally, Europe led the green bond market in 2023, accounting for over 50 percent of total issuance, with the Asia-Pacific and

North America following at 32 percent and 11 percent, respectively. The top issuing countries were the United States, China, and Germany, contributing 16 percent, 13 percent, and 10 percent to the total volume.

The green bond market has seen not only a diversification in issuing regions but also in the sectors financed, with energy, transport, and buildings comprising 77 percent of the usage of proceeds. The market also observed a trend toward larger deal sizes, with those over USD 500 million increasing their share significantly. While primarily dominated by advanced economies, there is potential to expand the green bond market in emerging and developing economies (EMDEs), which would require enhanced third-party certification, uniform guidelines, aligned taxonomies, streamlined regulations, and better financial product design to facilitate growth.

Blue bonds, a subset of green bonds, are innovative financing instruments dedicated to funding sustainable water-related initiatives, including the sustainable use of maritime resources. They channel funds specifically toward ocean-friendly projects such as coastal climate adaptation, marine ecosystem management, offshore renewables, marine pollution prevention, sustainable fisheries and aquaculture management, marine biodiversity conservation, and sustainable coastal tourism. These bonds exclusively support critical clean water resources protection and associated sustainable activities.

As of the end of 2023, blue bonds worth USD 6.8 billion had been issued, representing 0.2 percent of overall GSS+B issuance since 2019, when the first blue bond was issued. The ocean economy is expected to double to USD 3 trillion by 2030, employing 40 million people as compared to 2010. Innovative financing solutions are key to enhancing ocean and coastal preservation and increasing clean water resources, and blue financial instruments have significant potential to help reach these goals. Trade association ICMA, together with four international institutions, developed in September 2023 a global practitioner's guide for bonds to finance the sustainable blue economy. Based on input from financial market participants, the marine industry, and global institutions, the guide provides information in areas such as evaluating the environmental impact of blue bond investments and the steps needed to facilitate transactions that preserve the market's integrity.

4.3.2.1.1 Biodiversity Instruments As awareness of the link between biodiversity loss and climate change grows, biodiversity considerations are increasingly incorporated into climate finance mechanisms. Investments are now more frequently directed toward projects that offer dual benefits for climate mitigation and biodiversity conservation, such as NbS like forest and wetland restoration. Additionally, the development of biodiversity markets for trading conservation credits and enhanced transparency through initiatives like the Taskforce on Nature-related Financial Disclosures (TNFD) are designed to attract private investment into biodiversity projects. Innovative financial instruments, including blue bonds and biodiversity offsets, also play a role.

Globally, investors, financial institutions, and bond issuers are showing growing interest in biodiversity finance, which draws on diverse funding sources – public, private, and philanthropic – and uses financial instruments such as green bonds, biodiversity offsets, payments for ecosystem services (PES), conservation trust funds, and eco-taxes. This form of finance seeks to preserve and sustainably manage natural habitats, species, and genetic diversity, underscoring the essential role of biodiversity in sustainable financial strategies.

Following COP15 and the launch of the Global Biodiversity Framework (GBF), and coupled with influence of the TNFD, bond issuances targeting biodiversity protection and restoration have increased significantly. In 2022, sixty bonds were issued with proceeds dedicated to biodiversity projects. Europe led with forty-six deals, focusing on national biodiversity strategies, flora and fauna conservation, forest protection, and Natura 2000 sites, which protect threatened species habitats.[9]

Biodiversity and blue economy financing through use-of-proceeds bonds still significantly lag behind climate-related issuance. Yet, these areas are crucial for clean transition as they closely align with climate mitigation and adaptation objectives. The GBF, adopted in Montreal in December 2022, emphasizes the need for significant increases in financial resources for biodiversity. Financial flows into global biodiversity conservation nearly tripled from 2012 to 2019, reaching approximately USD 130 billion. However, to reverse biodiversity decline by 2030, the funding gap for the broad range of actions under the Convention on Biological Diversity (CBD) is estimated to be around USD 700 billion annually. The effectiveness of biodiversity finance relies on scaling investments, enhancing funding mechanisms, and ensuring governance. Tools like the IFC's Biodiversity Finance Reference Guide are essential for targeting investments to mitigate biodiversity loss.

Transition bonds, while sharing characteristics with green bonds, are specifically designed to finance the shift of high-carbon industries and companies toward lower carbon emissions and more sustainable operations. These bonds, which can be either sustainability-linked or use-of-proceeds, are particularly intended for issuers in hard-to-abate sectors such as mining, steel, cement, aviation, and shipping. Their key attribute is supporting projects that, while not always *green*, facilitate climate transition and include a broader range of sectors and activities under the transition label.

The Climate Bonds Taxonomy, which outlines assets and activities aligned with a 1.5-degree pathway, supports financing under either green or transition labels. In 2022, the Climate Bonds

---

[9] Additionally, funds were allocated for aquatic and marine protection, addressing overfishing and supporting marine biodiversity recovery. In Asia-Pacific, bond issuances have supported broad biodiversity efforts, including habitat and wetland recovery. Notable examples include a CNY 1 billion bond from China and sovereign green bonds from Hong Kong SAR (HKD 20 billion) and Singapore (SGD 2.4 billion), all dedicated to enhancing natural areas.

Initiative introduced specific criteria for basic chemicals, cement, hydrogen production, and steel, helping entities in these sectors determine suitable assets, projects, and expenditures for inclusion in green or transition bond issuances.

To provide a comprehensive picture of use-of-proceeds instruments, we finally mention two last bond types: social bonds and sustainability bonds. *Social bonds* are instruments that raise funds for projects that address or mitigate a specific social issue and/or seek to achieve positive social outcomes, such as improving food security and access to education, healthcare, and financing, especially but not exclusively for target populations. Social bonds channel their proceeds toward projects that deliver significant social benefits, primarily targeting specific underserved groups. The Social Bond Principles set by ICMA mirror those of the GBP and were updated in June 2020 to adapt to the evolving market, including broader social project categories and target demographics in response to the COVID-19 pandemic. *Sustainability bonds* combine the objectives of green and social bonds, raising funds for environmental and social projects. The ICMA's Sustainability Bond Guidelines incorporate the fundamental aspects of both Green and Social Bond Principles.

4.3.2.2 Performance-based Green Financial Instruments

Sustainability-linked bonds are performance-oriented financial instruments that differ from green bonds as their terms, such as interest rates, are directly tied to the issuer's achievement of specific sustainability targets. These targets are defined by Key Performance Indicators (KPIs) and aim for ambitious yet achievable goals at the corporate level. As outlined by the ICMA's Sustainability-Linked Bond Principles, released in June 2020, SLBs are not restricted by use of proceeds like traditional green and social bonds. Instead, they link borrowing costs to attaining predefined ESG targets, financing general corporate purposes, and emphasizing the importance of clear, quantifiable sustainability objectives in their structuring, disclosure, and reporting standards.

Sustainability-linked bonds (SLBs) raise general-purpose finance with terms, such as coupon step-ups or occasionally step-downs, linked to the achievement of predefined, time-bound Sustainability Performance Targets (SPTs). These targets adjust the interest rate based on the issuer's success or failure in meeting specific sustainability goals, making SLBs future-oriented and performance-dependent instruments.

Since the first SLB was issued in December 2018, the market has rapidly evolved, marked by a diverse and growing pool of issuers. After a surge in 2021 as markets rebounded post-COVID, issuance has faced challenges due to adverse global market conditions in 2022, which impacted capital markets broadly and raised concerns about the credibility of SLBs. Nonetheless, the dominance of nonfinancial corporates, which account for 84 percent of the cumulative issuance, continues, although public sector entities have also begun entering the market. Notably, Chile and Uruguay issued their first sovereign SLBs in 2022.

The geographical distribution of issuances shows Italy, France, and Germany as leading issuer domiciles. While the majority of SLBs have historically targeted reducing scopes 1 and 2 GHG emissions, there is a growing push to include scope 3 emissions and factors like gender diversity. Emerging markets are increasingly participating, with countries like Brazil, South Africa, Turkey, Morocco, Indonesia, and Chile contributing more to the market.

Despite some stagnation post-2021, the SLB market is showing signs of maturation and expansion. In 2022, the aligned SLB volume grew by 95 percent, and the quality of bonds improved significantly, with 35 percent of the issued amount being aligned in 2023 compared to just 14 percent in 2022. This evolution suggests a potential for further growth as the market diversifies across more currencies, issuer domiciles, and issuer types, becoming increasingly robust and inclusive.

The environmental effectiveness of SLBs can be undermined when the financial penalties for missing SPTs are relatively modest. This dynamic suggests a critical need for more substantial penalties to ensure that SLBs drive significant environmental improvements rather than merely serving as a cost-effective financing option for issuers. So far, cases of issuers failing to meet their SPTs have been rare; however, when they do occur, they raise doubts about the ambition of the targets and whether the standard 25-basis-point coupon step-up provides enough incentive for compliance. The combination of a high likelihood of meeting targets and minimal repercussions for missing them can make SLBs appear no different from standard, unlabeled bonds to some investors. Instituting stronger penalties would help ensure that SLBs attract capital and effectively enforce stringent environmental commitments for greater impact.

4.3.2.3 Other Sustainable Finance Instruments

Debt-for-nature swaps are debt relief schemes primarily aimed at sovereigns, where a creditor voluntarily cancels or reduces the debt in exchange for the debtor's financial contribution to a conservation project. Thanks to guarantees from higher-rated third parties on the newly swapped bonds, these typically feature lower spreads than the government's standard (senior unsecured) bonds. Typically, an international conservation organization might purchase a portion of a country's debt at a reduced rate on the secondary market, agreeing to cancel it provided the country commits to investing a specified amount in local environmental projects such as reforestation, wildlife protection, or the establishment of national parks. In 2023, Ecuador signed the world's largest debt-for-nature swap deal, acquiring USD 1.6 billion of debt for USD 644 million. In return, the government committed to disbursing USD 18 million annually for 20 years to support conservation efforts in the Galapagos Islands.

Green loans are an alternative financing mechanism designed to fund projects with positive environmental impacts; similar to green bonds, their use of proceeds should fall within the environmental or climate criteria. *Blue loans* are financing instruments that earmark funds exclusively for ocean-friendly projects and critical clean water resources protection. Unlike green bonds, green or blue loans are usually smaller, privately arranged, and often lack transparency due to their bilateral nature, making it challenging to access information about the deals, such as loan amounts, terms, and uses of proceeds. According to the Climate Bonds Initiative, which tracks these loans on a best-efforts basis, USD 10.4 billion in green loans were issued in 2022. Green loans represented 2 percent of the total loan market that year, with 70 percent of the volume coming from Asia-Pacific and Europe, each accounting for 35 percent.

Green Sukuk, Islamic financial certificates similar to bonds, are structured to fund environmentally friendly projects in compliance with Sharia law and have been growing globally as a pivotal tool for sustainable development, particularly in the areas of renewable energy and climate resilience. Malaysia, a leader in Islamic finance, launched its first green sukuk in 2017, followed by Indonesia, which has funded various sustainable projects. The Middle East has also seen a significant uptake, with countries like Saudi Arabia and the United Arab Emirates aligning their Islamic finance sectors with global sustainability goals, as evidenced by the surge in green and sustainable sukuk issuance to USD 5.5 billion in 2023. These instruments adhere to Climate Bond Standards certification, supporting projects ranging from solar parks to EVs, underpinning their environmental commitments. The role of Islamic finance in facilitating the clean energy transition was further highlighted at the COP28 summit, underscoring its increasing contribution to global sustainability efforts, with the Middle East now accounting for nearly half of the global green sukuk issuance.

Finally, recent initiatives promote the development of *green equity*, whereby investors use equity stakes in clients to foster environmental sustainability and align projects with climate goals. An example is when development or climate funds take equity in financial intermediaries and require them to scale climate lending and reduce exposure to polluting assets. In some frameworks, greening equity involves mandating limits on fossil investments and using equity influence to ensure climate compatibility.

4.3.3 GSS+ Market Developments

While recent developments in the GSS+ fixed-income market has grown rapidly (Figure 4.10), investors continue to face challenges such as regulatory ambiguity, limited transparency, and the presence of a "greenium" – a higher price premium for GSS+ bonds than traditional bonds. As of 2023, GSS+ bonds reached a cumulative volume of USD 5.5 trillion, with 80 percent aligned with the Climate Bonds Initiative (CBI) methodology. Green bonds represent 63 percent of this total, with emerging market issuances accounting for 16 percent. With increasing attention to biodiversity and social risks, there is growing investor interest in innovative structures like debt-for-nature swaps, blue bonds for marine conservation, and orange bonds for gender-focused initiatives. With the European Green Bond Regulation (Regulation 2023/2631) entering into force in December 2024, the EU green bond standard marks a maturing market with stronger requirements for transparency, accountability, and validation.

GSS+ issuance accounted for 13 percent of total bond issuance in 2022 and 2023, reflecting a longstanding positive correlation with conventional bond issuance over the past decade. Historically led by

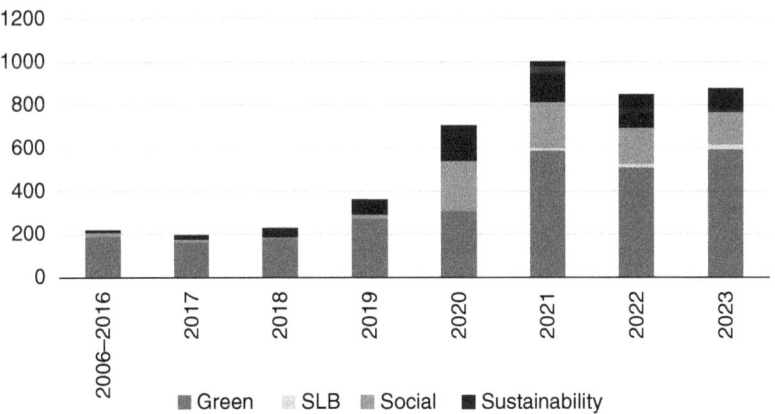

FIGURE 4.10 GSS+ issuance by category (USD billion)
Source: CBI

high-income countries, the GSS+ market is now witnessing greater participation from lower-income countries. In 2023, North American issuance declined for the second consecutive year, reflecting less favorable sentiment toward ESG investing. Emerging markets experienced a 45 percent increase in issuance to USD 209 billion, notably in countries outside China, underscoring their commitment to climate and social goals.

The Middle East and Latin America saw substantial expansion, recording growth rates of 150 percent and 56 percent, respectively. Additionally, the Asia-Pacific region now represents 25 percent of total GSS+ issuance, its highest proportion to date, driven by new entrants like India, which issued its inaugural sovereign green bond in 2022.

In 2023, the green, social, and sustainability (GSS+) bond markets, including SLBs, saw robust growth. Total GSS+ issuance rose to USD 870 billion, a 3 percent increase from the previous year, with green bonds leading at USD 587.6 billion, up 15 percent. However, social and sustainability bonds faced declines of 7 percent and 30 percent, respectively. SLB issuance rebounded impressively in the past year, surging by 83 percent to reach USD 22.8 billion compared to USD 11.7 billion recorded for 2022. This robust performance reflects increasing market acceptance and strong regulatory support, particularly in Europe, contributing 46 percent to the total GSS+ issuance.

The currency diversity in GSS+ issuance also increased, with less than 70 percent of bonds issued in euros and US dollars for the first time in 2023 (Figure 4.11). Ten different currencies represent at least 1 percent of the market, reflecting the growing financial participation of regions like Asia-Pacific, Latin America, and the Middle East. The trend toward greater currency diversification shows an expanding global participation in the GSS+ market, especially from issuers in emerging markets such as Mexico and South Korea, increasingly opting to issue bonds in local currencies.

The broader economic context also played a crucial role in shaping the GSS+ market dynamics. The easing of inflationary pressures

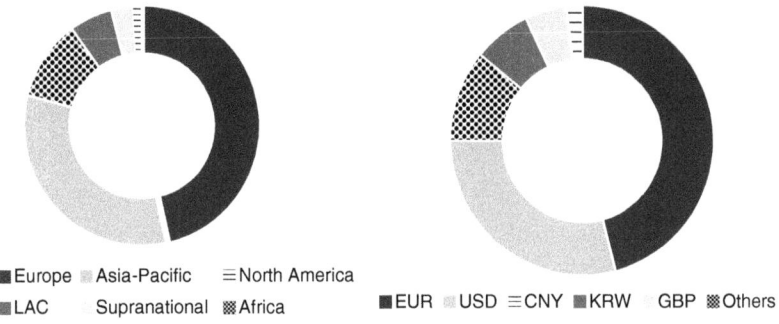

FIGURE 4.11 Regional and issuer currency distribution of the GSS+ deals in 2023

and relatively stable economic activity helped sustain market growth. Looking forward, the GSS+ market is expected to continue its expansion, supported by increasing public investment in climate mitigation and adaptation as governments strive to reach net zero targets by 2050. This structural support is particularly significant in emerging markets, where investment shortfalls around the energy transition are larger, and the green premium is wider. As these markets deepen their engagement with GSS+ instruments, they connect local borrowers directly to a growing pool of international capital that prioritizes ESG criteria, setting the stage for continued growth in sustainable finance.

The growth in GSS+ issuance is expected to continue, supported by high investor demand, the increasing adoption of sustainable taxonomies and transparency initiatives, and expanding issuance from emerging markets. Enhanced regulatory efforts to establish standardized sustainable finance guidelines across jurisdictions also deepen market access for developing economies and attract significant investment capital. To fully unlock the potential of this nascent market and meet the financial needs of emerging markets transitioning their economic models, a collaborative effort involving financial supervisors, governments, investors, borrowers, and multilateral development institutions is crucial.

4.3.4 GSS+ Market Dynamics and Pricing

In the long run, we expect GSS+ bond issuance to continue to be structurally supported by two major drivers. Firstly, we foresee increasing public spending as governments strive to reach net zero targets by 2050. Secondly, we expect investor demand for GSS+ instruments to outpace supply. This dynamic is likely to be even more pronounced in emerging markets, where financing gaps for the energy transition are particularly large. Still, the green premium – or *greenium*, meaning the lower yield on GSS+ instruments compared to equivalent conventional bonds – remains wider. On the positive side, investors in ESG and green investment funds tend to maintain their investments even after periods of underperformance, indicating a more resilient and dedicated support base for sustainable assets.

The analysis of the pricing dynamics of GSS+ bonds shows how these bonds offer pricing advantages for issuers and investors compared to traditional bonds. Based on 110 green bonds with a combined volume of USD 124.6 billion, CBI constructed yield curves for 50 nonsovereign bonds, finding that 16 bonds (32 percent) were priced on or inside their secondary market yield curves (CBI, 2023).[10] Of the bonds that achieved a *greenium* (green premium), 12 were denominated in EUR and four in USD. CBI noted that the green label is particularly attractive due to its dedicated investor base and liquidity, allowing investors to sell more easily. The analysis also highlighted that 66 percent of green bonds were allocated to investors with green or responsible investment mandates.

4.4 GREENIUM

Green, blue, biodiversity, and climate transition bonds share core financial characteristics with conventional bonds, including seniority, maturity, and credit rating. They are treated equally alongside other similar-ranking instruments from the issuer in bankruptcy

---

[10] cbi_pricing_h1_2023_01f.pdf (climatebonds.net)

situations. Their distinctive feature lies in their compliance with internationally recognized standards and guidelines for climate transition funding, which underscores their role in supporting environmental and sustainability goals while offering the same financial security as traditional bonds.

Investing in green financial products enables investors to align their portfolios with global decarbonization efforts and meet ESG reporting requirements, reflecting a commitment to combating climate change. This alignment positions investors to enhance returns potentially and provides reputational benefits and access to more favorable investment terms, known as *greenium*. This greenium often results in lower yields for green bonds than conventional bonds, compensating for the higher transaction costs associated with issuing green bonds – such as compliance with stringent regulations, independent reviews, and annual audits on progress. CBI defines *greenium* differently, referring to the phenomenon where a bond is sold in the primary market at a higher price – and thus a lower yield – compared to the existing debt of the same issuer in the secondary market, akin to a new issue concession. This metric serves as a proxy to determine if the green label can secure cheaper funding for the issuer.

Such a concept of *greenium* is now well-documented in financial literature. Most research has focused on primary markets with mixed results. Tang and Zhang (2018) and Flammer (2021) found no greenium in global corporate green bonds, while Larcker and Watts (2019) observed no greenium in the US municipal bond market. Conversely, Ehler and Packer (2017) and Kapraun et al. (2021) identified a significant greenium of about 20 basis points for corporate green bonds. All studies concur that green bonds with external reviews consistently display a greenium, with factors like currency and issuer country affecting credibility. Specifically, EUR-denominated and EU-issued green bonds trade at a greenium, unlike Chinese green bonds (Kapraun et al., 2021). Fatica et al. (2021) also found that green bonds from UNEP FI financial institutions are issued with a greenium.

When examining secondary market performance and comparing new-issue spreads of green bonds with those of conventional bonds issued in different years, the findings vary widely. Zerbib (2019) examined the pricing of green bonds in secondary markets and reported evidence of a small but statistically significant greenium, equivalent to about −2 basis points across a broad sample of bonds. The effect was found to be more pronounced for financial and low-rated bonds. Hachenberg and Schiereck (2018) use a similar method and find a significant green premium of −3.9 basis points for A-rated bonds, though the premium is negative but insignificant for the overall sample. Baker et al. (2018) extend the traditional CAPM to include preferences for green bonds in the US market, confirming that green bonds are issued at lower yields than comparable conventional bonds. They also note that green bond ownership is more concentrated, attributed to a subset of investors favoring green investments. Karpf and Mandel (2017) found a green bond discount, with green bonds carrying a positive yield differential of about 8 basis points. However, the authors suggest that this gap reflects differences in bond characteristics rather than the green label itself. Meanwhile, Ehlers and Packer (2017) and Kapraun et al. (2021) documented that green bonds generally perform similarly to conventional bonds.

Pietsch and Salakhova (2022) analyze green bonds issued in the euro area from 2016 to 2021, using the ICMA GBP definition, and create a comparable control group of conventional bonds. First, they observe a greenium of approximately 4 basis points across the full sample, though it is only significant at the 10 percent level. Second, this greenium is driven by green bonds with higher credibility. Specifically, green bonds with external reviews show a statistically significant greenium of 5.3 basis points. Green bonds issued by environmentally focused firms and UNEP FI banks exhibit even more significant greeniums of 22.2 and 17.38 basis points, respectively. Third, the greenium's economic and statistical significance grows over time, particularly for green bonds issued by banks. Green bonds from alternative energy firms consistently trade at a greenium throughout the period. Lastly, the authors find that the greenium for green bonds issued by banks is driven by increased demand from retail investors.

The resilience of green bonds is particularly notable during periods of economic instability, as observed during the 2020 pandemic when green bonds showed enhanced stability and outperformed conventional bonds. This resilience is supported by a dedicated investor base that prioritizes long-term sustainable investment, maintaining demand and price stability even during turbulent times. Additionally, the wider green premium in emerging markets compared to developed economies indicates a robust investor appetite, making it cheaper for governments and corporations to raise capital through green bonds.

4.5 CONCLUSION

Globally, regulatory frameworks supporting sustainable finance are becoming more diverse and sophisticated, reflecting a broader array of policy measures. Yet these efforts cannot succeed in isolation. They must be embedded within national sustainable development strategies and aligned with fiscal, technological, and industrial policies. Such integration is essential to building a robust sustainable finance ecosystem that engages all actors across the investment value chain – asset owners, managers, exchanges, issuers, and regulators.

Harmonizing and aligning corporate sustainability accounting and reporting frameworks is vital for scaling up climate finance and enhancing market efficiency. Implementing holistic strategies incorporating sustainability into investment practices, alongside new tools like taxonomies, standards for sustainable financial products, climate disclosure requirements, and carbon pricing mechanisms, represents critical steps toward a green transition. Regional initiatives to standardize policies already illustrate the benefits of broader international convergence based on established standards and practices. In countries with less developed regulatory and standard-setting systems, targeted technical assistance will be critical to building market structures that can support sustainable finance.

The effectiveness of regulatory frameworks and initiatives play a decisive role in shaping and expanding the GSS+ bond market. Improving transparency, accountability, and impact verification strengthens the market infrastructure for scaling climate finance. The private sector's engagement, crucial for expanding climate finance, relies heavily on robust support from governments and international institutions. This includes enhancing the attractiveness of projects through various incentives and risk mitigation strategies, utilizing tools like guarantees, risk insurance, and blended finance mechanisms. Taken together, these strategies are central to mobilizing private finance – a theme discussed further in Chapter 7.

5 Central Banks, Climate Change, and Price Stability

5.1 INTRODUCTION

As seen in Chapter 3, climate change and the ecological transition entail significant risks for the economic and financial systems, pushing central banks to step in and stabilize price and output fluctuations that could be related to such risks. By managing climate change-induced economic and financial fluctuations, central banks can play a critical role in preventing these financial and economic risks or mitigating their impact. As an independent national authority, a central bank conducts monetary policy to keep inflation under control and deliver on the price stability objective. The primary mandate of central banks that pursue *inflation targeting* policies is to keep inflation in check, close to a predetermined target. By stirring policy interest rates, central banks modify supply and demand conditions, which in turn enable them to reach a new equilibrium that ensures price stability, fosters economic growth, and promotes maximum employment. Climate change may endanger this price stability objective by triggering inflationary pressures and price volatility due to extreme weather events (e.g., surging food prices after a flood) or transition policy (e.g., a carbon tax). Such climate-related economic effects could affect the central bank's ability to deliver on its price stability mandate in the future and become highly relevant for the conduct of monetary policy (Bolton et al., 2020; Boneva et al., 2022; Drudi et al., 2021).

A comprehensive assessment of climatic risks on inflation is, therefore, an important element in guiding the mitigation and adaptation efforts of governments, as well as informing monetary policy concerning the risks posed by climate change. It is, therefore, important for central banks to correctly assess the sign and the magnitude of these effects. Climate change is a tragedy of horizons in the sense that its effects can lead to long-term structural upheavals beyond economic cycles, beyond political cycles, and, finally, beyond the monetary policy horizon. Indeed, climate change also modifies long-term variables that are also key for central bankers, like potential output or the natural rate of interest. As seen in Chapter 1, extreme weather events and global warming could reduce the stock of capital and alter labor productivity, *in fine* lowering overall supply. On the other hand, the overall supply impact of ecological transition is less clear. Mitigation policies make obsolete some parts of the capital stock due to technological inadequacy or GHG emission intensity. This loss of potential output could be offset by the supportive impact of the green transition on new capital accumulation and technological innovation. These supply aspects of the ecological transition are of great importance for central bankers due to their direct influence on natural interest rates and the room for maneuvering of monetary policy. Transition policies, such as carbon tax, could also create stagflationary episodes (higher inflation and lower growth), creating a difficult trade-off for central banks aiming at stabilizing both prices and output.

Because climate-related risks will affect the objective of price stability, the vast majority of central banks plan to integrate, respond, and act to continue to deliver on this objective. This requires a better understanding of the effects of climate change and mitigation policies on price developments and designing appropriate policy reactions. In addition, central banks may also adapt their instruments and monetary policy operations to fully integrate climate risks and align their operational framework with ecological targets.

5.2 CLIMATE CHANGE AND MACROECONOMIC STABILIZATION CHALLENGES FOR CENTRAL BANKS

Most central banks' monetary policy objective is to keep inflation low, stable, and predictable. Under all likely scenarios of a clean transition, climate change will impact the economic and financial ecosystem in which central banks operate. Transition policy uncertainty and

5 CENTRAL BANKS, CLIMATE CHANGE, AND PRICE STABILITY

increased economic volatility arising from climate risks will complicate central banks' assessments relative to the output gap and inflation.

Per its direct influence on inflation and output developments, climate change tends to challenge central banks in ensuring price stability and anchoring inflation expectations. The materialization of both physical and transition risks could significantly alter price developments in the short to medium term.

5.2.1 Differentiating the Inflationary Impact of Climate-Related Risks

The ECB Executive Board member Isabel Schnabel (2022) summarized the potential impact of the climate-related risks on inflation, pointing to three new sources that must be addressed: climateflation, fossilflation, and greenflation (Table 5.1).

- *Climateflation:* Extreme weather events cause supply chain disruptions in ecosystem services-dependent sectors (agriculture, fisheries, forestry, energy, and tourism).
- *Fossilflation:* Higher volatility and increased inflation caused by a disorderly green transition: A contraction of fossil fuel supplies unmatched by efforts on demand (oil and gas shortages) and carbon taxes and prices.
- *Greenflation:* Inflation caused by increased capital investment to comply with climate objectives: The demand for critical materials and resources necessary to the energy transition (lithium, cobalt, nickel, graphite, and manganese) has increased unmatched by supply.

So far, greenflation has a much lower impact on final consumer prices than fossilflation and the transition to a low-carbon economy is not responsible for the rise in energy prices observed in 2022.[1] However, during the transition period, the adoption of low-emission

---

[1] Main drivers of the global surge of inflation in 2022 can be summarized as surging food and energy prices after the invasion of Ukraine, supply pressures due to renewed waves of Covid in China, as well as excess global liquidity arising from a decade of low interest rates and ultra-accommodative monetary policy in advanced economies.

Table 5.1 *Inflationary impact of climate-related risks*

	Physical risks	Transition risks	
	Climateflation	Fossilflation	Greenflation
Definitions	Pressures from Climate change on ecosystem services that are necessary to economic activities. Economic losses in climate-related sectors	The mismatch between supply contraction and strenuous demand creates upward pressure on fossil fuel prices and increased volatility	Green technologies require significant amounts of metals and minerals (e.g., copper, lithium, and cobalt) Strong demand exceeding supply capacities puts pressure on prices
Causes	Global warming and changes in weather patterns (chronic and acute natural hazards) jeopardize harvests	Carbon pricing or regulation Decreasing exposure of financial investors to fossil fuel industries leading to an increase in costs	Rising demand and constrained supply in transition critical minerals
Examples	Between April 2020 and December 2021, coffee prices increased 70% after droughts and frost destroyed crops in Brazil, the world's largest coffee-producing country.[2]	Between April and May 2022, fossil fuel-related items – transport and household energy – contributed about 20% to India's annual rate of inflation.[3]	Between December 2020 and November 2022, the price of lithium has been multiplied by close to 15.

[2] www.theguardian.com/environment/2022/jun/28/climate-crisis-food-shortages
[3] Report published by Cambridge Econometrics "Fossil Fuel Prices and Inflation in India."

technologies by a growing number of industries is expected to cause greenflation, which could lead to upward pressure on prices for a wide range of products (Schnabel, 2022). We will see below that these expected inflationary effects are far from consensus.

5.2.2 Climate Change and Impact on Prices

Extreme weather events and other physical risks associated with climate change can lead to substantial output losses, necessitating central bank intervention to mitigate economic fluctuations and stimulate growth. These challenges are particularly pronounced for emerging markets, especially in Africa, where monetary authorities often have fewer financial resources compared to their counterparts in developed countries, and the vulnerability to extreme weather events, such as droughts and floods, is more pronounced. The materialization of the physical risks related to climate change could trigger similar dynamics to negative supply shocks, encompassing aspects such as capital destruction, reduced labor supply, and decreased productivity. These factors collectively diminish potential output, contribute to economic overheating, and heighten inflationary pressures. Some industrial sectors are more vulnerable to the inflationary impact of climate-change-related events, in particular those depending on ecosystem services such as agriculture, fishery, forestry, energy with hydropower, or even tourism. For example, the impact of severe droughts or floods can result in a significant increase in food prices, thereby eroding the purchasing power of vulnerable households.

Countering such challenges with the traditional monetary policy toolbox may prove difficult, as demonstrated by the food and energy price spikes observed after Russia's invasion of Ukraine. Food prices hit a new all-time high in 2022, driven by vegetable oils and cereal price increases (Figure 5.1). Central bankers will face an intricate trade-off between stabilizing inflation and promoting economic growth in the context of climate-related disruptions. While an interest rate hike might partially mitigate supply-driven inflation, it could

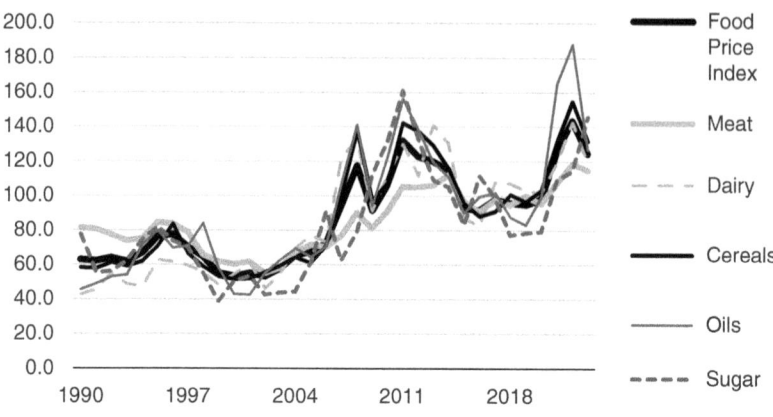

FIGURE 5.1 Food price indices (2014–2016 = 100)
Source: FAO

simultaneously impede credit expansion and exert downward pressure on economic activity.

While the increase in food prices after 2020 was mainly driven by a robust demand in the recovery from COVID-19 and the Russian invasion on Ukraine, the IPCC report on Impacts, Adaptation and Vulnerability (IPCC, 2022), underlined that "Climate change has caused regionally different, but mostly negative, impacts on crop yields, quality, and marketability of products (high confidence)." Agriculture is not the only sector to suffer from climate change, "Economic damages from climate change have been detected in climate-exposed sectors, with regional effects to agriculture, forestry, fishery, energy, and tourism (high confidence)." In these exposed sectors, even if climate-related events are not putting durable upward pressure on food prices, they increase price volatility in most cases.

Recent work has started to quantify the relationship between climate and inflation, generally by exploiting large datasets of price inflation and relating them to changes in weather conditions. Parker (2018) studied the potential effects of various natural disasters on consumer price inflation and found historical impacts of storms and floods on inflation. Faccia et al. (2021) focused on large temperature deviations as exogenous shocks and identified short-term inflationary impacts from hot summers, with stronger effects in emerging market economies. Mukherjee and Ouattara (2021) studied the effects of changing annual temperatures and found impacts that persist for a number of years. Ciccarelli et al. (2023) took a VAR approach to study the effects of different temperature shocks in the four largest euro area economies on prices. They found upward impacts on inflation from both increasing average temperatures in summer, which are more pronounced in warmer countries, and from increasing temperature variability. They also find an inflationary impact on services from hotter summers in warmer euro area countries, presumably due to impacts through food prices and a sensitivity of tourism-related services to hotter temperatures. The inflationary impact on other components of the harmonized price index was found to be less persistent and, at times, also negative. Accounting for heterogenous impacts across seasons and baseline climatic and socio-economic conditions, Kotz et al. (2024) find that hotter-than-usual summers can increase inflation for several months, usually through impacts on food prices. For example, they report that the 2022 extreme summer heat increased the food inflation in the euro area by around 0.7 percentage points cumulatively after one year.

The literature also provides mixed evidence regarding the impacts of other types of (catastrophic) extreme weather events or environmental degradation on different inflation components or on the medium-term inflation outlook (e.g., Parker, 2018; Ciccarelli and Marotta, 2024). The overall balance on headline inflation between negative supply shocks on agriculture and occasional negative demand shocks on other components is not always clear ex ante.

Kotz et al. (2024) also find that upward pressures from rising temperatures on inflation are estimated to be larger in warmer months and countries, but the impact can be insignificant in colder months and countries. Nonlinearities are found regarding inflation impacts from higher temperatures (Faccia et al., 2021; Ciccarelli et al., 2023; Kotz et al., 2024; also see above). Due to this nonlinear relationship, the inflation impact of climate change is especially set to increase during extremely hot summers. Moessner (2022) found nonlinear impacts of annual precipitation changes, regarding other variables besides temperature.

Kotz et al. (2024) also apply empirical elasticities to the temperature–inflation relationship to temperatures projected by physical climate models and find that – ceteris paribus – future average warming would also put further pressure on inflation. The impact of extreme heat on food inflation in Europe, noted above, is projected to be 50 percent greater under the levels of warming expected by 2035.

5.2.3 The Debate around the Transition-Induced Risks to Price Stability

While the transition to a low-carbon economy will most likely increase inflation in the short to medium term, the magnitude of the inflationary impact depends on the policy path chosen. As seen in Chapter 3, there is no global carbon price that truthfully reflects the environmental cost of emissions. The implementation of such a carbon price, which takes into account the environmental cost and incentivizes a forceful shift toward green energies, would naturally make fossil fuels more expensive (the so-called *fossilflation* – see above). As economies transition toward renewable energies, they could face energy inflation for a prolonged period. Although the prices of renewable energies have dramatically reduced over the past years, transforming the entire infrastructure and production facilities will take decades. In the meantime, countries that have fallen behind the transition curve will be the most affected by fossil inflation. Given the urgency to step up the decarbonization efforts to meet the goals of the Paris climate agreement, in contrast with short-lived energy price hikes in the past, fossil fuel prices could keep rising and stay elevated for a protracted period. Carbon tax policies, as well as changes in global demand for fossil fuels, will certainly amplify the fluctuations in oil and gas prices. This price volatility could affect inflation down the road (through import prices and changes in export demand) and alter medium-term inflation expectations.

Price pressures could also be associated with the transition to cleaner energies. The transition toward greener production technologies requires an intensive consumption of inputs in metals and minerals such as copper, lithium, nickel, and cobalt. The switch to low-emission technologies will certainly generate upward pressure on the prices of these specific inputs. Given the time needed to develop new mines, supply, and transport bottlenecks for these products will most probably generate inflationary pressures in the short and medium run. While attracting less attention from central banks than fossil fuel prices, strong mineral price fluctuations, as observed since the beginning of the 2000s, can also affect overall price levels. In this respect, Boer et al. (2021) find that inflation-adjusted prices of lithium, copper, cobalt, and nickel could reach "peaks similar to historical ones but for an unprecedented, sustained period of roughly a decade" (Boer et al., 2021, pp. 4–5). While the pass-through of such prices to overall inflation has been low so far, the inflationary impact of mineral prices might become larger, should materials shortages could intensify supply bottlenecks. While the share of metal in final consumption is marginal, the contribution of mineral price changes to inflation mainly comes from their impact on the production and distribution chains. As they are mostly relevant to industry, their effect on inflation would be greater in countries with a large industrial sector.

Beyond the production of decarbonized energy, the green transition requires major adaptations of the economic system. Underlying structural transformations of production may be hampered by certain obstacles that adversely affect activity and inflation. In the labor market, for example, the reallocation of labor to low-carbon activities, or the need for upskilling in sectors that require major transformations (construction, transport, etc.), may produce labor shortages and lead to both wage increases and unemployment (Girard et al., 2022). In the market for goods and services, the transition requires carbon-based goods and services to become more expensive than other goods and services, causing uncertain effects on inflation. Consequently, the development of low-carbon technologies, especially in renewable energies (production and use), could have disinflationary effects. Continued uncertainty about future transition policies would negatively affect both prices and activity.

The potential consequences for activity and inflation during the transition may, therefore, vary significantly depending on the shocks considered. A typology of potential shocks – linked to both supply and demand – is necessary to properly assess the implications of transition risks for price stability and growth. Such shocks could have an inflationary impact, particularly in the case of a negative supply shock, especially if this occurs in a disorderly fashion. Conversely, certain shocks could have a disinflationary effect, in the event of heightened uncertainty or financial disruption linked to stranded assets.

Transition-related developments can be classified as supply or demand shocks, which can be both positive and negative. A positive demand shock – the one generally presented in ordered/optimistic scenarios – could have a positive effect on economic activity, but also inflationary implications. On the other hand, negative demand shocks – triggered by uncertainty or financial market turbulence – could be disinflationary and recessionary. On the supply side, positive shocks could stimulate economic growth and reduce inflation if they stimulate innovation and productivity. On the contrary, if the shocks are negative, triggered by for example, by higher costs due to carbon taxation or stranded assets, stagflationary episodes could appear.

Figure 5.2 depicts various standard scenarios corresponding to representative cases of transition-related shocks as follows:

- A first group of scenarios focuses on the deterioration of supply conditions, which could lead to stagflation (rising inflation accompanied by falling growth). This first category could be represented by an abrupt increase in carbon pricing or a sudden tightening of environmental regulations.
- A second category focuses instead on shocks that can negatively affect demand, and thus lead to deflation (simultaneous decline in inflation and growth or financial market turmoil due to stranded assets).

5 CENTRAL BANKS, CLIMATE CHANGE, AND PRICE STABILITY

	Inflation	
Negative supply-side shocks		**Positive demand-side shocks**
Disorderly carbon taxation (sudden and/or unanticipated)		**Boom in green public investment** financed by carbon taxation
Sudden tightening of environmental regulations		Boom in green private expenditures coupled with a **"green bubble"** (e.g., shortage of metals and minerals required by green technologies)
Negative demand-side shocks		**Positive supply-side shocks**
Confidence crisis due to **uncertainty on transition policies**		**Large green private capital expenditures** increase potential output without crowding-out other investment (but crowding out consumption)
Financial turmoil, initiated by stranded assets, leading to tightened financing conditions		**Green innovation** boosts aggregate productivity

FIGURE 5.2 Climate transition: a wide diversity of shocks, which can coexist
Source: Allen et al. (2023)

- A third category looks at the transition as a succession of positive shocks to demand, triggered, for example, by sustainable public investments or a boom in green assets (*green bubble*) with a positive effect on growth and inflation.
- The last category is based on the assumption of an improvement in supply, thanks to elevated private capital expenditure with no crowding out of other investments or the diffusion of green innovation to the overall economy, which increases output with no inflationary effects.

Introducing a carbon tax in advanced economies or significantly increasing the global carbon price to reflect the genuine environmental cost of emissions could serve as a powerful incentive for transitioning to cleaner energies. However, such transition policies may also result in elevated global fossil fuel prices and heightened short- to medium-term volatility. This poses a notable inflation risk, particularly for Central European countries with substantial and fossil fuel-intensive manufacturing sectors within the EU. Conversely, implementing a carbon tax on goods entering the EU would adversely impact the price competitiveness of emerging market exporters to Europe, especially those in neighboring North Africa.

Current empirical literature, mainly focused on the inflationary effects of carbon taxes, has so far not shown any significant effect of such taxes on inflation. Counterfactual exercises on the reaction of consumer prices after the implementation of carbon taxes do not point to rapid inflation, even suggesting deflationary effects (Konradt and Weder di Mauro, 2023). Moreover, energy prices tend to rise slightly in carbon-taxed economies, before oscillating around zero. Conversely, food prices are found to decline modestly, and core Consumer Price Inflation (CPI) inflation has fallen persistently since the implementation of the carbon tax. Another study (McKibbin, Konradt and Weder di Mauro, 2021) examines the interaction between climate change policies and monetary policy in the euro area (see Chapter 3 for details about European transition policies). Their findings highlight that under observed monetary policy reaction, the inflationary effects of the carbon tax in euro area countries have been contained. The only significant increase in the HICP (of around 0.8 index points) occurred in the first two years after the introduction of the tax. At the same time, however, the impact on core inflation tended to be negative. Thus, carbon taxes mainly affected relative prices rather than the general price level. Producers appear to have absorbed part of the carbon tax into their margins since consumer price inflation was lower than producer price inflation. A final study (Ciccarelli and Marotta, 2024) associates transition risks with technological shocks that reduce both the level of emissions and economic damage over the business cycle. The effects of this shock show that energy prices rise faster and more sharply, peaking between one and two years; food prices peak after one year, and finally, the CPI reacts only marginally in the first few years after implementing the carbon tax.

While the various empirical studies minimize the inflationary risks associated with the transition process, these empirical assessments are based on past observations of periods during which the transition was only modest and carbon price increases were limited. These past studies may, therefore, ignore transmission mechanisms that will emerge in the future when transition risks start to materialize. More importantly, the swiftness and effectiveness of transition policies determine the timing and severity of their impact on output and price development. When policies are gradual and credible, the output-inflation trade-off would be small. If the transition to clean energy generation is delayed, the costs in terms of inflation increase and output losses will be much greater (IMF, 2022).

Finally, and more fundamentally for central banks, it is necessary to understand how the different price dynamics discussed above could alter inflation expectations. If not properly anticipated, the transition to carbon neutrality could also lead to a rapid succession of shocks, increasing price volatility. This increased volatility could disrupt the decisions of economic agents, weaken inflation expectations and therefore constitute a significant challenge for the conduct of a monetary policy in response to the challenges of transition. Moreover, as shocks related to climate change are likely to affect food and energy prices the most, inflation expectations of households tend to particularly overweigh the changes in these prices. This key aspect of energy inflation could potentially amplify the second-round effects and trigger a wage-price spiral.

5.3 IMPLICATION FOR THE CONDUCT OF MONETARY POLICY

There is no consensus about how monetary policy should respond to the price pressures induced by climate change and mitigation policies. Some fear that monetary policy will hinder the development of a less carbon-intensive economy if it responds to energy price inflation with restrictive monetary policy. Indeed, interest rates directly affect the cost of capital, and any increase to combat overall inflation would penalize or disincentivize investment in clean technologies. At the same time, the central banks need to maintain price stability to deliver on their primary mandate, which may give rise to challenging trade-offs.

5.3.1 *Climate Change and the Transmission of Monetary Policy*

As discussed in Chapters 2 and 3, climate change and its mitigation may significantly affect key macroeconomic variables and the

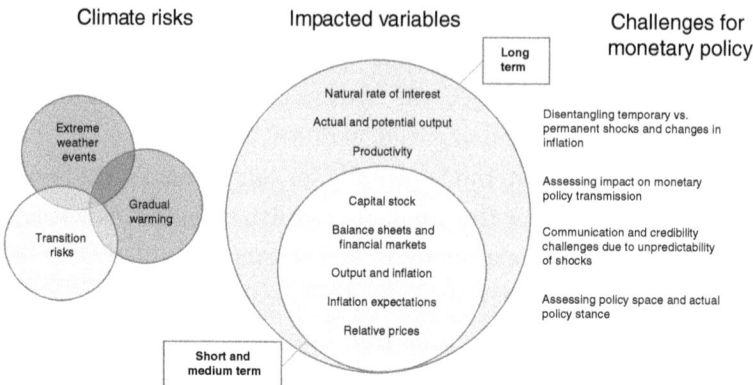

FIGURE 5.3 Climate risks, macroeconomic variables, and challenges for monetary policy
Source: NGFS (2020)

financial system. Central banks should actively integrate climate-related risks into their operational framework as well as monetary policy decisions and strategies.

Even if the economic and financial impacts of climate change currently remain uncertain, it is likely that these impacts will lead to shocks that significantly alter supply and demand conditions as well as quantity and price equilibria. In addition, climate change will certainly disturb financial markets and create shifts in asset prices. The risks associated with climate change could challenge central banks in meeting their price stability and financial stability objectives.

Monetary policy decisions, such as interest rate policy, affect economic activity and prices by affecting financial conditions, financial institution balance sheets, asset valuations, and agent's inflation expectations (Figure 5.3).

Under the normal functioning of the economic and financial environment, the change in the official interest rates is directly transmitted to money-market interest rates and also indirectly to lending and deposit rates of commercial banks. Expectations of future policy interest-rate changes also determine medium and long-term interest rates. To illustrate, the central bank's reaction to an economy

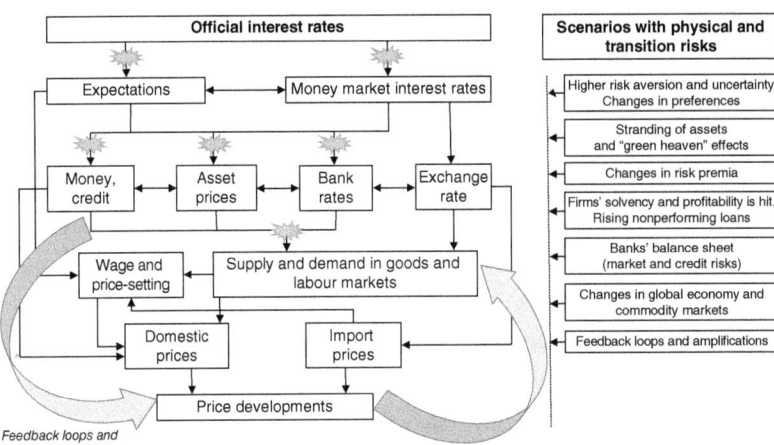

FIGURE 5.4 Monetary policy transmission under climate change strains
Source: NGFS (2020)

giving signs of overheating would certainly be raising interest rates to put a break on spending and borrowing. Conversely, the central bank would cut interest rates to boost economic activity in the context of an economic slowdown and overcapacity (positive output gap). The well-functioning of these traditional transmission channels is essential to the effectiveness of the monetary policy action.

The climate-related physical and transition risks could limit the policy space of central banks and even impair some of the monetary policy transmission channels (Figure 5.4). Taking the traditional interest rate channel, the fall in natural interest rates induced by climate risks (see Section 5.2.2) may weaken the transmission of policy rates to market rates by reducing the room for maneuver of conventional monetary policy when rates are close to the zero (effective) lower bound.

The credit channel will certainly be the most affected by climate risks, which could be a concern for central banks of the economies where this is the predominant transmission channel of monetary policy. Stranded assets resulting from low-carbon policies or climate hazards could dramatically increase the credit risk and trigger defaults in securities and loan portfolios as well as reduce asset values. By affecting the balance sheet of financial intermediaries, these climate-related developments could restrain banks' lending capacity to the economy. In addition, climate risk could increase the risk premiums of exposed companies and increased borrowing costs may create additional financial frictions, preventing an effective transmission of monetary policy. Finally, climate hazards and new transition policies may affect the net present value and probability of default of assets pledged to central banks to participate in central bank monetary policy operations, hence reducing collateral values.

Climate change could also weaken the asset price channel of monetary policy transmission. Extreme weather events and transition policies could alter real estate property prices. These risks would also affect the valuation of certain companies in the financial markets and, therefore, potentially loosen the relationship between key interest rates and equity prices. Falling asset values may also constrain banks to reduce their credit supply to comply with regulatory capital ratios. The materialization of climate risks would also affect the country's exchange rate, potentially making the exchange rate channel less sensitive to changes in policy rates.

Expectations are another key channel that could be altered by climate risk. Although climate-related damages to household and corporate balance sheets could materialize over time, economic agents may anticipate them and adapt their behavior straight away. The weakening of the expectations channel occurs when shocks move inflation expectations away from the target defended by the central bank. If climate shocks become persistent (linked, for example, to global warming or to transition policies that permanently modify relative sectoral prices), they could generate second-round effects, in particular via wages, hence increasing inflationary pressures in the medium term.

Climate change is likely to have a disproportionate impact on certain regions and sectors due to the presence of nonlinearities. Areas that are already hotter are projected to be more affected by increasing temperatures. In the case of a monetary union, this will result in asymmetric impacts on inflation in different member countries, which could pose a challenge for the transmission of a single monetary policy. In the European case, if extreme weather events become more severe and frequent, climate migration and refugees within Europe may increase due to these asymmetric impacts. Even with more benign effects on European countries, climate migration from outside of Europe should be expected, as climate impacts are greater in other parts of the world. However, it is possible that some regions may experience a net benefit, although this is far from certain.

5.3.2 Assessing the Monetary Policy Space

The economic repercussions of climate change can impede central banks' ability to assess the stance of monetary policy. This reflects the potential of climate change to alter an economy's productive capacity, commonly referred to potential output. Additionally, climate change can impact the neutral interest rate, thereby affecting the overall stance of monetary policy. Evaluating these concepts in real-time is already challenging under normal circumstances, and climate change exacerbates this complexity by introducing additional uncertainties.

The Natural (or Neutral) Interest Rate (NIR) or R^* is a key variable that guides central banks' monetary policy stance considering the economy's position in the economic cycle. The NIR corresponds to the real interest rate that is consistent with stable inflation in an economy that grows at its potential with full employment. Although the NIR is unobservable and difficult to estimate, climate change affects most factors that determine natural rates. Table 5.2 presents the expected impact of climate change on the key drivers of the natural rate, namely growth, technological progress, savings behavior, risk premia, and fiscal policy.

Despite the incomplete state of knowledge and high uncertainty regarding the overall net impact, it is likely that climate change will further intensify the persistent downward pressure on natural interest rates observed over the past decades. For instance, output losses,

Table 5.2 *Climate change and natural interest rate*

Channel	Potential impact of climate change
Growth	Lower NIR as climate change might discourage labor supply, lower labor productivity, and shift age composition of population. Higher NIR for countries attracting migration flows as climate change increases their labor supply.
Technology	Lower NIR through the diversion of resources away from innovation and toward mitigation and adaptation. Higher NIR as environmental regulation may foster the search for efficiency gains and encourage innovation.
Savings behavior	Lower NIR through increased preference for savings driven by (i) greater income inequality (the poorest part of the population is typically more exposed to the consequences of climate change), and (ii) higher uncertainty about the future.
Risk premium	Lower NIR as climate change could increase preference for holding safe assets.
Fiscal policy	Higher NIR as government debt rises because of increased mitigation and adaptation investment, or higher expenditure to cover health and other costs of natural disasters.

Source: NGFS (2020)

lower productivity, or more limited labor supply due to severe and more frequent climate hazards would reduce the natural interest rate, hence constraining the policy space of central banks by bringing policy interest rates close to the zero (or effective) lower bound. Although efforts to accelerate the transition to climate-sustainable growth could result in major technological advances and very significant productivity gains, the longer these efforts are delayed and limited, the more likely it is that climate change will adversely affect natural interest rates. In sum, by bringing natural interest rates down, climate change will reduce rather than increase the *space* available to central banks and challenge them in the conduct of the conventional monetary policy via interest rate cuts.

5.3.3 Monetary Policy Trade-Offs and the Limits to the Look Through Policy

An escalation in the frequency and severity of these negative supply shocks is likely to heighten the volatility in headline inflation and affect inflation expectations. While monetary policy could effectively respond to demand shock by using the tools at its disposal, supply shocks are more difficult to counter. Central banks' response to this type of shock may imply an undesirable trade-off between stabilizing inflation and stabilizing fluctuations in activity.

Generally speaking, monetary policy decisions require the identification of three dimensions: the nature, persistence, and magnitude of the shocks affecting the economy. In terms of identifying the nature of the shock, a demand shock – whether positive, such as an increase in *green* investment, or negative, such as higher uncertainty about transition policies – can theoretically guarantee stable prices for a change in the output gap (*divine coincidence*[4]). On the other hand, a negative supply shock (e.g., a carbon tax implemented in a haphazard manner) is considered more difficult to resolve as a trade-off, as monetary policy faces a dilemma between stabilizing output gap fluctuations and stabilizing inflation. As for the persistence of the shock, a temporary shock, that is, one unlikely to affect inflation in the medium term, should similarly not trigger a monetary policy reaction. Unlike a permanent shock, where its effects could spread to the rest of the economy over a medium- to long-term horizon, a temporary shock is a short-term shock, for which monetary policy offers neither the right instruments nor the right policy to respond to its effects. Finally, with regard to the size of shocks, the larger the shock, the more likely monetary policy is to act.

---

[4] A situation where the pursuit of achieving price stability automatically leads to stabilization of activity without the need for separate policy measures.

In short, monetary policy can afford to look *through* or *beyond* any shock if it is considered temporary, small in scale, and without any trade-off between price stability and economic activity growth. On the other hand, if the central bank considers the shock to be more persistent and likely to have second-round effects on wages and inflation and to de-anchor inflation expectations, it may become increasingly difficult to look *through* such shocks.

We examine in more detail two opposite cases of threats to price stability due to climate change mitigation: a negative supply shock causing *stagflation* (higher inflation and lower output) and a negative demand shock leading to deflation.

5.3.3.1   The Case of Stagflation

The stagflation case corresponds to negative supply shocks. In the context of the transition, these shocks could relate to the inflationary effects of carbon taxes or tighter regulation that put upward pressures on carbon-intensive energy prices. This could be represented below (Figure 5.5), where the clean energy transition (*Transition shock*) restricts supply (from S to S'). With the demand curve (D) unchanged, the supply shock leads to a new equilibrium with higher inflation (from P to P') and lower output (from Y to Y').

This situation leads to a difficult trade-off for central bankers. This is even more so for central banks with the so-called *dual mandate*, like the Federal Reserve, which implies the pursuit of two objectives: price stability and maximum sustainable employment. A restrictive monetary policy to combat higher inflation would penalize economic activity, threatening the second objective by curbing labor market dynamics.

When confronted with an adverse supply shock, central banks face critical questions: Is the shock transitory or persistent? What are the consequences for monetary policy? Which measure of inflation should be stabilized (headline or core inflation)?

Let us first recall the difference between headline and core inflation:

5 CENTRAL BANKS, CLIMATE CHANGE, AND PRICE STABILITY

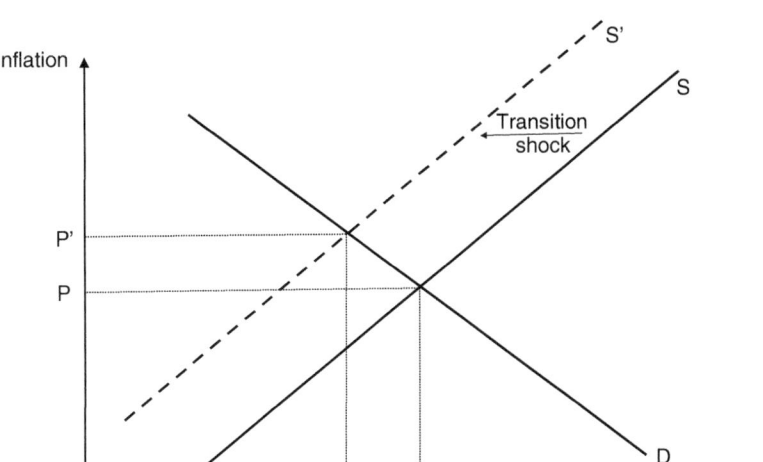

FIGURE 5.5 Dominant negative supply shock

- Headline inflation (or broad inflation) is the inflation related to all the economy's commodities, goods, and services. Corresponds to the CPI inflation (*all items*)
- Core inflation (underlying inflation) is the inflation of all the goods and services except the volatile food and energy prices (e.g., oil and gas)

When considering the conduct of monetary policy, many central bankers focus on core inflation. The Federal Reserve, for example, pays particular attention to the growth rate of the core personal consumption expenditure (PCE) deflator, which excludes food and energy prices. In its 2021 strategy review, the ECB maintained the headline Harmonized Index of Consumer Prices (HICP) as the designated index for assessing the price stability objective in the euro area. The index will continue to serve as the primary index for monetary policy purposes. The evaluation of the appropriateness of the HICP is based on four criteria: timeliness, reliability (e.g., infrequent revisions), comparability (over time and across countries), and credibility.

In low-income and developing countries, the share of the budget allocated to food is, on average, higher than in emerging or advanced economies. Food consumption accounts for around 44% (and in some cases over 60%) of household consumption in low-income and developing countries. By comparison, food consumption accounts for 27% of emerging economies and 16% of advanced economies. The sensitivity of overall inflation to changes in food and energy prices is, therefore, much stronger in low-income countries.

An increase in energy prices directly concerns headline inflation. While core inflation remains unaffected by energy-related components, it should theoretically not respond to such price increases. Nevertheless, core inflation can be indirectly influenced by the rise in production prices and potential second-round effects. Alp et al. (2023) show, in selected advanced economies, that the pass-through of oil price to headline inflation is a gradual and enduring process. The impact builds up over approximately 8 quarters following the oil price increase. A 10% permanent immediate increase in oil prices raises the energy CPI itself by 2.3% after two quarters. Pass-through to core inflation is slow but long-lasting, with the effect building over about eight quarters after the oil price increase. Taking into account the relative importance of core products in the overall CPI basket, their analysis suggests that the second-round effects of a 10% increase in oil prices would raise headline CPI by almost 0.15% at its peak. Including the effect on the energy CPI, a 10% increase in the price of oil raises headline CPI by almost 0.4% in total.

In normal times, the increase in oil prices is not permanent. Holm-Hodula and Hubrich (2017) show that in such a normal regime, oil price shocks trigger only limited and short-lived adjustments in headline inflation. In the adverse regime, by contrast, oil price shocks are followed by sizeable and sustained macroeconomic fluctuations, with inflation moving in the same direction as the oil price. The responses of inflation expectations and wage growth point to second-round effects as a potential driver of the dynamics characterizing the adverse regime.

For the central banks, endorsing a benign view is supported by the argument that some temporary increase in oil prices should not justify a tightening of monetary policy. Such tightening, achieved through higher interest rates, could adversely impact economic activity, disposable incomes, and the profits of households and firms. However, if the escalation in energy prices becomes entrenched in inflation expectations, it may give rise to second-round effects, thereby reinforcing the existing inflationary pressures.

From a monetary policy standpoint, it is essential to evaluate the comparative validity of these divergent assessments. Based on statements from policymakers in different jurisdictions, central banks typically consider adjusting the monetary policy stance only in the latter scenario. This situation arises when oil price fluctuations start influencing inflation expectations, posing a potential risk of causing lasting impacts on actual inflation dynamics. In contrast, in the absence of such second-round effects, central banks are inclined to maintain the existing monetary policy stance, effectively *looking through* the fluctuations in energy prices.

In the face of a transient energy price shock, employing a *looking through* policy is deemed appropriate. This approach is justified by the expectation that inflation will revert to its equilibrium level after the shock, if inflation expectations are well anchored.

Due to the lags in the transmission of monetary policy, it becomes impossible for central banks to counter transitory and unexpected shocks. Consequently, adopting a *looking through* approach becomes the most fitting reaction, with central banks relying on their credibility to ensure that agents correctly align their expectations with the central bank's view.

The economic costs of inflation arise primarily when prices exhibit rigidity, distorting relative prices and diminishing the signaling role of individual prices in conveying scarcity. This disruption hampers the efficient allocation of resources. However, oil prices demonstrate flexibility as they adjust to reflect oil scarcity, providing a signal for both firms and households to reduce their oil demand. It is, therefore, by stabilizing core inflation (which is sticky) that the benefits of price stability are the largest. Generally speaking, real consumption experiences an increase when monetary policy focuses on stabilizing core inflation compared to when it targets headline inflation. Additionally, the real interest rate is lower under core inflation stabilization, which proves beneficial for financing initiatives such as green projects essential for the transition. Aoki (2001) studies oil-price-driven supply shocks within a two-sector New Keynesian model with a flexible-price sector (oil), and a sticky-price sector (non-oil goods). He finds that the optimal monetary policy is to target sticky-price inflation (i.e., core inflation). In this case, there is no trade-off since stabilizing core inflation also stabilizes the output gap.

In the context of energy transition, the increase in the cost of carbon-intensive sources of energy becomes more permanent and expected. This sets it apart from traditional energy-price shock as the transition introduces important upside risks to the baseline projection of inflation over the medium term, with a systematically higher-than-expected contribution from energy costs to inflation.

Climate-related inflation is likely to have its most immediate impact on food and energy prices. However, households tend to overestimate the importance of these price rises when shaping their inflation expectations. Consequently, this type of inflation has the potential to magnify second-round effects, possibly triggering a wage-price spiral. The resulting higher and more volatile inflation in the short and medium term alters how households and businesses plan for the future due to the impacts of climate change. Furthermore, government actions can directly influence inflation expectations as economic actors respond to announcements of new policies and regulations to reduce greenhouse gas emissions. If inflation expectations may eventually become deanchored and drift up, possibly accompanied by second-round effects leading to higher broad inflation, the central bank may need to abandon the *look through* stance. Hence, in line with Schnabel (2022), the escalation in energy prices might necessitate a shift away from a *looking through* policy. Schnabel contends that "[headline inflation] best represents households' expenses and thus provides the best guide for fully and effectively protecting their purchasing power." Moreover, deviating from a *look-through* policy to adopt a tighter monetary policy stance would signal a strong commitment of the central bank to price stability. This, however, poses a difficult trade-off as the tightening of monetary policy could impair growth and employment by raising the financing conditions of households and firms.

Dupraz et al. (2022) find that *looking through* greenflation shocks yields benefits. Stabilizing core inflation maximizes a key advantage of price stability: enabling the price system to guide resource allocation by signaling scarcity (e.g., of oil) and stabilizing the output gap (following Aoki, 2001). While headline inflation, inclusive of oil prices, rises more spontaneously, stabilizing it necessitates a tighter monetary policy stance to bring aggregate demand below potential. Importantly, *looking through* doesn't mean keeping policy rates unchanged; monetary policy is tightened, albeit to a lesser extent. The benefits persist even with a risk of inflation expectations deanchoring. However, failing to stabilize core inflation at the target entails significant and enduring costs. Therefore, monetary policy should react promptly and decisively, even when focusing on core components.

At the heart of the challenge lies the risk of deanchoring. The earlier conclusions remain valid as long as the central bank ultimately succeeds in fully stabilizing headline or core inflation. Otherwise, there are significant costs to not stabilizing inflation (as inflation expectations persistently rise). If agents' expectations of core inflation depends on the past evolution of headline inflation, stabilizing core inflation will imply above-target headline inflation, which feeds into higher expected core inflation. This would add pressure to core inflation, which monetary policy needs to counteract through a negative output gap.

In conclusion, whatever the strategy chosen, the energy transition – by implying a persistent rise in energy prices – puts upward pressure on inflation – directly on headline measures and indirectly on core measures. To maintain its credibility and keep inflation expectations well anchored, central banks need to react earlier and more strongly than for a standard temporary energy price shock, which leads to economic costs (lower income and consumption). In this case, the central bank might have to respond quite aggressively to bring inflation expectations back to target. The key judgment, therefore, is how long can the central bank risk above-target inflation before inflation expectations become deanchored. This is impossible to say with certainty, but the more persistent the shock, the less advisable a *look through* strategy becomes.

However, the implementation of a tighter monetary policy stance could be hampered by two issues:

- The subsequent tightening of financing conditions could jeopardize the development of *green-friendly* energies and activities, which require significant investments;
- Labor and capital reallocation across industries during the transition may be costly in terms of global output (creative destruction), leading to an unpleasant trade-off for central bankers (higher prices and lower economic activity).

In both cases, an efficient policy mix (monetary and fiscal policy) becomes crucial.

5.3.3.2 The Case of Deflation

The deflation scenario arises from negative demand shocks attributed to the energy transition (Figure 5.6). In this context, a decline in aggregate demand occurs (from D to D′), contributing to reduced output (from Y to Y′) and, subsequently, lower inflation (from P to P′). This phenomenon occurs when demand weakens while the supply remains constant, impacting overall economic output and inflation rates.

Deflation can create a vicious cycle for the economy, as it can cause a decrease in spending and investment, which in turn leads to lower economic growth and higher unemployment rates.

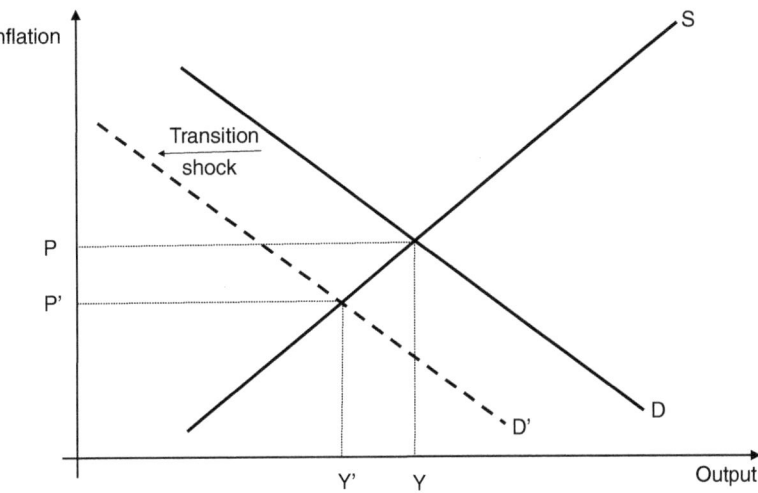

FIGURE 5.6 Negative demand shock

The so-called *deflationary spiral* depicts a scenario in which declining prices trigger a chain reaction, causing a reduction in economic activity, declining wages, a sluggish circulation of currency, increased cash hoarding due to its rising purchasing power, and a greater challenge in debt repayment. This, in turn, results in defaults, further currency destruction, and a continuous cycle of falling prices.

Regarding the action of the central bank in such a situation, several questions arise: What are the consequences for monetary policy? Does monetary policy have the capacity to respond to such a shock? Central banks can use monetary policy to halt a deflationary spiral and spur demand. However, if monetary policy efforts fail, due to greater-than-anticipated weakness in the economy or because target interest rates are already zero or possibly below zero (called the effective lower bound or ELB),[5] a deflationary spiral may occur even with an expansionary monetary policy in place.

---

[5] ELB refers to the point (possibly below zero) at which further cuts in the main monetary policy interest rate no longer provide stimulus to aggregate demand and GDP, or at which some adverse effects, such as in the financial sector, can arise. The ELB is therefore the limit to how low interest rates can go.

The deflationary impact of transition could lead to increases in instances where ELB is binding, especially if the natural rate of interest, R* (see Section 5.3.2), is lower. The clean transition, while narrowing the policy space for conventional monetary policy and increasing the probability of hitting the ELB, could undermine the effectiveness of monetary policy transmission. As traditional tools face limitations, integrating unconventional monetary policy (UMP) measures into the ordinary monetary policy toolkit becomes a compelling argument in the face of evolving economic challenges (Drudi et al., 2021).

The potential deflationary impact of a transition policy, such as a carbon tax, stems from the heightened costs associated with emission-intensive energy inputs. As firms manufacturing goods experience an increase in the cost of carbon-intensive energy sources, they are likely to curtail their demand for such inputs. Due to the limited substitutability between inputs (capital and labor) and energy in the production process, firms are inclined to diminish their demand for these inputs. This reduction not only affects labor income (wages) and capital income (interest rates) at an aggregate level but is also exacerbated by the insufficient compensatory effect of the rise in green energy production. Therefore, both consumption and investment experience a decline, resulting in an overall contraction in GDP. The decrease in inflation aligns with the diminished aggregate demand, prompting the central bank to lower the policy rate, possibly reaching the ELB.

Addressing a deflationary transition policy, particularly during situations triggered by events like a carbon tax, confidence crisis, or financial turmoil, requires an adjustment in the policy mix. When the impact is intensified by the frequency of the central bank being constrained by the ELB on the policy rate, a tailored policy mix becomes imperative to effectively navigate and counteract the deflationary pressures. In terms of monetary policy, the central bank may engage in the purchase of long-term sovereign bonds for monetary policy purposes. This strategic move, aimed at lowering long-term interest rates, would support aggregate demand, thereby sustaining economic activity and inflation. Consequently, the combined efforts of fiscal measures and UMPs assume a significant role in mitigating transition risks and bolstering the overall economic activity.

5.3.3.3 *Assessing the Monetary Policy Trade-Off*

Transition policies may generate a trade-off between inflation and employment objectives. Del Negro et al. (2023) underscore the nuanced interplay between pricing flexibility and climate policy design in shaping the balance between inflation and employment objectives. The existence and magnitude of this trade-off hinge on how flexible prices are in the dirty and green sectors relative to the broader economy. Additionally, the nature of climate policies, whether they involve taxes or subsidies, further influences the characteristics of this trade-off.

In theory, in a scenario where prices are flexible, the central bank could effectively attain any desired aggregate inflation rate without encountering trade-offs. Rapid adjustments in relative prices, reflecting taxes or subsidies, would ensure that the overall price level aligns with monetary policy decisions without imposing real activity costs. However, the presence of price rigidities, where prices do not adjust instantaneously but instead take time to do so, complicates the central bank's task and introduces a trade-off between inflation and economic activity. This trade-off arises because in order to achieve low inflation (or deflation) in the sticky-price sector to counterbalance high inflation in the dirty sector, the central bank needs to cool the economy. If the central bank is unwilling to pursue this course of action, it may be compelled to tolerate temporarily elevated inflation. Even if dirty-sector prices are not completely flexible, this result still holds as long as they are less rigid than prices in the rest of the economy. Del Negro et al. (2023) show that this is empirically true for the US economy, as the mean price frequency change in the dirty sectors is higher than in the rest of the economy, illustrated by a positive correlation between price flexibility and CO_2 emissions.

In summary, the green transition becomes inflationary only when policies deliberately raise prices in the dirty sector, typically through mechanisms like carbon pricing. However, if prices in the green sector demonstrate greater flexibility compared to the broader economy, climate policies involving subsidies to green sectors – such as electric vehicles or renewable energy – rather than taxes on dirty sectors, could potentially have a disinflationary impact. This reversal follows the same logic discussed above: subsidies lower relative prices for goods and services, while taxes raise them.

5.3.4 Strategic Implications

The inflationary impact of climate change and the increased price volatility pose key challenges to central banks' objective of price stability and their monetary policy strategy. Climate change tends to increase the uncertainty surrounding the macroeconomic diagnosis on which the central banks rely for conducting monetary policy.

Many economies entrust their central banks with the primary objective of ensuring price stability, commonly measured by a specific inflation level that is publicly communicated to anchor inflation expectations. In the context of inflation targeting, flexibility comes into play as the central bank endeavors to achieve the target level over the medium term. This flexibility involves the central bank *looking through* short-term price volatility that may arise from various economic shocks, focusing on the overall trajectory of inflation rather than reacting to transient fluctuations.

Within this framework, central banks are tasked with evaluating how the transition to a low-carbon economy introduces risks to their mandate of ensuring price stability. This involves a careful analysis of the potential impact of the transition on inflation and an assessment of how well the central bank's objectives align with the evolving economic landscape shaped by the clean transition. Additionally, central banks should delineate a tolerance band for deviations from their inflation target attributable to contributions from energy to headline inflation.

The complex ways in which climate change affects different elements of the inflation-targeting framework may require central banks to reconsider the design of their monetary policy regimes (McKibbin et al., 2017; Dees and Weber, 2020). Specifically, there may be a need to reassess the strategy concerning the chosen measure for the inflation target, including the choice between a target expressed as a level or interval, the timeframe within which the inflation target must be achieved, and the actual level of the target. Integrating these crucial implications of climate change into monetary strategy is currently under discussion among major central banks.

5.3.4.1 Inflation Measure Chosen as Inflation Target

Core inflation, known for its lower volatility and heightened responsiveness to monetary policy signals, contrasts with the more fluctuating and less reactive nature of an overall price index. However, the latter is often deemed more representative and understandable, thereby enhancing its ability to anchor the expectations of economic agents. The impact of climate change, which is anticipated to amplify inflation volatility directly or through transition policies, may prompt central banks to reassess the trade-off between the credibility and representativeness of the target index.

In this context, central banks might need to break with the prevailing consensus that monetary policy should look through rising energy prices, as they might need to respond to them to ensure price stability over the medium term. A wide number of elements make a case for a departure from a *looking through* policy. In the past, central banks have typically looked through energy price shocks for various good reasons. As discussed in Section 5.2.1, in the past, these energy price shocks tended to be short-lived. In this case, a monetary policy response, such as an interest rate hike, would not be effective and would run the risk of amplifying the negative effect of rising energy prices on aggregate demand and output. Furthermore, the prolonged lags in policy transmission could lead to a situation where inflation decreases as a delayed response to policy action, just as the initial upward shock has subsided. However, the urgency and scale of necessary climate action, such as the swift implementation of a global carbon tax, might extend the duration of energy price shocks beyond the typical timeframe. This higher for longer energy inflation could potentially modify, or even deanchor, inflation expectations, considering the greater importance given to food and energy in consumer baskets. Finally, the potential emergence of second-round effects stemming from energy inflation, such as impacts on wage-setting mechanisms, is another factor that necessitates careful consideration of energy inflation.

5.3.4.2 Choice between a Target Expressed as a Level or as an Interval

In a world where climate-related shocks are more frequent and substantial, the merits of inflation targeting, incorporating both a reference level and a tolerance band, could gain added significance. In the event that inflation experiences heightened volatility due to these shocks, a reference level becomes instrumental for clearly communicating the central bank's objective in the medium term to anchor expectations. At the same time, including a tolerance band communicates that the level is not an absolute target to be strictly followed. This approach offers increased flexibility to the central bank in handling temporary shocks and mitigating fluctuations in economic activity.

5.3.4.3 Horizon Over Which the Inflation Target Must be Reached

In the presence of a supply shock, a more extended time horizon to achieve the inflation target tends to mitigate the volatility of interest rates, as well as the decline in production and employment. However, a prolonged target horizon raises concerns about the credibility of the central bank if observed inflation frequently deviates from the target level over this extended period. In practical terms, the challenges

5   CENTRAL BANKS, CLIMATE CHANGE, AND PRICE STABILITY   201

posed by climate change underscore the heightened importance of clear and transparent communication regarding the policy direction of central banks.

5.3.4.4   *Choice of the Level of the Inflation Target*

If climate change were to amplify the factors pushing the NIR down, the relevance of the target level might regain attention. In response to such scrutiny, central banks must exercise caution against targeting an inflation level that is excessively low, as this poses the risk of substantially limiting their flexibility. All other things being equal, the probability of the policy rate hitting its effective floor is higher when climate-related shocks impact an economy with an already relatively low natural interest rate, influenced by other structural factors.

5.3.5   *Divergence in Approaches toward Climate Change across Central Banks*

Climate change has become a notable area of divergence between the major central banks, in particular between the US Federal Reserve (Fed) and European Central Bank (ECB), despite their historical tendency to use similar tools, frameworks, and policy objectives. While the Fed has limited its approach to climate change to basic climate policy norms, recognizing some relevance of climate change to its monetary and prudential objectives, but refraining from endorsing decarbonization, the ECB has demonstrated a deeper recognition of the profound challenges climate change poses to achieving its central banking objectives. As noted by DiLeo et al. (2023), the highly polarized and partisan discourse on climate change in the United States, driven by a powerful domestic fossil fuel industry, has resulted in the Federal Reserve embracing only a limited version of essential climate norms. This represents a notable departure from the ECB's proactive approach to climate issues. Notably, the ECB has adopted proactive climate policy standards, incorporating climate change criteria into its asset purchase programs and implementing extensive supervisory interventions to ensure that financial institutions take climate risk into account.

Other central banks have also shown some engagement in the greening of monetary policy operations. For instance, the Bank of England has taken actions to green its Corporate Bond Purchase Scheme (CBPS). The goal is to achieve a 25 percent reduction in the weighted average carbon intensity (WACI) of the CBPS portfolio by 2025, and full alignment with net zero by 2050. Firms will now need to meet climate-related eligibility criteria for their bonds to be purchased by the CBPS, with purchases of eligible firms' debt being *tilted* toward the stronger climate performers within their sectors. The extent to which purchases are tilted toward or away from a firm will depend on the strength of its climate performance, assessed against four metrics: the emission intensity of its activities, its progress in reducing emissions, having published a climate disclosure and having an emissions reduction target (with more credit if this is third-party verified).

5.3.6 Promoting Actively the Energy Transition: Operational Challenges

Including climate change considerations in central bank actions will require significant adjustment of central banks' primary operational functions that they undertake to implement monetary policy. Central bank mandates generally steer clear of actions targeting specific entities like firms, households, sectors, or geographies, and they typically refrain from systematically using monetary tools to support government policy actions (Dikau and Volz, 2021). The ECB and the Bank of England have been pioneers in incorporating climate-related policies into their operational frameworks. Extending these policies to a wider range of central banks would require addressing underlying data gaps and establishing a universally accepted green taxonomy. While green central banking initiatives in developing countries mostly focus on reporting and disclosure, the People's Bank of China stands out by introducing green instruments into its operational framework.

This review focuses on three key policy areas: credit operations, collateral policies, and asset purchases.

Through the *lending channel*, central banks have the potential to implement green lending initiatives. This involves linking the interest rate on lending facilities to commercial banks' commitment to addressing climate change or the decarbonization of their business models. In essence, this approach entails directing financing operations to favor low-carbon and environmentally sustainable borrowers. Commercial banks can then convey this practice to their customers, contributing to the overall greening of the economy. Adjusting credit operations through the refinement of counterparty eligibility criteria can influence lending behavior, encouraging financial institutions to originate or invest more in low-carbon and sustainable assets. Notably, central banks in Japan and China have already introduced various credit incentives to support green projects. The ECB has also signaled the potential consideration of green-targeted lending operations in the future, particularly when its policy becomes expansionary again.[6]

Going into greater detail, these *green* initiatives can be operationalized by linking the interest rate for central bank *lending facilities* to a counterparty's climate change mitigation contribution and/or the decarbonization level of its business model, relative to a relevant benchmark (refer to Measure (1) in Table 5.3). Additionally, the central bank could implement varying interest rates for counterparties based on the proportion of low-carbon or carbon-intensive assets pledged as collateral, or by establishing a credit facility, potentially at concessional rates, accessible exclusively against low-carbon assets (refer to Measure (2)). Another avenue could involve making access to lending facilities contingent on a counterparty's disclosure of climate-related information (refer to Measure (3)).

Central banks could also alter their *collateral frameworks* to align with climate objectives and incentivize asset allocation favoring low-carbon projects. Adjusting collateral policy in alignment

[6] Schnabel (2023).

with climate objectives represents a crucial avenue for central banks. Collateral policy defines the scope of assets that can secure central bank credit operations, along with the corresponding risk control measures. The central bank can enhance its climate-conscious approach by applying haircuts that more accurately reflect climate-related risks (refer to Measure (4)). Additionally, the central bank could implement negative screening, excluding otherwise eligible *dirty* collateral assets or adjusting eligibility criteria based on the carbon performance of underlying assets (refer to Measure (5)). Conversely, positive screening may involve accepting sustainable collateral and encouraging banks and capital markets to support environmentally friendly projects and assets (refer to Measure (6)). The central bank could further mandate counterparties to pledge collateral that complies with a climate-related metric at an aggregate pool level (refer to Measure (7)). In 2018, the People's Bank of China expanded its eligible collateral to include green loans and green bonds. The National Bank of Hungary has also introduced incentives for green securities. Looking ahead, the ECB has outlined plans to incorporate negative screening, climate-related disclosure requirements, and haircuts into its collateral program, starting in 2026.

Central banks can align their balance sheets with the objectives of the Paris Agreement through asset purchase programs. This approach supports green bond markets and increases the proportion of clean assets in their balance sheets. An example of this commitment is seen in the Bank of England, which has pledged a 25 percent reduction in the weighted average carbon intensity of its corporate bonds portfolio by 2025, with a goal of complete alignment with net zero by 2050. Similarly, since the end of 2022, the ECB has taken steps to tilt its corporate bond holdings toward issuers with better climate performance by reinvesting redemptions. For now, the ECB follows only a flow-based tilting approach by adjusting its reinvestments of corporate bonds based on a climate score that reflects issuers' carbon intensity, their decarbonization plans, and the quality of their climate-related disclosures.

In a bid to green their balance sheets, central banks have the option of purchasing green assets from both public and private sectors. This strategic move aims to lower interest rates on sustainable activities or reduce credit spreads. In the context of quantitative easing (QE) policies, the central bank could tailor asset purchases based on climate-related risks and criteria applied at the issuer or asset level (refer to Measure (8)), or exclude assets or issuers failing to meet climate-related criteria from such purchases (refer to Measure (9)).

Green asset purchases have primarily focused on corporate bonds, and extending this approach to greening public sector asset holdings poses more challenges. For instance, in the case of the ECB, sovereign bond purchases adhere to the capital key, constraining the feasibility of tilting strategies based on countries' carbon intensities. The overall supply of green sovereign bonds is currently insufficient compared to the size of central banks' sovereign bond portfolios. Additionally, a key obstacle is the lack of a reliable global taxonomy and sovereign rating framework to assess whether sovereign bonds align with the goals of the Paris Agreement.

Overall, the outlined options for incorporating green practices into central bank operations would not only encourage borrowers to enhance their disclosures and decrease carbon emissions but also serve as a positive example for other financial institutions through responsible lending, collateral, and asset purchase practices. Beyond that, these green initiatives would benefit central banks by diminishing their balance sheet exposure to climate risks. Particularly in emerging market economies, central bank green policies are poised to play a pivotal role in advancing the green and sustainable bond market by boosting demand for environmentally sustainable financial products and subsequently lowering their yields.

The evaluation of these diverse measures must consider four key criteria: consequences for monetary policy effectiveness, contribution to mitigating climate change, effectiveness as a risk protection measure, and operational feasibility. Table 5.3 compares the different policy options in relation to these criteria. Concerning the

Table 5.3 Comparative assessment of policy options

Criteria	Credit operations			Collateral				Asset purchases	
	(1) Adjusting Pricing to Lending Benchmark	(2) Adjusting Pricing to Collateral	(3) Adjusting Counterparties' Eligibility	(4) Haircut adjustment	(5) Negative screening	(6) Positive screening	(7) Aligning collateral pools	(8) Tilting	(9) Negative screening
Consequences for monetary policy effectiveness	Minimal	Negative	Strongly negative	Minimal	Negative	Positive	Minimal	Minimal	Negative
Contribution to mitigating climate change	Strongly positive	Positive	Positive	Positive	Positive	Strongly positive	Strongly positive	Strongly positive	Positive
Effectiveness as risk protection measure	Minimal	Minimal	Positive	Positive	Positive	Negative	Positive	Positive	Positive
Operational feasibility	Negative	Negative	Minimal	Negative	Minimal	Minimal	Negative	Negative	Minimal

Source: NGFS (2020)

consequences for monetary policy effectiveness, several options risk curtailing the scope of central bank operations and the policy space, especially if they involve excluding counterparties from credit operations. Only positive screening in collateral policy stands out as the option with potentially positive implications for the effectiveness of monetary policy operations.

Regarding the contribution to mitigating climate change, while all measures are assessed to yield positive implications, a few options may prove more impactful than others. Notably, measures focusing on (i) adjusting the pricing of targeted credit operations, (ii) positively screening collateral, (iii) aligning collateral pools, and (iv) tilting asset purchases. These measures would typically leverage and foster market mechanisms.

In terms of effectiveness in risk protection, many reviewed options are expected to better shield central bank balance sheets against escalating financial risks, particularly those that directly reduce risk exposure to issuers or counterparties. Finally, it is crucial to note that all options necessitate significant changes to central bank operational frameworks. Factoring in climate-related considerations may involve procuring additional specialist climate data, adapting Information Technologies (IT) and reporting systems, revising internal processes, and rewriting operational terms and conditions.

5.3.7 What are the Risks of Proactive Measures?

Central banks should be mindful that their actions in favor of climate change could also bear some additional risks. Focusing on issues that are outside their primary remit could undermine their own credibility. As long as policy decisions align with the mandate to uphold price and financial stability, the risk of mission creep remains minimal. However, adopting a *green* monetary policy or incorporating climate change into their mandate could jeopardize the independence that underpins their institutions (Issing, 2019). Even if environmental concerns fall under secondary objectives, central banks should be mindful of managing expectations.

Confronting challenges associated with climate change may involve policy considerations that extend beyond the typical responsibilities of central banks and financial regulators. Governments and supranational entities possess a broader toolkit to actively promote the low-carbon transition and address physical risks associated with climate change. Central banks risk compromising their credibility and reputation in their core activities when they publicly hold themselves accountable in areas with limited capability and information accuracy. In emerging and developing markets where financial resources are limited to tackle climate change, this mission expansion could make central banks more vulnerable to heightened political pressures, posing a potential threat to their autonomy and credibility.

Sir Paul Tucker, a former deputy governor of the Bank of England, highlighted the potential impact of climate change on financial stability during a House of Lords select committee: "One thing that is said about climate change and central banking is that climate change could be very bad for financial stability, and I agree. Wars, including civil wars, are very bad for financial stability, too. Should central banks ration the provision of credit to suppliers of arms manufacturers?"[7]

Additionally, there are legal constraints that central banks must navigate when supporting the transition to a greener economy. Green monetary policies, encompassing collateral and QE, must align with the central banks' mandates, particularly in upholding price stability. For instance, the ECB operates within the framework of the Treaty on the Functioning of the European Union (TFEU) and the ESCB/ECB Statute. The TFEU states that the primary objective of the ECB is to maintain price stability, and policies related to climate change can be justified if they contribute to this primary objective. Furthermore, the ECB is tasked with supporting economic policies in the Union, one of which involves the protection and improvement of the environment's quality (Art.3(3) of the Treaty on European

---

[7] https://committees.parliament.uk/oralevidence/1653/pdf/

Union). The TFEU includes a *consistency clause*, urging Union institutions to avoid decisions that contradict policies promoted by other institutions. In this context, the ECB could argue for a green monetary policy, as long as it does not compromise price stability, recognizing that the primary responsibility for environmental policies lies elsewhere in the Union.

In addition, while considering climate concerns, the ECB must observe the general principles of EU law:

- *Principle of Proportionality:* Any measures taken must be proportionate to the objectives, avoiding actions that exceed what is deemed necessary for addressing climate issues effectively.
- *Principle of Institutional Balance*: The ECB's climate-driven actions should not be interpreted as a transfer of responsibilities designated by the Treaties to other Union institutions. Article 192 of the TFEU designates the European Parliament and the Council as competent to address environmental objectives.
- The principle of *equal treatment* necessitates that the differential treatment of assets or counterparties must have a clear and objective justification, such as being based on criteria related to climate change considerations.
- Principle of *Open Market Economy (Market Neutrality)*: The ECB is obligated to operate in accordance with the principle of an open market economy, fostering free competition and facilitating the efficient allocation of resources. While the Eurosystem should refrain from measures that unduly disrupt market functioning or restrict competition, it's important to note that this is not an absolute prohibition of ECB interference. If necessary to pursue its primary or secondary objectives, the ECB may intervene while considering the principle of market neutrality.

5.4 CONCLUSION

Climate change introduces unique and complex risks to the macroeconomic environment, significantly influencing central banks' policy frameworks and actions. Both the physical impacts of climate change and the transitional adjustments required to mitigate its effects can lead to inflationary pressures, complicating the task of macroeconomic stabilization. The challenges are complex as central banks face different types of inflationary impacts stemming from climate-related risks. Physical risks, such as extreme weather events, can disrupt supply chains and reduce agricultural outputs, leading to price increases in affected sectors. Meanwhile, transition risks associated with shifting toward a low-carbon economy, such as changes in energy costs or regulatory compliance costs, can also create upward pressures on prices. These dynamics necessitate a nuanced approach from central banks, requiring them to differentiate and respond to various sources of inflation.

As a result, central banks must navigate a complex landscape where traditional tools and strategies may need to be adapted to account for the influence of climate change. This includes reconsidering the transmission mechanisms of monetary policy, as climate-related risks may alter the effectiveness of interest rates and other instruments. The potential for climate change to constrain the monetary policy space, limiting the effectiveness of standard policy responses, is a crucial consideration for central banks globally. Moreover, there are strategic implications for central banks, as they need to balance short-term stabilization goals with long-term climate risks, which may require more proactive measures.

From an operational perspective, while some central banks are actively integrating climate considerations into their monetary policy frameworks, there remains key challenges, such as data limitations and the need for new modeling techniques. Moreover, central banks must remain cautious against the potential risks of proactive measures, such as unintended consequences on financial stability or credibility risks if actions are perceived as overstepping their traditional mandates. Clear communication and a measured approach to managing these risks are therefore key.

6 Risks to Financial Stability and Prudential Policy

6.1 INTRODUCTION

Financial stability is crucial for sustainable economic growth. In response to the Global Financial Crisis (GFC) of 2007–2008, prudential policies have been strengthened to maintain this stability. The Basel III framework, developed by the Basel Committee on Banking Supervision (BCBS), introduced stricter capital requirements, enhanced liquidity standards, and improved risk management practices for banks globally. These measures are designed to bolster the resilience of financial institutions against shocks, ensuring they have sufficient buffers to absorb losses during periods of stress. Additionally, prudential policies encompass a range of tools and frameworks aimed at preventing excessive risk-taking, monitoring systemic risks, and promoting transparency in financial markets. By fostering a stable and well-regulated financial system, prudential policies not only protect depositors and investors but also contribute to the overall resilience of economies, enabling them to better navigate future challenges, including those related to climate change.

As seen in Chapter 5, central banks can play a critical role in dealing with climate-related risks and their impact on our economies. In addition to the conduct of monetary policy, central banks in some jurisdictions are also in charge of safeguarding the stability of the financial system. In other cases, the institutions responsible for monetary policy and banking supervision are independent. The diversity of existing systems reflects the historical evolution of individual institutions and the specific circumstances of each country. Economic theory and examining institutional arrangements do not indicate that any single model is intrinsically more efficient than all the others. In any case, to guarantee the effectiveness of the monetary policy and preserve its transmission to the economy, central banks and supervisory authorities should ensure that the financial system is stable and resilient. History (e.g., the US sub-prime crisis in 2007–2008, the euro area sovereign debt crisis in 2011) has shown that price stability is a critical but insufficient condition to guarantee financial stability. Therefore, in addition to the economic pillar (price and macroeconomic stability), central banks and supervisory authorities also aim to prevent the emergence of financial vulnerabilities and their diffusion to the financial system (banks and financial markets). Taking into account the links between monetary conditions and the resilience of the financial system, the task of financial supervision becomes key, whether it is operated within the central bank's policy space or conducted by an independent supervisory authority.

The impacts of climate change influence the financial stability objective of central banks and weigh on financial conditions. Extreme weather events cause damage to physical assets, such as real estate properties, production facilities, and infrastructure, but also result in the loss of human life. With an increase in the frequency and severity of these weather events, these types of physical damages are likely to result in higher losses for insurance companies, severe deteriorations in household and corporate balance sheets and increased debt defaults that could endanger the financial sector.

A late and abrupt transition to a low-carbon economy could also destabilize financial systems. These financial risks can take the form of *stranded* assets when capital is invested in projects that are not compatible with the transition to a low-carbon economy or exposed to increased physical risks. This situation could also lead to stranded values when markets revalue risky assets in line with the transition policy decisions. This sudden reassessment of climate risks could have a negative effect on the balance sheets of financial market participants, with potential consequences for risk premia and credit conditions, and once again threaten the overall stability of the financial system.

The transmission of climate-related risks to the financial system is multifaceted and complex (see Chapter 3), thus requiring the adaptation of standard supervisory tools to this new type of risk. Such an assessment depends upon reviewing and innovating across a wide range of tasks, from identifying risks and measuring exposures to quantifying them. Once risks have been assessed, it is necessary to raise awareness among financial actors and design policy actions to prevent these risks, notably in terms of prudential responses, whether they target individual financial institutions or system-wide stabilization goals.

6.2 TRANSMISSION OF CLIMATE-RELATED SHOCKS TO THE FINANCIAL SYSTEM

Physical and transition risks can materialize as financial risks in five main channels, often accompanied by second-round and spillover effects (Figure 6.1). Through their impact on sovereigns, nonfinancial corporations, and households, climate-related risks are transmitted to financial institutions through credit, market, liquidity, insurance, and operational risks. Feedback loops and second-round

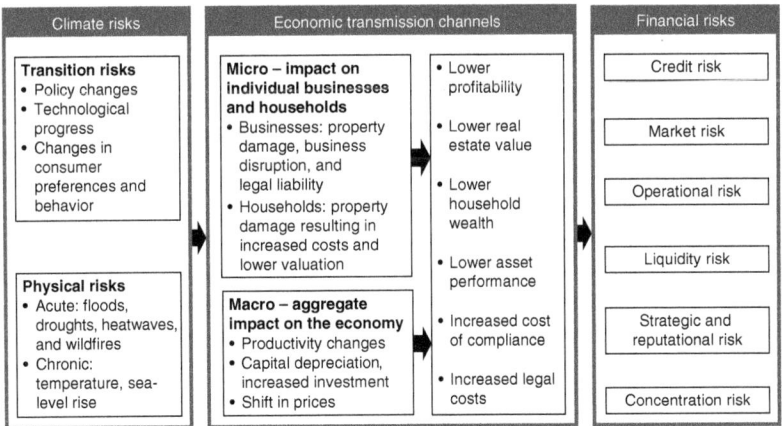

FIGURE 6.1 Channels and spillovers for materialization of physical and transition risks
Source: Walther (2023) based on EBA and NGFS

effects on the nonfinancial sector can mitigate or amplify those impacts. Contagion within the financial sector can also threaten financial stability.

Before exploring these mechanisms in detail, we need to review how to measure the exposures of financial systems to climate risks. The physician Lord Kelvin said:

> When you can measure what you are speaking about, and express it in numbers, you know something about it; but when you cannot measure it, when you cannot express it in numbers, your knowledge is of a meager and unsatisfactory kind: it may be the beginning of knowledge, but you have scarcely, in your thoughts, advanced to the stage of science, whatever the matter may be.[1]

Policymakers lack crucial data to gauge the effectiveness of climate policies – from emission reduction incentives to resilience regulations. Without comprehensive, comparable data, the assessment of what works and where adjustments are needed remains difficult. Efforts such as the Data Gaps Initiative at the G20 level aim to enhance official statistics, including climate data and indicators covering income, wealth, and financial inclusion, ensuring they are more detailed and timely for informed policymaking. In this section, we will review the challenges in measuring the exposures of financial systems and financial institutions to climate risks, both physical and transition, including banks and insurance companies.

6.2.1 Measuring Exposures of Financial Systems to Climate Risks

An effective risk management framework for banks and supervisors is necessary to limit the economic and financial impacts of climate risks on banking institutions. Before quantitatively assessing such impacts, as a first step, mapping and measuring climate-related

---

[1] Popular Lectures and Addresses vol. 1 (1889) "Electrical Units of Measurement," delivered 3 May 1883.

exposures and any area of risk concentration is to be performed. These are fundamental components of an effective risk governance framework (Basel Committee on Banking Supervision (BCBS), 2015). While the inclusion of climate-related financial risks into risk management frameworks shares many similarities with standard processes of risk assessment, the exceptional features of climate-related financial risks pose some key challenges (BCBS, 2021a, 2021b).

Starting with physical risks, the impacts of weather-related hazards on production facilities (land, plants, and machines) and activities that generate financial flows must first be defined. Such impacts are usually assessed using damage functions (see Chapter 1) that link the increase in temperature with losses in capital stocks and economic activity. Similarly, transition risks are measured with models that translate policy actions to decarbonize the economy into economic costs. As those risks are likely to increase in the future, these assessments are forward-looking in nature and rely on scenario analyses.

Banks are exposed to climate-related financial risks through their relationships with their customers and counterparties: corporates, households, sovereigns, and other financial institutions. When assessing the impacts of the role of climate-related risks in these relationships, banks (and supervisors) need to calculate exposures with a sufficient level of granularity, accounting for the heterogeneity in their portfolios. For physical risks, as extreme weather events occur at the regional or local level, geographical distribution and heterogeneity have to be taken into account. For transition risks, accounting for sectoral heterogeneity in exposures is key (i.e., a bank exposed to sensitive sectors, like petroleum production, is more at risk than another one financing green activities). Intrasectoral heterogeneity is also crucial to account for different carbon intensities, energy efficiency, or adaptive expenditures. Heterogeneity in country exposures not only matters as differing policy and regulatory regimes but also the macroeconomic conditions (such as high indebtedness and unsustainable fiscal deficits) influence the overall vulnerability to climate risks.

The assessment of climate-related financial risks, therefore, requires developing new datasets to complement the traditional data sources used in financial risk analyses. Such climate-specific data are not yet fully available or are of inadequate quality, for example, regarding historical depth, level of granularity, reliance, and comparability (NGFS, 2022a). Three broad categories of data are necessary for a satisfactory assessment of climate-related financial risks (BIS, 2021):

- data identifying physical and transition risk drivers, used to quantify economic consequences of climate change and identify at-risk geographical locations or sectors exposed to transition policies.
- data describing the vulnerability of exposures to climate-related risk factors, including physical vulnerability (e.g., geospatial vulnerability of business facilities to weather events) and transition sensitivity (e.g., exposures to economic activities according to the classification *Climate Policy Relevant Sectors* – see Battiston et al., 2017).
- financial exposure data to project cash flows, valuations, or prices, including data on portfolio composition (e.g., asset holdings or loans) and relevant information on counterparties (e.g., adjustments to the probability of default (PD) and loss-given-default (LGD) parameters in the credit valuation process or revenue forecasts).

Policymakers and supervisors have identified three key building blocks to make climate-related data available, comparable, and reliable (Figure 6.2 and NGFS, 2022a). First, firms need to disclose climate-related risks through their existing reporting processes. Since 2017, the Task Force for Climate-related Financial Disclosures (TCFD), at the request of the Financial Stability Board (FSB), has issued recommendations to companies and other organizations to help them improve transparency on the actual and potential impact of climate change on their activities. While disclosing such information has been done so far on a voluntary basis, a rapid convergence toward a common and consistent set of global disclosure standards is necessary to deploy mandatory disclosures on the prudential front. In 2021, the IFRS Foundation announced a plan to establish a sustainability

6 RISKS TO FINANCIAL STABILITY AND PRUDENTIAL POLICY

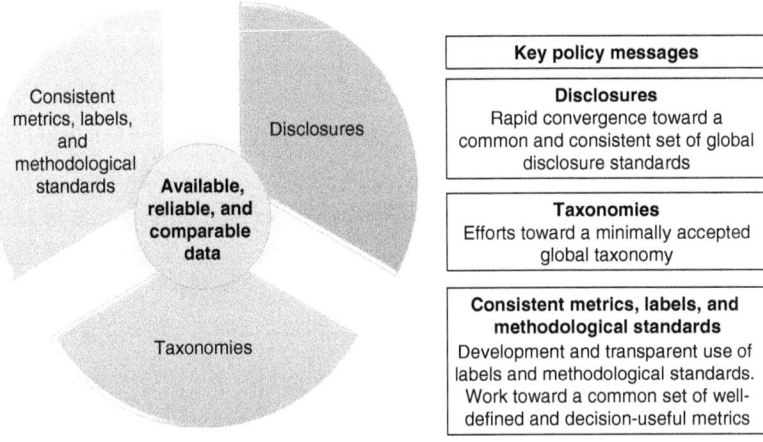

FIGURE 6.2 Bridging the climate data gap
Source: NGFS (2022a)

standards board with support from the International Organization of Securities Commissions (IOSCO) and build on existing frameworks, such as the TCFD. An adequate disclosure framework also requires mechanisms for verifying and auditing climate-related financial disclosures are essential to improve data reliability and comparability.

Second, to properly classify activities as green and nongreen, there is a need to set up a minimally accepted global taxonomy (and sustainable finance classifications). A green taxonomy is a classification system that establishes a list of environmentally sustainable economic activities. The taxonomy is instrumental in preventing *greenwashing* as a communication and marketing strategy (see more details in Chapter 4). More importantly, it forcefully helps companies, investors, and policymakers to make more informed decisions, to become more climate-friendly, to mitigate market fragmentation, and ultimately to allocate investments where they are most needed to reach climate goals. Currently, different jurisdictions are establishing different, separate taxonomies for green finance (e.g., the EU Taxonomy in 2020). The convergence of different taxonomies over time will not only be important in ensuring consistency in climate-related disclosures but also for the consistency and comparability of credit ratings.

Finally, certification labels and methodological standards play a crucial role in delivering well-defined metrics that are practical for decision-making. A certification label is a label or symbol indicating that compliance with standards has been verified and its use is usually controlled by the standard-setting body issuing the label (e.g., Energy Performance Certificates or ISO standards). Certification is especially crucial for issuing sustainable financial instruments such as green/blue bonds or for incentivizing capital allocation to sustainable instruments (see Chapter 4). The certification of environmental labels is still in progress: They need to be harmonized across regions, and the information they certify should be made comparable, homogeneous, and easily available.

6.2.2 *Exposure of Financial Institutions to Physical Risks*

Banks stand at the center of capital allocation, and one of the most critical dimensions of the transition to a climate-resilient economy is how the financial sector, particularly banking institutions, manages climate-related risks and opportunities.

The dangers posed by climate change can arise from two types of risks: long-term risks associated with gradual changes in climate patterns, such as rising temperatures, and short-term risks associated with more frequent and/or severe weather events, such as tropical cyclones, storms, floods, and droughts. Financial institutions and financial systems face these risks directly, making proper assessment essential. Such assessments must account for the country's specific context and address existing information gaps.

There are several factors that contribute to the risks associated with climate change. These include the *hazards* associated with each peril that a region is exposed to, which are influenced by climate change; the *exposure* of assets and systems to these perils, which depends on the geographic location and various dynamics such as

Table 6.1 *Assessing impacts of acute physical climate risk*

Category	Description
Hazard	• Hazard associated with each peril to which a region is exposed. • Influenced by climate change and other environmental dynamics.
Exposure	• Exposure to perils based on geographic location of assets and systems. • Influenced by dynamics such as population and economic growth and migration.
Vulnerability	• Translation of hazard intensity into expected damage or loss for exposed assets and systems. • Influenced by factors such as construction quality, building codes, and other socioeconomic vulnerability factors.
Financial, social, and macroeconomic	• Mechanisms through which direct and indirect losses manifest at the financial or macroeconomic level. • Influenced by macroeconomic variables and structure of financial system, and moderated by various transmission channels.

Source: World Bank

population and economic growth; the *vulnerability* of exposed assets and systems; and the *mechanisms* through which the risks manifest at a financial or macroeconomic level (NGFS, 2022b).

When modeling physical climate-change risks, three critical factors must be considered (Table 6.1):

Exposure Level: This involves estimating the potential share and composition of the population or the value and properties of assets at risk. It helps assess how much exposure exists.

Hazard Description: The hazard component describes the physical characteristics of weather-related events, including their frequency and intensity. For instance, heat waves, storms, floods, and other natural disasters fall under this category.

Vulnerability: This factor relates to how susceptible the exposed entities (people, assets, etc.) are to weather-related damages. Vulnerability combines information about changes in hazard with the level of exposure. It accounts, in particular, for adaptation efforts as mitigation factors to limit the impact of physical risks.

Importantly, an increase in the frequency and intensity of weather-related catastrophes does not necessarily imply a corresponding increase in physical risk. For instance, if no properties or people live in affected areas or if sufficient preventive measures are in place, the damages caused by an event may be limited or negligible.

The impact of climate change, both from gradual changes in climatic conditions and acute events, can affect financial institutions in several ways (NGFS, 2019):

- *Business and operational risks*: Weather-related events can disrupt financial services (e.g., damages to IT servers after flooding or to office buildings and collateral).
- *Credit and counterparty risks*: Physical damages can affect the debt repayment capacity and collateral values of borrowers (Stenek et al., 2011), including sovereigns (Kraemer and Negrila, 2014). Lenders may face a higher likelihood of clients defaulting on payments, which could lead to an increase in the proportion of impaired loans in their portfolio. Capital (property, land, or equipment) held by lenders as collateral could also lose value. Banks may suffer write-downs or devaluations of collateral assets in the real estate and tourism sectors if they are located in areas of high risk from sea-level rise. For example, if real estate assets held as security are located in a flood-prone area, their value is likely to be reduced if floods become more frequent. Agricultural producers who experience losses from shifting climate patterns or increased extreme weather events may be at higher risk for delinquency and default. Commercial or industrial customers who face higher costs from physical risks may lose significant revenue if their prices are no longer competitive in global markets. Furthermore, institutions may be exposed to increased liabilities associated with the financial guarantees they provide to their clients.
- *Market risks*: The physical impact of climate change could affect an investment's value and expected return. If climate change damages an

investment, the investor may experience a decrease in capital gains realized on equity sale due to the investment's negative reputation.
- *Legal and liability risks*: If climate change is not managed, it can result in an increase in all types of corporate risks discussed earlier, as well as an increased risk of damage to third parties from investment projects. This, in turn, may lead to disputes between investment institutions and their clients, as well as between institutions and third parties such as local communities, co-investors, and project end-users. The approach to climate-risk disclosure and management is moving from voluntary initiatives to mandatory obligations, as demonstrated by recent changes (or proposed changes) to laws and regulations that require such disclosures. These new requirements build on the existing obligation for company directors to report material future risks to shareholders in their annual reports. Additionally, some lawyers now recognize that sufficient information on climate change exists to justify its inclusion in strategic and operational decisions, suggesting it may soon carry *legal significance* in court. (LCCP Finance Group 2009, quoted in Stenek et al., 2011)

6.2.3 Transition Risks, Asset Stranding, and Market Risks

The four financial risk categories mentioned above are also considered in most transition risk assessments: (1) business and operational risk as well as reputation risk from investing in emission-intensive assets or financing polluting activities; (2) credit and counterparty risks as the energy transition can affect the profitability of exposed sectors; (3) market risk resulting from revaluation of transition-related assets; and (4) legal and liability risk coming from climate-related losses.

The financial stability impact of the transition is especially related to the issue of asset stranding (see Chapter 3). Stranded assets would be removed from the balance sheets of their owners, at least in part, potentially impacting financial markets adversely (van der Ploeg and Rezai, 2020). The uncertainty surrounding future transition developments could lead to financial disturbances. As the transition becomes clearer (or is credibly announced), investors recognize that existing high-carbon investments may not yield expected returns, leading to significant asset devaluations, especially if climate policies are stringent, the transition occurs rapidly, or reallocation costs are substantial (Daumas, 2024).

The transmission of asset stranding to financial institutions could be amplified by contagion. In production networks, these spillovers could adversely impact nonfinancial companies or financial institutions that were not initially exposed to transition risks. Within financial markets, amplifiers are linked to common exposure to similar risky assets or interactions across financial institutions (Battiston et al., 2017) or institutional sectors (Stolbova et al., 2018).

Former Bank of England Governor Mark Carney popularized the term *climate Minsky moment* in his 2005 seminal speech, describing the sudden shift in investors' expectations of future climate policies and the resulting forced sale of assets, as risks were reassessed. A Minsky moment refers to a tipping point that triggers a market collapse, often arising from regulatory blind spots where underlying risks go unrecognized or unmitigated. Named after economist Hyman Minsky, it describes a situation where overleveraged investors suddenly begin selling their assets, causing a sharp market decline. In the context of climate change, a *climate Minsky moment*, therefore, refers to a sudden and significant shift in financial markets or economic conditions triggered by the realization of the risks associated with climate change. This could include events such as a rapid reassessment of the value of fossil fuel assets, increased financial liabilities due to climate-related disasters, or a sudden change in investor sentiment toward environmentally sustainable practices.

To estimate the impact of climate-related risks on financial institutions, market-based stress-testing methodologies could be used to measure the effect of climate risk on asset prices. Using publicly available data, these stress tests assess institutions' expected capital shortfall in climate stress scenarios. Jung et al. (2021) propose a stress-testing procedure in three steps. The first step is to quantify the climate risk factor using a market-based measure, as previous studies suggest that climate risks are priced in the equity market (see Bolton and Kacperczyk, 2021; Engle et al., 2020). As their stress test focuses exclusively on transition risks, they assume that a large proportion of existing fossil fuel reserves will become stranded (see Chapter 3). This step relies on the stranded asset portfolio return as a market-based proxy measure for transition risk. The second step of market-based stress testing is to perform an econometric regression including financial institutions' stock returns (dependent variable) and the climate risk factor (explanatory variable), the so-called *climate beta*. This climate-related sensitivity parameter is expected to be positive for banks with large exposure to gas and oil loans and negative for banks with large exposure to renewable energy, for example. Finally, the third step is to compute the climate systemic risk indicator – called CRISK by Jung et al. (2021), which is a function of a given financial firm's size, leverage, and expected equity loss conditional on climate stress. This step is based on the same methodology as the systemic risk indicator (SRISK) of Brownlees and Engle (2017), with the climate risk factor added to the size and the leverage of banks as risk drivers.

The stress scenario that Jung et al. (2021) consider is a 50 percent drop in the return on the stranded asset portfolio over six months (i.e., an adverse shock corresponding to the first percentile of the historical six-month return on the stranded asset portfolio). The study finds that the climate beta and CRISK substantially increased during 2020. In 2020, the aggregate CRISK of the top four US banks increased by USD 425 billion, corresponding to approximately 47 percent relative to their market capitalization. To isolate the effect of climate stress from the effect of market stress, Jung et al. (2021) also measure the marginal CRISK (i.e., the difference between CRISK and nonstressed CRISK) of the top four US banks and find that it reached USD 260 billion at the end of 2020 and remain elevated until 2021, suggesting that the effect of climate stress could be substantial. CRISK and marginal CRISK data are available from the V-Lab (NYU Stern). Figure 6.3 presents the series for the World

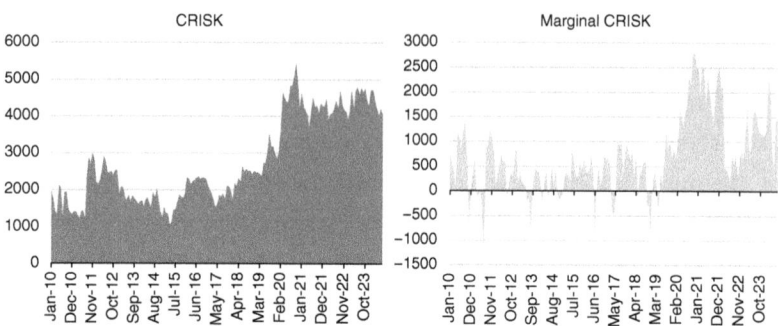

FIGURE 6.3 CRISK and marginal CRISK for World Financials
Source: V-Lab (2024) – V-Lab: Climate Risk Analysis Summary (nyu.edu)

Financials aggregate, showing a sharp rise in both CRISK and marginal CRISK from 2020, with marginal CRISK displaying a renewed increase in 2022–2024.

6.2.4 Climate Risks and Insurance/Reinsurance Sector

Private insurance should be the primary means of covering losses resulting from climate-related natural disasters and lowering their financial consequences on households and firms (see Table 6.2 for an overview of how climate change impacts insurance products). However, the anticipated rise in severe weather events, as projected by climate scientists, is posing challenges to insuring properties in certain regions, leaving many assets uninsured. A widening of such an insurance protection gap (IPG) could, therefore, create financial stability risks, reinforcing the risks to the banking sector detailed above.

Escalating climate-related catastrophic losses pose a significant threat to the liabilities of non-life insurers (see Table 6.3). These losses stem primarily from more frequent and severe natural disasters, including heat waves, wildfires, storms, and floods, which are expected to impact all property-related lines of business.

For insurance companies, transition risks mainly arise through their investment portfolios. While life insurers are primarily exposed to transition risks – since they generally do not insure properties vulnerable to physical risks – non-life insurers also face such risks on the asset side of their balance sheets. Market risks for insurance companies arise from potential impairments of financial assets due to the transition toward a low-carbon economy, leading to stranded assets and declining market values in carbon-intensive industry sectors (see Chapter 3). Credit risks could also emerge when counterparties' creditworthiness deteriorates, especially for companies inadequately accounting for transition risks. Both types of risk can negatively impact insurers' asset value, manifesting as equity price shocks or yield fluctuations (Gatzert and Özdil, 2023).

Climate events can heavily affect insurance liabilities, especially in property and business interruption lines, which cover damages to property, vehicles, crops, and related losses.

Natural catastrophes can also drive up mortgage insurance claims, a trend likely to intensify as weather events grow more frequent and severe, often requiring simultaneous responses. The impacts of climate-related hazards, however, differ across regions, limiting the diversification benefits of insurers' portfolios. If insurance liabilities are not priced accurately – particularly in the presence of knowledge gaps or overreliance on historical data – insurers may face heightened risks. In response, they might raise premiums or restrict coverage, ultimately shifting a greater share of the risk onto households, companies, and their lenders. This could also lead to a widening of the IPG, which is the difference between optimal insurance coverage and actual coverage in every country. In other words, the protection gap describes uninsured losses in any given country. This gap undergoes natural fluctuations and is influenced by many factors, including economic dynamics, shifts in GDP and population, and risks beyond climate change, such as cyber threats, pandemics, and changes in technology and behaviors.

In Europe, the IPG is at 35 percent, that is, only a third of losses from extreme weather events are insured. Globally, natural disasters generated about USD 313 billion in economic losses in 2022, yet less than half of this amount (USD 132 billion) was insured, leaving an

Table 6.2 *Climate change impacts on insurance products*

Product line	Description of nature of exposure to physical risks	Description of nature of exposure to transition risks
Life – Protection	Increased mortality due to higher frequency and severity of extreme heat events	–
Life – Investments/Savings	Higher frequency of policy lapses due to change in policyholder behavior.	–
Health/Medical (e.g., critical illness, long-term care, disability, hospital, and medical plans)	Increased morbidity, more frequent and longer duration of disability, and higher hospitalization rates due to weather changes.	–
Non-life – Property (e.g., commercial property, motor, and business interruption)	Increased damage to assets and business interruption from extreme weather events, i.e., floods, hurricanes, heat waves, wildfires, droughts, sea-level rise, erosion, or biodiversity loss	Lower insurability for businesses related to the use of coal-fired power plants. Higher premiums and claim costs due to a shift toward electric vehicles or to changes in energy efficiency regulation.
Non-life – Casualty (e.g., work injury compensation, general liability, financial lines)	Work-related or physical injuries to customers/employees arising from climate-related emissions in operations or productions; extreme weather events, pollution.	Increased probability of repayment defaults of companies in high-emission sectors as a result of policy and regulatory risks. Increased claims due to legal charges due to inaction or greenwashing.

(continued)

Table 6.2 *(cont.)*

Product line	Description of nature of exposure to physical risks	Description of nature of exposure to transition risks
Others (e.g., employee benefits, personal accident, and travel)	Changing demand from employees to counter effects of climate change, leading to increased claims.	Lower demand for products due to change in consumer behavior. Increased climate change litigation arising from the mismanagement of climate-related risks. Uncertain profitability due to insufficient underwriting in relation to insurance covering new technology (e.g., offshore wind projects).

Source: Adapted from Khoo and Yong (2023)

insurance protection gap (IPG) of 58 percent – still worryingly high, even if one of the lowest on record (Aon, 2023). Significant differences exist among countries and regions in terms of IPG. In the United States, the protection gap is the smallest and stands below 40% while it exceeds 60% in emerging economies. In Europe, the insurance gap surpasses 75%, while in the Americas, it is above 80%, and in the Asia-Pacific region, it hovers around 80% in Americas (see Figure 6.4).

Moreover, while reinsurance may mitigate risks on non-life insurance companies, global weather trends could also impact reinsurance premiums and conditions, potentially resulting in a reinsurance gap (EIOPA, 2022). Although part of the insured losses remains with the direct insurers (i.e., the companies that issue the policies), a substantial share is transferred to reinsurers. As weather-related events increase, reinsurers can increase their reinsurance premiums, leading to higher costs for insurance companies. Moreover, losses

Table 6.3 *Potential negative consequences of physical climate change risk on the nonlife insurance business*

Assets side	Liability side
• Impairment of property due to physical damages related to extreme weather events. • Impairment of asset values due to financial losses affecting the profitability of firms. • Creditworthiness deterioration of counterparties.	Potential impact on several Lines of Business (LoBs) such as fire and other damages to property, motor property damage, crop damage, marine and aviation transport (MAT) through, for instance: • *Reserving risk* (associated with estimating the amount of money that an insurance company needs to set aside to cover future claims) • *Pricing risk* (uncertainty and potential financial losses associated with setting premiums for insurance policies) • *Underwriting risk* (uncertainty and potential financial loss associated with predicting future claims) • *Reinsurance risk* (associated with the transfer of part of risk exposure to reinsurers)

Source: Adapted from EIOPA (2022)

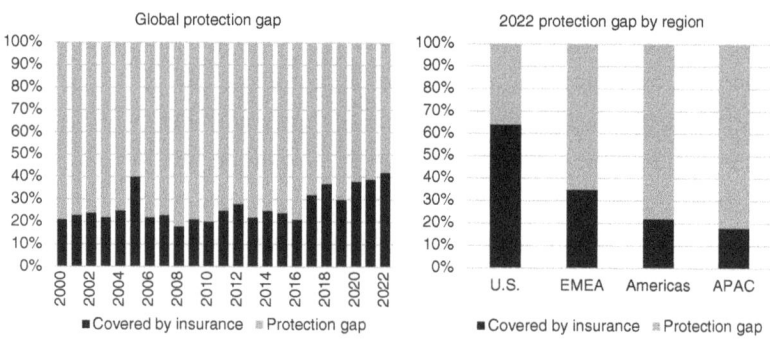

FIGURE 6.4 Protection gap
Source: Catastrophe Insight, Aon

could also remain uninsured, since the IPG also extends to the reinsurance market. This reinsurance gap partly reflects the high concentration of the reinsurance sector, which is dominated by a few large firms that absorb insurance risks onto their balance sheets. These firms may lack the capacity to meet rising market demand and face the same climate-related challenges as their clients, reducing overall reinsurance availability. As a result, insurers are left with larger unfunded liabilities in the insurers' balance sheets.

In addition to the simultaneous impact of climate risks on the assets and liabilities of non-life insurers, there is a possibility that a sharp increase in physical risks triggers an abrupt transition of the economy, acting as a "wake-up call" for governments that have so far remained passive in advancing the green transition. This, in turn, would lead to higher transition risks on the asset side, in addition to higher physical risks. BaFin (2020) emphasizes the significance of considering the interdependence between climate transition and physical risks, which consequently extends to the interdependence between assets and liabilities to be taken into account within asset-liability management.

6.3 CAN CENTRAL BANKS AND PRUDENTIAL AUTHORITIES PREVENT OR LIMIT THE THREAT THAT CLIMATE CHANGE POSES TO FINANCIAL STABILITY?

Governments have the principal responsibility for implementing a policy response to address climate-related challenges. Compared to central banks and prudential authorities, governments have a much broader range of tools and policies to prevent and mitigate climate-related risks (Chapter 2). While financial stability considerations require actions to address climate-related risks, there is so far no common agreement among central banks and prudential authorities on how they should include climate change in their supervisory framework and which boundaries they should respect.

6.3.1 Raising Awareness: Climate Stress-Tests

Actions aimed at raising awareness of climate risks involve central bankers' speeches or communication on climate-related issues. Central banks also promote climate risk management in the financial sector and, in particular, the disclosure of climate-related risks by creating momentum, including especially by supporting standards.

To reveal and highlight the exposure of banks to climate-related risks, central banks and supervisors have launched climate stress-testing exercises. These stress tests rely on climate scenario analysis, whose goals are both macroprudential – to understand and estimate financial system-wide risks – and microprudential – to look at specific risks to financial firms, including the impact on balance sheets and income statements.

6.3.1.1 Climate Scenario Analysis to Assess Financial Risks

As with *standard* stress test scenarios, climate scenarios are not forecasts, but hypothetical frameworks designed to explore a range of potential future environmental conditions and their impacts. They present extreme but plausible future outcomes that highlight certain significant aspects of the issues and challenges associated with climate change. The impacts selected should reflect the orders of magnitude involved, but the scenarios are not prejudgments of what is likely to happen or of what is desirable. On the contrary, these scenarios are voluntarily designed to be adverse to test the resilience of financial institutions to high-impact-low probability events (Boirard et al., 2022; Allen et al., 2022).

Most climate stress-testing exercises conducted by supervisory authorities rely on the work of the Network for Greening the Financial System (NGFS), these scenarios depict a variety of plausible futures. They are constructed through comprehensive modeling of energy, economic, and climate systems, offering a methodological framework that is well-adapted for integrating climate risks. The NGFS regularly publishes several transition reference scenarios featuring three different situations (see diagram in Chapter 1 – Figure 1.3). The first group of scenarios describes an *orderly* transition. In these scenarios, the transition would have started in 2020, featuring the proactive and gradual implementation of mitigation policies such as carbon taxes and support measures for renewable energy sources. As a positive side effect of this scenario, meeting climate commitments would reduce physical risks. The second family of scenarios sets out the response to a *disorderly* transition (delayed or sudden), requiring more stringent measures that would call for more disruptive adaptations. Finally, the third family of scenarios, referred to as Hot house world, reflects *business as usual*, with no additional transition measures from governments other than those already in place, leading to the aggravation of chronic physical risks and an increase in the frequency and severity of extreme weather events. Under such a scenario of inaction, transition risks, on the other hand, remain limited.

The NGFS scenarios show that while transition risk leads to a negative short-term impact on GDP in the Net Zero 2050 scenario, the cost-saving later on more than offsets these initial losses compared to a Delayed Transition or a Current Policies scenario. Acute physical risk is the most relevant source of risk in the short and long term. Since physical risk is unaffected by mitigation efforts in the short run, acute physical risk is similar across scenarios until 2040, with a strong surge in losses in Current Policies thereafter. Chronic physical risk becomes gradually more important over time. It causes the largest negative impact on GDP in the Current Policies scenario, with associated economic losses in 2050 being almost double what is implied by the Net Zero 2050 scenario (see Figure 1.8 in Chapter 1).

Similar to *standard* stress test scenarios, climate scenarios present extreme but plausible future outcomes that highlight certain significant aspects of the issues and challenges associated with climate change. Climate scenarios also display a number of specificities that differentiate them from the type of standard stress test scenarios used by supervisors to assess financial institutions' capacity to absorb losses in the face of adverse economic and financial shocks (see Table 6.4).

Unlike standard stress tests, climate scenarios rely on forward-looking data, as there is no historical precedent on which to build quantitative scenarios. The calibration of climate scenarios thus requires different expertise in various scientific fields. This is

Table 6.4 *The specificities of climate scenarios*

	Standard scenarios	Climate scenarios	
		Transition risks	Physical risks
Time horizon	Short and medium term	Short, medium, and long-term	Short, medium, and long-term
Types of variables	Economic and financial	Climate policies, technological innovations, behaviors	Climate policies, technological innovations, environmental changes
Shock calibration	Based on historical data	Little to no guidance from history	
Aggregation	National	Sectoral	Sectoral and geographical
Feedback loops	Macroeconomic models with financial frictions	Work in progress (e.g., interactions between public policy and the economy)	Climate–economy interactions
Discount rate	Not used	Important for long-term analyses	Important for long-term analyses

Source: Banque de France

skillfully illustrated by the work of the Intergovernmental Panel on Climate Change (IPCC) on climate scenarios and long-term socio-economic pathways. Climate change also imposes far longer time horizons than the three to five years generally used when performing standard stress test exercises. This poses additional challenges in terms of data availability and model uncertainty. Finally, in order to perform an economic assessment of the transition, the sectoral impacts of the structural transformations needed to achieve climate goals must be taken into account. Finally, firm-level heterogeneities must be incorporated into climate scenarios to precisely capture the impact of the most disruptive shocks.

Scenario analysis can help explore different possible paths into the future, such as the adoption of carbon taxes, changes in consumer behavior, and advancements in renewable energy technologies. However, these scenarios typically describe transition paths over long horizons, extending to 2050 or even 2060. Allen et al. (2020) show that while the transition shocks trigger larger changes at the sectoral level, the main macroeconomic variables (unemployment and GDP in particular) do not differ significantly across long-term scenarios. Beyond long-term challenges and trade-offs due to climate change and mitigation policies, policymakers, regulators, and financial institutions are also increasingly interested in analyzing the short-term impact of these policies on the real economy, individual financial institutions, and the broader financial system. The NGFS is also exploring short-term scenarios over a time horizon of three to five years (NGFS, 2023), in order to overcome limitations in macroeconomic and financial risk analysis stemming from the focus on long-term climate-economy relationships as captured in the long-run NGFS climate scenarios. While long-term scenario analysis is a useful tool for exploring the potential impacts of climate transition on a global scale, it may not provide an accurate picture of the effects of transition shocks in the short term. Major changes can unfold over short periods when rapid bifurcations occur, driven by unexpected policy shifts, technological breakthroughs, or sudden shifts in consumer behavior. These factors can significantly influence macrofinancial variables in the short term, creating temporary movements in economic activity, inflation, or financial prices that are usually ignored in long-term scenarios. Moreover, short-term scenarios can incorporate macro-financial shocks on top of climate shocks and zoom into sudden impacts and amplification mechanisms in the short to medium term.

The NGFS proposes five climate scenario narratives that describe the short-term dynamics associated with different transition and physical impacts (Table 6.5). These narratives are not meant to provide certainty but to illustrate a limited number of possible futures that can support resilience planning.

This approach is grounded in a close examination of the current global macroeconomic environment, the policy landscape, climate conditions, and the broader set of surrounding risks:

- Could the need to rapidly substitute away from traditional energy sources lead to an acceleration of efforts facilitating a move toward renewables? (Scenarios I and II)
- Could bottlenecks in the supply of fossil energy lead countries to delay climate policies and lock in fossil fuel-based technologies before suddenly transitioning? (Scenario III)
- What if severe natural disasters hit globally? (Scenario IV)
- What if the transition takes place but in a geographically fragmented fashion? (Scenario V)

Banque de France, the French central bank, was among the first institutions to develop short-term climate scenarios (Allen et al., 2023). These short-term scenarios reflect the diversity of transition shocks – increase in carbon and energy prices, increase in public or private investment in the low-carbon transition, increase in the cost of capital due to uncertainty, deterioration of confidence, accelerated obsolescence of part of the installed capital, and similar factors.

The scenario-based stress-test exercises can be performed following two approaches: bottom-up and top-down. In bottom-up exercises, the central bank or supervisor sets out the scenario and the methodology, and financial institutions run the scenarios on their balance sheet, using their internal data and models. The advantage of this approach is to ensure a consistent methodology across institutions, and this type of stress tests are relatively resource-light. The bottom-up scenarios have several other benefits for financial authorities: They allow them to gain insight into institutions' own methods and abilities to analyze climate-related risks; they improve institutions' own capabilities to perform climate scenario analysis; they foster data collection within institutions; and they increase awareness of the economic and financial implications of climate-related

Table 6.5 *Overview of short-term scenario narratives*

Scenario	Narrative
Highway to Paris	Elevated levels of uncertainty related to fossil energy supply lead governments to implement an ambitious mitigation pathway in a timely and anticipated fashion. There is a boom in green public investment, leading to a rapid reallocation of capital across sectors and internationally via cross-country capital flows and lending patterns. Technology shocks lead to a faster-than-anticipated transition, inducing disorderliness. Green prudential policies prevent financial turmoil, albeit with losses in some sectors due to stranded assets. **In line with reaching net zero by 2050.**
Green Bubble	Elevated levels of uncertainty related to fossil energy supply limit governments in their ability to implement ambitious mitigation policy. Green regulation overtakes government policies in driving the transition, leading to a glut of green private investment and the build-up of a green credit bubble. A sunspot (i.e., an unrelated random event) leads to the burst of the bubble, a sharp rise in risk premia, and a confidence crisis. **In line with reaching net zero by 2050.**
Sudden Wake-up Call	Elevated levels of uncertainty related to fossil energy supply limit governments in their ability to implement ambitious mitigation policy. Driven by an event that triggers a sudden change in public opinion (e.g., a severe natural disaster), an unanticipated and accelerated transition occurs. The abrupt policy change sets off shock waves through the economy and financial system: stranded assets in polluting sectors cause severe financial stress which propagates internationally via capital, trade, and financial flows. **In line with reaching net zero by 2050.**

(continued)

Table 6.5 *(cont.)*

Scenario	Narrative
Low Policy Ambition and Disasters	Severe acute physical disasters hit exposed jurisdictions. Investors price in a sizeable risk premium, which freezes private investment, and reduces their exposure to the jurisdictions and sectors whose assets are at greatest risk of disaster losses. Households consume less and save more due to the increase in uncertainty and insurance costs increase. **NOT in line with reaching net zero by 2050.**
Diverging Realities	The world as a whole aims to avoid the worst impacts of global warming. However, severe natural disasters in the EMDEs and LICs and a lack of external financing lead to recovery traps, i.e., a lack of fiscal space for affected regions to transition. Meanwhile, the disruption of transition-critical mineral supply chains originating in disaster-prone regions hampers the speed of the global transition. The sudden realization that the global transition is too slow to avoid a Hot house world leads to a sudden reassessment of future physical impacts globally. As a result, risk premia rise sharply. **NOT in line with reaching net zero by 2050.**

Source: Nowzohour and Dees (2024)

risks (Boirard et al., 2022). By contrast, a top-down exercise is run entirely by the central bank or supervisor, without the involvement of financial institutions. This approach allows for gaining insight into institutions' own methods and abilities to analyze climate-related risks. The top-down scenarios also ensure a consistent methodology across financial institutions, provide room for sensitivity analysis as assumptions and parameters can be easily adjusted, and reduce resource costs (Boirard et al., 2022). We detail both approaches in the following and summarize the results of a few prominent stress-testing exercises.

BOX 6.1: Bank of England's Climate Biennial Exploratory Scenario (CBES)

In 2021, the Bank of England ran its first exploratory scenario exercise on climate risk, involving the largest UK banks and insurers. The exercise included three scenarios exploring both transition and physical risks, considering two possible routes to net-zero UK greenhouse gas (GHG) emissions by 2050: an "Early Action" scenario and a "Late Action" scenario. A third "No Additional Action" scenario explores the physical risks that would materialize if policy action were insufficient to limit global warming under 2°C. Table B6.1.1

Table B6.1.1 *Summary of assumptions in the CBES scenarios*

Scenario	Early action	Late action	No additional action
Transition risks	Medium	High	Limited
Transition begins in	2021	2031	n.a.
Nature of transition	Early and orderly	Late and disorderly	Only policies that were in place before 2021
Peak UK shadow carbon price (2010 USD/tonne CO_2e)	900	1,100	30
Physical risks	Limited	Limited	High
Mean global warming relative to pre-industrial times by the end of scenario (°C)	1.8	1.8	3.3
Mean sea-level rise in the UK (m)	0.16	0.16	0.39
Impact on output	Temporarily lower growth	Sudden contraction (recession)	Permanently lower growth and higher uncertainty

gives, for each of these scenarios, the assumptions on the climate policy variable (carbon price), the physical consequences on climate in terms of temperature and sea-level rise as well as their impact on economic output.

Based on institutions' projections, the overall costs to banks and insurers from the transition to net zero should be bearable without substantial impacts on firms' solvency positions. This is because not all of the losses on insurers' investments would ultimately fall on shareholders. Firms' projections suggest that these costs will be lower if early, well-ordered action is taken. The loss estimates are based on the simplifying assumption that banks' and insurers' balance sheets stay fixed over the scenario horizon, which may, to some degree, overestimate the magnitude of final losses. In reality, the business models of banks and insurers are likely to respond to climate risks over time and mitigate some of the losses projected (Figure B6.1.1).

This first exercise has also revealed a lack of data on several aspects that participants need to review to manage climate risks. The quality gap across organizations in assessing and modeling these risks was very large, bringing the Bank of England to encourage all participating institutions to improve their climate risk management capabilities.

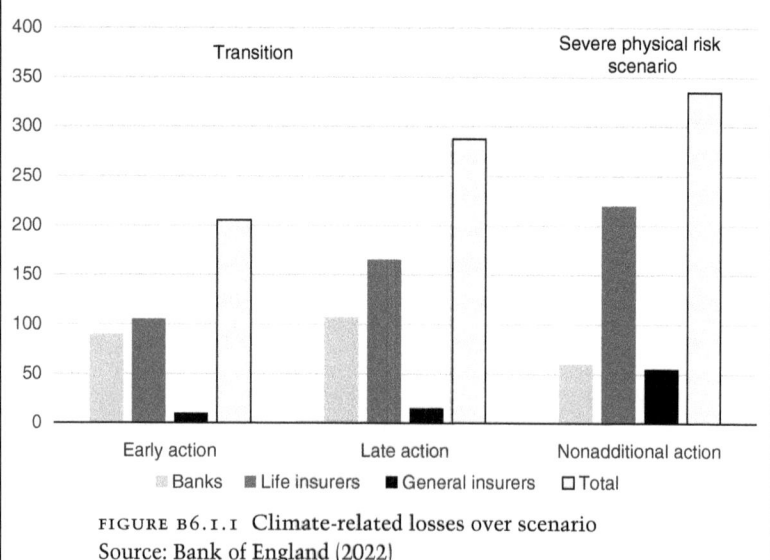

FIGURE B6.1.1 Climate-related losses over scenario
Source: Bank of England (2022)

6.3.1.2 Bottom-Up Climate Stress Tests

Bottom-up climate stress-test exercises have been conducted by ACPR-Banque de France (2021), the ECB-SSM (2022), or the Bank of England (2022 and Box 6.1). Based on the scenarios and assumptions used, the ACPR pilot exercise first showed that exposure and vulnerabilities for French institutions were *moderate* overall. About half of French financial institutions' exposures are in France and roughly three quarters are in Europe. These regions are generally less vulnerable to climate-related physical and transition risks than other parts of the world. However, according to the NGFS projections used in this exercise, exposures in geographical areas such as the United States (which accounts for about 9 percent of French financial institutions' exposures) seem to be more sensitive to transition risk. Furthermore, French institutions show relatively low exposures to the sectors most affected by transition risks, such as mining and quarrying, coking and refined petroleum products, and agriculture. Banks have been reducing these exposures gradually through 2050. Nevertheless, these sensitive sectors show the sharpest rise in risk, with probabilities of default and the cost of risk increasing significantly, including a threefold rise in the latter.

Looking at the distribution of impacts across the six main institutions, notable heterogeneity emerges. The interquartile range of the cost of risk – measuring the spread between the upper and lower quartiles of outcomes – was 11.5 basis points in 2019 but rises to 16.2 basis points (+40.8 percent) in the sudden transition scenario (15.6 basis points in the orderly transition scenario). This reflects varying rates of increase in credit risk (particularly corporate) across institutions depending on the scenario. For five institutions, the cost of risk increases by 2050 in the sudden transition scenario, ranging from +0.8 percent to +46.0 percent. The magnitude of the impact is closely linked to the share of sensitive sectors in each institution's corporate portfolio (see Figure 6.5).

In 2022, the European Central Bank conducted a constrained bottom-up climate risk stress test for the euro area. Banks assessed

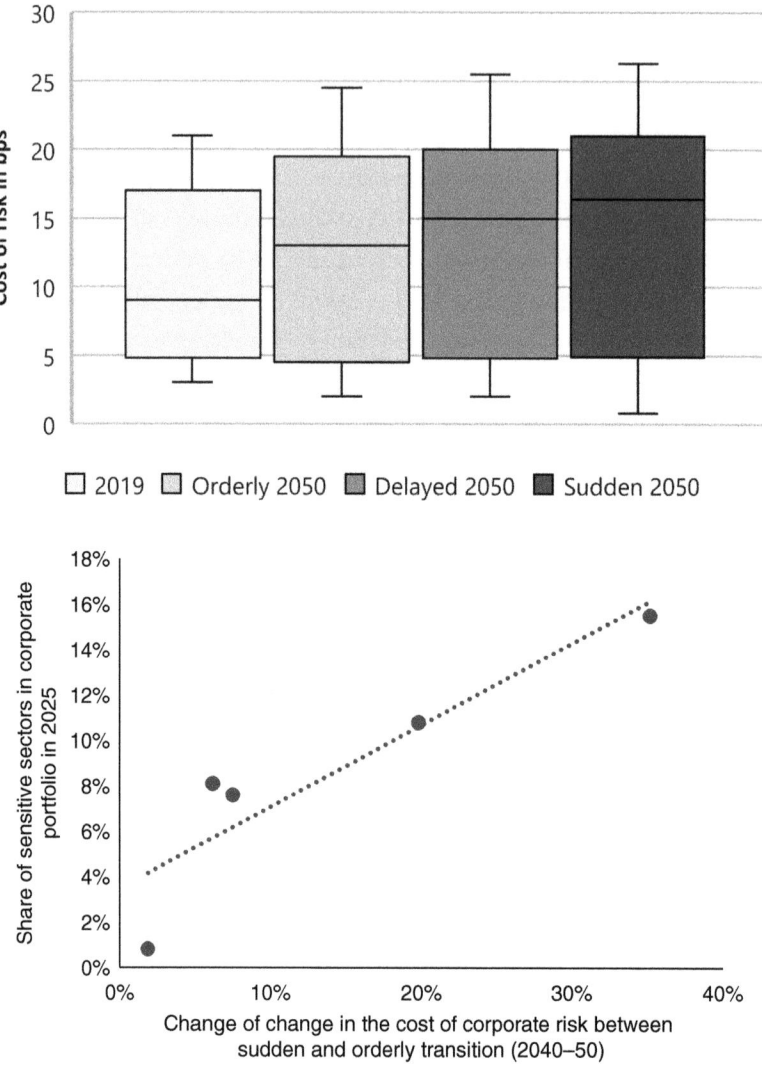

FIGURE 6.5 Dispersion of risk cost across institutions and correlation with the share of sensitive sectors in portfolios
Source: ACPR-Banque de France (2021)

the impact of transition and physical risks on corporate exposures and exposures secured by real estate. The results showed that banks are, to a varying degree, exposed to the materialization of physical risks. Taking the impact of physical and transition risks together, the projections of forty-one banks conducted by the ECB (2022) indicate a loss of around EUR 70 billion for the analyzed scenarios. These additional provisions amount to roughly one-third of the total exposure of participating banks. However, this figure likely underestimates the true impact of climate risk, given several factors – such as the reliance on relatively moderate scenarios compared to conventional stress tests, and the still preliminary state of available data and modeling techniques. Overall, these exercises reveal that climate risks are relevant for financial institutions, especially those that generate income from activities related to GHG-emitting industries. The financial institutions are also, to varying degrees, exposed to the materialization of acute physical risks (e.g., drought, heat events, or floods). The risks banks are facing in this regard are closely linked to the geographical location of their lending activities and could, in some cases, lead to nonnegligible losses (ECB, 2022). The results indicate that the risks are significant, but banks have the capabilities to withstand the shock.

6.3.1.3 Top-down Climate Stress Tests

Alogoskoufis et al. (2021) also developed a top-down economy-wide climate stress test that assesses the resilience of NFCs and euro area banks to transition and physical risks. The stress test, based on climate-specific scenarios, used climate and financial information for 4 million companies worldwide and mapped them to 1,600 consolidated banking groups in the euro area through granular loan and security holdings. The results of the ECB's economy-wide climate stress test showed that the short-term costs of the transition were lower than the costs of physical consequences of climate change in the absence of mitigation policies in the medium to long term. The results also indicate that while the average effects of climate risks would rise only moderately through 2050 in the absence of mitigation, the impacts are highly concentrated in specific regions and sectors. For corporates and banks most exposed to climate risks, the potential impact is severe, particularly without further mitigating policies. Rising costs from extreme weather events could substantially erode the creditworthiness of banks' clients.

In 2023, the ECB published a second top-down climate stress-testing exercise (Emambakhsh et al., 2023). One of the novelties rests on the design of three plausible short-term transition risk scenarios: The *accelerated transition* scenario assumes a jumpstart of the transition with rapid and severe increases in energy prices; the *late-push transition* scenario assumes that the green transition starts in 2026 and is intense enough to achieve emission reductions by 2030, and the *delayed transition* scenario also assumes that the transition starts in 2026 but more gradually and slowly, missing therefore the emission targets set in the Paris Agreement.

Transition risks would be the most impactful under the late-push scenario, with large differences across sectors (the largest increases in credit risk would occur in the electricity, mining, and manufacturing sectors). Due to energy price shocks and associated lower profits, firms' probabilities of default (PDs) would increase (especially in the mining and manufacturing sectors, where the change PD is twice as large as the increase in other sectors). In the mining and manufacturing sectors, the median PD would increase by 1 percentage point, respectively (0.6 pp on aggregate), and the 75th percentile would increase by 3.2 and 2.3 pp, respectively (1.4 on aggregate). Banks' credit risk would also increase in the transition process, especially for banks exposed to the most vulnerable firms. The exercise distinguishes, in particular, large from small banks (i.e., significant institutions – SI – from nonsignificant institutions – non-SI). The increase in the aggregate PDs of corporate loan portfolios would be larger at the beginning of the transition under the accelerated transition scenario, peaking at 50 percent and 60 percent above the starting point in 2026 for non-SI and SI, respectively. From 2026 onwards, the change in median PD under the late-push transition scenario becomes higher by 100 and 70 percent in 2030 for non-SI and SI, respectively. Credit risk would start to recover in the second half of the time horizon under the accelerated and late-push transition scenarios, given that the peak of the transition would have been reached by then. By contrast, under the delayed transition scenario, there would be a continuous increase in credit risk until 2030, due to the slower pace of emissions reductions through 2050, resulting in greater physical risk. Expected losses (at the one-year horizon) would amount between 0.7 percent and 0.9 percent of total loan exposures for the median significant institution in 2030 under the three transition scenarios. This share would exceed 2 percent for the banks most vulnerable to transition risk, that is, twice as high as the median bank under the late-push scenario.

In summary, the climate stress testing exercises show that an accelerated transition to a carbon-neutral economy would bring significant benefits to businesses, households, and the financial system, compared to a late transition scenario. Credit risk would increase during the transition in all scenarios, but would be particularly high in the case of late and abrupt action as envisaged in the late transition scenario. The scenarios have very different long-term implications for physical risks. In the case of a late transition, businesses and households could be more vulnerable to physical risks in the long term.

6.3.1.4 *Nonlinearities and Second-Round Effects*

Physical and transition risks may trigger complex, nonlinear chain-reaction effects with associated tipping points and irreversible impacts (see Bolton et al. (2020) for further details). Although limited information is available on potential nonlinearities associated with climate change, it is highly probable that the risk is underestimated. However, the existence of *tipping points* with the breach of biophysical thresholds (like the loss of the Greenland ice sheet), with irreversible effects on climate change, would considerably affect the overall banking system. As described by Bolton et al. (2020), *green swan* events may trigger nonlinearities and have far-reaching consequences on banks, including profitability and charter value. A new emerging literature considers the increasing likelihood of the simultaneous breach of several tipping points.

According to a literature review (BCBS, 2023), the financial system may amplify initial climate shocks, notably through uncertainty channels. Battiston et al. (2017) show that second-round effects can be of comparable magnitude to first-round effects, with fire sales being a key factor in triggering a fall in asset prices, which affects the value of banks' portfolios, leading to an even larger sell-off. Ahnert and Georg (2018) find that information contagion increases systemic risk when banks are subject to common exposure. Aldasoro et al. (2017) show that contagion spreads through interbank linkages, fire sales, and liquidity hoarding, based on a network model of the interbank market. The exposure to common asset classes of different market participants, interdependencies among financial institutions, and potential fire-sale dynamics could amplify the impact of climate risks on banks. Roncoroni et al. (2021a) study how the structure of a financial network and market conditions affect financial stability in the European banking system. They detect two channels of financial contagion: direct interconnectedness via a network of interbank loans, bank loans to nonfinancial corporates and retail clients, and security holdings, and indirect interconnectedness via overlapping exposures to common asset classes. They uncover a strongly nonlinear relationship between diversification of exposures, shock size, and losses due to interbank contagion. They also demonstrate the potential for contagion effects to amplify first-round stress test results due to interconnectedness. In an extension, Roncoroni et al. (2021b) analyze the effects on financial stability of the interplay between climate transition risk and market conditions. They identify conditions under which total losses of the financial system are large, even if the direct exposure to shocks is small. They also show that the combination of distress contagion and common exposure contagion gives rise to losses larger than the sum of individual contributions.

6.3.1.5 Insurance Stress-Tests

Climate stress tests for insurance companies remain limited, whereas such exercises for banks have already become widespread.

As part of its climate pilot exercise, ACPR included insurance companies, considering separately property and human health damages. In the scenario used in this exercise, natural disasters are projected to double between 2019 and 2050, including a surge in vector-borne infections and in air pollution impacts on health. The results of the exercise showed that vulnerabilities associated with physical risk were far from negligible. Based on information provided by insurers, the cost of claims could rise five- to sixfold between 2020 and 2050, driven by the growing scale and frequency of natural disasters. Over the same period, insurance premiums are projected to increase by 130% to 200% – equivalent to an annual rise of about 2.8% to 3.7%, depending on the category.

The main hazards contributing to this increase in claims are the risks of drought on the one hand and flooding on the other, as well as the greater risk of cyclones in the overseas territories. The increase in claims highlights an insurability risk in certain parts of the country. As yearly pricing reviews are common in the insurance industry, insurers are relatively protected against an increase in loss ratios caused by natural disasters. However, the long-term horizon used in these tests includes an expected twofold increase in climate disasters, with a widening IPG, as uninsured losses are expected to be multiplied by 2.6. In 2023, the ACPR conducted a second climate exercise, restricting its scope to the insurance sector, which revealed significant vulnerabilities to both physical and transition risks, particularly under short-term stress scenarios.

In 2022, EIOPA conducted its first climate stress test to assess the impact of climate-related risks on the European occupational pension sector. This exercise focused, therefore, on the asset side of insurance companies that could be particularly vulnerable to transition risks. The results showed that European Institutions for Occupational Retirement Provision (IORPs) hold significant exposure to transition risks, with assets declining by 12.9 percent – equivalent to valuation losses of around EUR 255 billion – after the materialization of the shock. Despite this, post-shock funding ratios for defined benefit (DB) schemes remained above 100 percent in most Member States, supported by strong pre-shock positions. By contrast, defined contribution (DC) schemes remained balanced by definition. Notably, while more than 90 percent of IORPs incorporate ESG factors into their investment policies, they still face challenges in directing funds toward climate risk-sensitive categories.

Given their diverse and interlinked nature, EIOPA (2022) also highlights the need for a comprehensive assessment of both physical and transition risks in a climate stress test. Campiglio et al. (2023) also highlight the significant economic costs of accumulation effects resulting from a sudden transition after a climate-related natural disaster. Gatzert and Özdil (2023) conducted a climate risk scenario analysis, including dependencies between assets (climate transition risks) and liabilities (physical climate risks) in an asset-liability management setting. The analysis is based on NGFS scenarios and aims to assess how transition and physical risks can accumulate on the balance sheet and potentially impact a nonlife insurer's profitability and default risk. They show that while physical climate risks seem to be manageable by risk-adjusted pricing and adequate reinsurance, a combination of physical and transition risks could have a large impact on non-life insurers' default risk. The sensitivity of insurance companies to these combined risks would depend on asset allocation, particularly if investments are large in high-carbon assets.

6.3.2 Prudential Responses

Since climate-related risks should be integrated into risk-management strategies of financial institutions, prudential authorities must also adapt their policy framework to safeguard the resilience of financial systems against the materialization of those risks.

6.3.2.1 Impact on Supervision and Microprudential Policy

Climate-related risks are implicitly covered in the mandates of supervisory authorities on safeguarding the safety and the soundness of the financial sector and preserving overall financial stability. Leveraging their prudential and/or financial stability mandate, supervisors can incorporate climate-related risks in the scope of their supervisory activities. For instance, the BCBS report on climate-related risk drivers and their transmission channels highlights that these drivers affect banks through traditional risk categories, namely credit, market, liquidity, operational, and underwriting risks.

Supervisors have made significant progress over the past years in issuing guidance on how banks, insurers, and other financial institutions should consider climate-related and environmental risks. Supervisory expectations and guidance on including such risks cover a wide range of action areas, from governance, business strategy, risk management, and scenario analysis to stress testing and disclosure. However, further progress is warranted in advancing Pillar 1, which oversees minimum capital requirements. The lack of reliable data and the need to develop proper methodologies to assess climate-related risks are the major impediments to the completion of the climate extension. The setting of Pillar 1 capital requirements is also hampered by a lack of common definitions, classifications, and taxonomies and evidence of risk differentials between *green* and *non-green* assets.

Pillar 2 of the Basel framework pertains to bank-specific additional capital requirements to cover risks underestimated or not covered by the minimum capital requirement of Pillar 1. As a complement to Pillar 1, the Pillar 2 framework provides a natural platform for integrating climate risks into supervision, drawing on its forward-looking tools, its capacity to capture risks not fully addressed under Pillar 1, and its greater flexibility. Pillar 2 tools include the banks' Internal Capital Adequacy Assessment Process (ICAAP) and the insurers' Own Risk and Solvency Assessment (ORSA), which produce essential outputs such as capital requirements to cover material risks that firms are exposed to. However, scenario and sensitivity analyses, and stress testing still need further development before supervisors can fully integrate them into the review process and use them as a basis for formal supervisory measures where appropriate.

6.3.2.2 Possible Macroprudential Responses to Climate Risks

Macroprudential policy that targets the systemic dimensions of climate risks is essential for addressing both climate-specific and more traditional externalities (ECB/ESRB, 2022). It complements the microprudential approach, which focuses on the bank-specific aspects of climate risk supervision (Baranović et al., 2021). By adopting a system-wide perspective, macroprudential tools can help prevent the build-up of risks arising from the collective lending decisions of financial institutions (Figure 6.6). In this sense, they are particularly well suited to tackling the negative externalities of excessive lending to high-carbon projects.

At present, none of the existing macroprudential instruments are readily deployable to address climate risks. Adaptations of the traditional instruments, together with the development of new tools, are pivotal for completing the supervisory framework. The Systemic Risk Buffer, in its sectoral application, could be, for instance, used to contain the build-up of risk concentration and, at the same time, enhance the resilience of banks against the materialization of

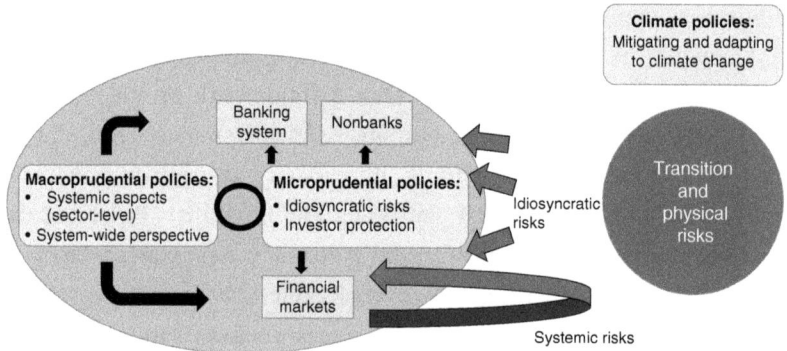

FIGURE 6.6 Integrating climate-related risks into micro- and macro-prudential policies
Source: ESB/ESRB (2022)

climate risks. Concentration limits could also incentivize banks to reduce the concentration of their exposure to carbon-intensive sectors (transition risks) or to geographical regions exposed to physical risks. Another possible macroprudential tool is the sectoral application of the leverage ratio, which would restrict the use of leverage to finance assets more exposed to climate risk. While such adaptations of the macroprudential framework are still under discussion, two countries (the UK and Canada) have considered developing new macroprudential policies to tackle climate-related risks. The Bank of England and the Prudential Regulation Authority have proposed an *escalating* climate buffer, which is based on a risk assessment of the materiality of future system-wide transition and the physical risks associated with climate change. Canada's financial regulator is also considering a new set of capital buffers to ensure that federally regulated financial institutions can endure an abrupt transition to a green economy.

Finally, when applying measures that are individually justified from a macroprudential perspective, it is important to carefully consider their potential unintended consequences, interactions with other climate policies as well as the consistency with the broader regulatory framework.

6.3.2.3 *Regulations for Insurers*

Reduced availability and affordability of insurance coverage against climate risks are a major concern for policymakers and many insurance regulators. As climate-related events grow more frequent and severe, and exposures increase, insurers face rising costs. In response, they may scale back coverage, raise premiums, or adopt both measures. Some supervisors are particularly concerned with the withdrawal of insurance coverage from critical economic sectors such as agriculture or real estate (Khoo and Yong, 2023). To cope with the challenges posed by climate change on insurance, insurers may need innovative designs, like impact underwriting. Including product adaptation measures and sharing information on risks can also contribute to clients' awareness and risk reduction measures. There is a trend of premium increases, exclusions, and withdrawal of non-life insurance coverage in certain geographical locations following extreme climate risk events, and overpricing of climate-related insurance products can also be a supervisory concern. Reinsurance is one of the most important tools insurers rely on to manage climate-related exposures from the policies they underwrite. The recent tendency of some reinsurers to limit their exposure to climate-related perils is therefore a source of concern for supervisors.

Rising climate protection gaps threaten financial stability and place a heavier burden on governments, both through greater macroeconomic risks and higher fiscal spending to cover uninsured losses. Regulators therefore need to take action to address this gap and mitigate catastrophe risks from climate change. Such actions should expand insurance coverage and strengthen adaptation measures, with the following main objectives (ECB/ESRB, 2023): help provide prompt insurance claim payouts following a disaster; incentivize risk mitigation and adaptation measures; be complementary to existing insurance coverage mechanisms; require the sharing of costs and responsibilities across the relevant stakeholders to ensure *skin in the game* and reduce moral hazard; and lower the share of economic losses from major natural disasters borne by the public sector over the long term.

If private (re)insurance should be the first line of defense to cover losses from climate-related natural disasters, financial markets may also be used to transfer risks via catastrophe bonds (CAT bonds) and thus support the reinsurance of such risks (Figure 6.7). CAT bonds provide two key benefits: (i) diversification as an alternative source of capital and (ii) a lower premium for overall coverage. Furthermore, CAT bonds could potentially combine impact underwriting with impact investing. To overcome residual limits to insurability, governments may need to step in with solutions adapted to national circumstances, such as public–private partnerships (PPPs)

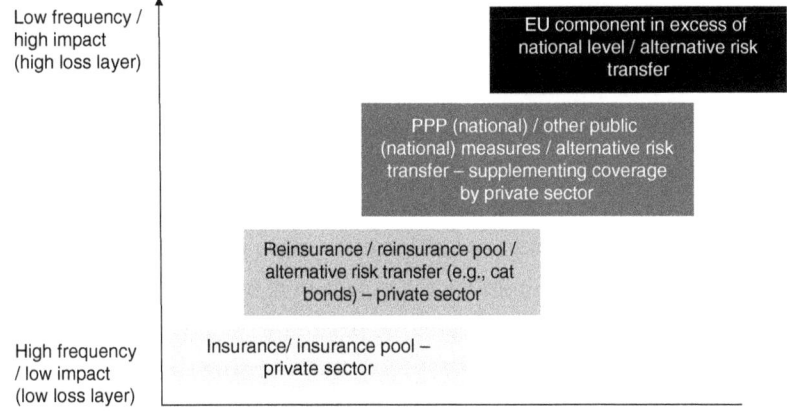

FIGURE 6.7 A ladder approach to catastrophe insurance
Source: ECB-EIOPA (2023)

or ex-ante public backstops. In the context of the EU, this could be reinforced by coordination efforts.

While higher private insurance coverage is beneficial and desirable, insurance provision should be carefully designed to ensure that it encourages adaptation and reduces vulnerability to climate-related catastrophes over time. Insurers should provide incentives for risk reduction and adaptation by, for example, promoting risk awareness and providing risk-based incentives linked to premiums (e.g., via impact underwriting). Such measures would directly reduce preventable damages from catastrophes and increase resilience, while also supporting insurability and helping to limit the risk of a widening IPG.

6.4 CONCLUSION

Climate change poses complex and multifaceted threats to the financial system, affecting a broad spectrum of sectors and institutions. Preserving overall economic stability requires a clear understanding of these risks and effective measures to mitigate them. This entails accurately gauging the exposure of financial systems to climate risks, including both physical risks – such as the damage from natural disasters to assets and infrastructure – and transition risks, which capture the financial implications of moving toward a low-carbon economy. Transition risks can trigger asset stranding and market disruptions as fossil fuel–dependent industries confront declining demand and stricter regulations. These vulnerabilities are especially acute in the insurance and reinsurance sectors, which face direct impacts from the increasing frequency and severity of climate-related events.

Central banks and prudential authorities play a crucial role in safeguarding financial stability in the face of these challenges. One of the primary strategies highlighted is the implementation of climate stress-tests. These tests are vital tools for assessing the resilience of financial institutions and systems to potential climate shocks. By simulating various scenarios, these stress-tests help to identify vulnerabilities and prepare for possible financial disruptions. Beyond risk assessment, prudential responses are also necessary, including enhancing regulatory frameworks, promoting better risk management practices among financial institutions, and encouraging the integration of climate considerations into financial decision-making. These measures are essential for preventing or limiting the threats posed by climate change to financial stability.

At the same time, while climate change introduces new risks to financial stability, it also offers an opportunity to strengthen the resilience of the financial system. By embracing these challenges and taking decisive action, central banks and prudential authorities can help ensure that the financial sector remains robust in the face of a changing climate.

7 Challenges in EMDEs and Ways to Overcome Them

7.1 INTRODUCTION

Emerging markets and developing economies (EMDEs) face significant challenges in attracting the capital necessary to meet their climate and development goals. A successful green transition in these economies requires substantial investment to decarbonize key sectors, estimated at a minimum of USD 1 trillion annually. Investment needs become even higher when spending is included for adaptation and building resilience. Climate impacts are increasingly threatening vulnerable populations in EMDEs, who have typically contributed little to the problem and who often lack the resources to adapt. A just transition is essential to ensure that the shift toward a low-carbon economy is fair and inclusive, providing support for those affected and creating opportunities for sustainable development.

Despite the need for substantial investment to scale up renewable energy and reduce emissions, EMDEs currently receive only a small fraction of the required funds. Moreover, climate financing to EMDEs is mostly public, concentrated on mitigation rather than adaptation, and primarily delivered in the form of debt. Various barriers, including high sovereign credit risk, currency fluctuations, regulatory uncertainties, and specific project risks, exacerbate the climate investment gap in EMDEs. Constrained public resources, combined with the magnitude of investment required, imply that a large share of future climate investments must come from the private sector to meet the Paris Agreement targets and protect vulnerable populations in EMDEs. Innovative financial strategies and de-risking instruments like blended finance have been developed to overcome obstacles to private investment. By strategically using concessional funds, these financial instruments enhance the attractiveness of climate projects to private investors, helping to mobilize and scale up private capital effectively for climate initiatives.

Addressing pressing climate investment needs in EMDEs requires a global and coordinated approach beyond national capabilities. Global policy coordination is essential to tackling the intertwined challenges of climate finance and sustainable development. Coordinated efforts promote equitable resource allocation, prevent carbon leakage and negative economic spillovers on EMDEs from regulatory advancements in advanced economies (AEs). Efficiently channeling resources toward key development and climate goals is essential. Achieving this requires stronger partnerships among governments, International Financial Institutions (IFIs), philanthropic organizations, and the private sector. IFIs play a critical role by leveraging their expertise and resources through the project cycle to reduce risks and support both development and climate agendas in EMDEs. Effective clean energy projects demand a deep understanding of development processes, infrastructure challenges, and credit risks, which IFIs such as Development Financial Institutions (DFIs) and Multilateral Development Banks (MDBs) can provide. Improving local ecosystems through capacity building and creating supportive environments to tap into domestic private capital is important to enhance climate investment and mobilize private capital. Clearer strategies and transition plans may help many EMDEs to provide better direction, particularly for the private sector. Simplifying and standardizing taxonomies and reporting will make climate finance data more accessible and facilitate greater investment flows.

7.2 OVERVIEW OF CLIMATE AND FINANCING CHALLENGES IN EMDES

While high-income economies have historically contributed the majority of emissions, EMDEs are now expected to be major future emission sources due to rapid population growth and increased energy demands. Promoting energy transition in these regions is vital to enhancing resilience to climate shocks and delivering immediate health benefits such as improved air quality and reduced pollution-related healthcare costs and premature deaths.

Moreover, agriculture is a critical sector for economic growth and employment in EMDEs. Yet it remains highly vulnerable to climate change, posing serious food security challenges and increasing import costs for economies already strained by hard-currency shortages. Historical data from 1964 to 2007 indicates that droughts and extreme heat have reduced global cereal production by about 10 percent on average, emphasizing the urgent need for enhanced resilience strategies (Lesk, Rowhani, and Ramankutty, 2016). Further, Zhao et al. (2017) analyzed the impact of global temperature increases on major crop yields. This study found that each degree Celsius rise in global temperature could reduce global wheat yields by 6 percent, rice by 3.2 percent, maize by 7.4 percent, and soybeans by 3.1 percent (Zhao, Liu, and Piao, 2017).

According to the African Development Bank, climate change is causing Africa to lose between 5 percent and 15 percent of its GDP per capita annually. These projections underscore the urgent need for robust climate adaptation and mitigation strategies to protect economic stability. According to S&P (2022), lower- and lower-middle-income countries face average losses 3.6 times greater than those of higher-middle and higher-income nations. Economic losses are likely to be higher and more persistent in countries with limited adaptive capacity, weaker institutions, and constrained financial resources.

7.2.1 How Large are the Financing Needs in EMDEs?

The Independent High-Level Expert Group on Climate Finance (IHLEG, 2023) report estimates that to meet the Paris Agreement and related development goals, USD 2.4 trillion is needed in EMDEs (other than China) by 2030 for climate-related investments. This represents, a fourfold increase from current levels. Addressing climate change requires aligning global energy demand with clean energy supply, a fundamental aspect of the Paris Agreement, and requires an incremental annual investment of USD 1,800 billion from current

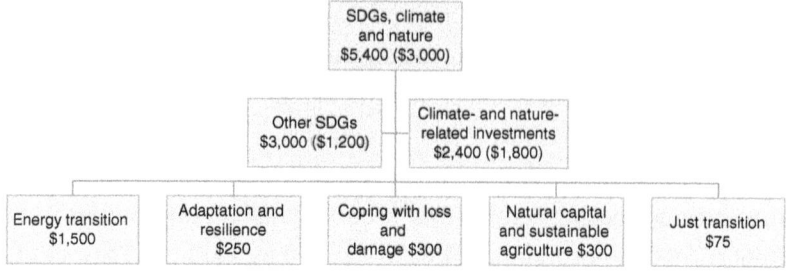

FIGURE 7.1 Investment needs for climate and sustainable development (USD billion per year by 2030)
Source: IHLEG (2023)
Note: Incremental investment from current levels is indicated in parentheses.

levels (Figure 7.1). Beyond the clean energy transition, EMDEs require funding for various initiatives to support long-term sustainable development. These include investments in adaptation and resilience to climate change, addressing loss and damage, sustainable agriculture, afforestation, conservation, and biodiversity, and ensuring a just transition.

The bulk of the financing needed for climate and nature-related investments by 2030 in EMDEs should be directed toward the energy transition, with USD 1,500 billion annually allocated to facilitate the shift toward cleaner and more sustainable energy sources. Additionally, USD 300 billion should be required to address the unavoidable impacts of climate change that have already occurred, categorized under coping with loss and damage (see further). Similarly, another USD 300 billion must be directed toward promoting practices that protect and enhance biodiversity and ecosystem services, focusing on natural capital and sustainable agriculture. Ensuring that communities and ecosystems can withstand and adapt to the impacts of climate change should demand USD 250 billion, earmarked for adaptation and resilience. Lastly, USD 75 billion should be dedicated to ensuring that the shift toward a low-carbon economy is fair and equitable for all affected populations, known as the just transition.

The International Energy Agency (IEA) (2023) emphasizes the urgent need to triple global renewable energy capacity to 11,000 gigawatts (GW) by 2030 to keep the global temperature increase within the 1.5°C limit, which is crucial for mitigating the most severe impacts of climate change. To significantly reduce carbon dioxide emissions, it is essential to substantially increase climate finance and scale up renewable energy technologies like solar and wind. However, there is a significant clean energy investment gap and EMDEs, excluding China, are left behind in the clean energy transition. Despite global clean energy investments reaching an all-time high in 2023, driven largely by growth in solar PV and electric vehicles (EVs), more than 90 percent of the increase in such investment since 2021 has occurred in developed economies and China. In 2022, low- and lower-middle-income countries accounted for only 7 percent of clean energy spending (IHLEG 2023).

Investment needs estimates vary based on assumptions and uncertainties in climate impact modeling, but they consistently underscore the immense scale of the challenge (Table 7.1). The United Nations Conference on Trade and Development's 2023 World Investment Report states that developing countries need around USD 1.7 trillion annually for green transition. However, they secured only USD 544 billion in 2022. The IEA-IFC's 2023 estimates indicate that to align with the Paris Agreement, annual investments in clean energy in EMDEs must more than triple from USD 770 billion in 2022 to between USD 2.2 and USD 2.8 trillion by the early 2030s, maintaining similar levels through 2050. Excluding China, this increase becomes even more dramatic, potentially rising sevenfold from USD 260 billion to between USD 1.4 and USD 1.9 trillion annually.

Public investments alone are insufficient to cover these extensive financing needs. Given limited public resources and constrained fiscal positions in most EMDEs, a substantial portion of the climate funding should come from the private sector. According to a joint report by the IFC and IEA (2023), the private sector must provide two-thirds of the financing for clean energy projects in emerging and developing economies, excluding China. Currently, annual private

Table 7.1 *Investment needs estimates in EMDEs to align with climate targets*

Source	Time horizon	Annual investment needs
The United Nations Conference on Trade and Development's (2023)	Current	USD 1.7 trillion
International Energy Agency (IEA), World Bank, and World Economic Forum (2021)	Through 2030	Over USD 1 trillion
IHLEG (2023)	Through 2030	USD 1.5 trillion only for clean transition, USD 2.4 trillion for total climate action (excluding China)
IEA-IFC (2023)	Through 2030	USD 2.2–USD 2.8 trillion USD 1.4–USD 1.9 trillion (excluding China)

funding for clean energy in these regions amounts to USD 135 billion and would need to increase to as much as USD 1.1 trillion annually within the next decade.

EMDEs have achieved remarkable progress in development over the last three decades. The global poverty rate has dramatically decreased from 38 percent in 1990 to 8.5 percent by 2019, reducing the number of people below the World Bank's extreme poverty line from over 2 billion to approximately 660 million. Life expectancy and educational attainment have also improved significantly. However, recent global crises, including the COVID-19 pandemic and geopolitical tensions, have reversed some of these gains, pushing Sustainable Development Goals (SDGs) further out of reach and exacerbating issues such as energy access and indebtedness. If not addressed, climate change also risks further reversing development achievements. The adverse impacts of climate change disproportionately affect the poorest and most vulnerable populations, such as women, children, the elderly, indigenous communities, and displaced populations, who often have the least resources to adapt to environmental shifts. Low-income communities with limited resources to adapt and recover face greater exposure and sensitivity to climate hazards, resulting in more significant social and economic impacts (Hallegatte & Rozenberg, 2017).

Most EMDEs find it difficult to allocate the necessary funds for clean energy and climate-resilient investments, exacerbating their vulnerability to climate shocks and hindering progress toward sustainability goals. Navigating climate challenges in developing nations requires balancing priorities: promoting economic growth and poverty alleviation while reducing greenhouse gas (GHG) emissions. The impacts of climate change, such as extreme weather events, directly induce poverty by destroying assets and forcing vulnerable families into costly coping strategies, such as slashing essential expenditures like health and education. These measures can profoundly affect long-term outcomes, particularly harming children in areas plagued by poverty and conflict. Moreover, climate change introduces emerging risks, notably heightening threats to coastal cities once considered secure. To foster effective resilience, it is crucial to integrate considerations of future climate conditions into ongoing development initiatives.

Acting on climate change in EMDEs offers immense opportunities to stimulate economic growth and productivity and create jobs. Climate-resilient infrastructure and sustainable practices can boost productivity. The World Bank (2025) highlights that investments in climate-smart agriculture can increase agricultural productivity, which is critical for economies heavily reliant on this sector. Improved infrastructure and energy systems can also enhance overall economic efficiency and competitiveness. Reducing air pollution through cleaner energy sources can lead to significant health benefits, reducing healthcare costs and improving labor productivity. The United Nations (2025) finds that every dollar of investment in renewable energies creates three times more jobs than in the fossil fuel industry. The IEA (2021) estimates that the transition toward net-zero emissions will lead to an overall increase in energy sector jobs: While about 5 million jobs in fossil fuel production could be lost by 2030, an estimated 14 million new jobs would be created in clean energy, resulting in a net gain of 9 million jobs (IEA, 2021). The IFC finds that from 2020 to 2030, an estimated USD 10 trillion in investment opportunities in select Emerging Markets (EMs), including China, could create over 213 million new jobs globally (IFC, 2021). Finally, investing in climate adaptation and resilience can mitigate the economic impacts of extreme weather events and climate-related disasters. Every dollar invested in resilient infrastructure can yield up to USD 4 in economic benefits by avoiding disaster-related losses and reducing recovery costs.

7.2.2 Climate Justice and Loss and Damage Fund

The politics of climate finance recognize that while the Global North has significantly benefited from fossil fuel use, the Global South faces more severe climate hazards such as droughts and storms, and higher levels of vulnerability. This perspective holds that the Global North has both a moral responsibility and a greater capacity to support climate change mitigation and adaptation efforts in the Global South.

Originally coined in the 1980s within US trade unions, the concept of just transition has recently gained traction for ensuring that all societal groups are included in the shift to a net-zero future. The International Labour Organization (ILO) defines a just transition as greening the economy in a fair and inclusive way that creates decent work opportunities without leaving anyone behind. A just transition aims to make the move to low-carbon economies equitable and inclusive, addressing environmental concerns as well as the structural changes brought about by globalization, labor-saving technologies, and the shift to service-based economies. In EMDEs, this involves maximizing the social and economic benefits of climate action while minimizing challenges such as job losses and poverty.

EMDEs are particularly vulnerable to the inequalities of the transition due to their less diversified economies, dependence on fossil fuels, and limited skill-generation capabilities. This necessitates inclusive and equitable transition strategies that protect vulnerable communities from the disruptions of moving away from carbon-intensive industries.

Responsible investors increasingly recognize the importance of a just transition. A mismanaged transition in coal- or oil-exporting countries with undiversified economies could lead to significant fiscal, financial, and political challenges. To address these vulnerabilities and ensure a just transition, investments in people and infrastructure are essential. This includes education, lifelong learning, training, skills development, and social protection measures for the most vulnerable. Complementing this effort, the loss and damage fund is set to provide crucial financial support to nations disproportionately affected by climate change, addressing the resulting inequities.

The concept of loss and damage complements the efforts of *just transition* by providing financial support to nations disproportionately affected by climate change. *Loss and damage* in climate change refers to the irreversible impacts that cannot be avoided through mitigation or adaptation efforts. It encompasses both slow-onset processes like sea-level rise and desertification, as well as extreme weather events such as floods and cyclones. These impacts are particularly severe in the Global South, including Africa and small island states, where they cause both economic and noneconomic damages.

The establishment of the Loss and Damage Fund during COP28 marked a significant advance in climate finance. The fund aims to address the disproportionate effects of climate change faced by countries with minimal contributions to global GHG emissions. It was kick-started with an initial pledge of about USD 700 million, which is far less than the estimated USD 580 billion needed by 2030 to address climate-related damages in these regions.

This initiative represents a critical step toward compensating for losses that can no longer be prevented or mitigated. The Loss and Damage Fund represents a step forward in addressing global climate justice. The African continent is a good example – Africa has contributed less than 4 percent to global GHG emissions, yet it is the most vulnerable to the impacts of climate change. The fund's establishment, however, highlighted ongoing challenges, including the need for substantial increases in financial pledges and the development of mechanisms to mobilize and allocate these funds effectively.

Key issues such as funding sources, eligibility criteria, and project specifics were debated at COP29, where countries agreed on a new collective finance goal of at least USD 300 billion annually by 2035, with aspirations to scale to USD 1.3 trillion. A proposed Climate Finance Action Fund and the operationalization of the Loss and Damage Fund remain under discussion, highlighting persistent debates on climate justice and the historical responsibility of the Global North.

7.2.3 *Financial and Fiscal Challenges Specific to EMDEs*

Investments aimed at achieving climate and sustainable development targets, particularly in clean electrification, grid infrastructure, and efficiency, are projected to drive a significant increase in public spending by the early 2030s. However, the public funding capabilities of EMDEs are dramatically constrained by recent global crises, currency fluctuations, high fiscal deficits, and the end of the G20's debt service suspension, which has intensified pressure on already debt-laden countries. The significant rise in global public debt, which has tripled since the mid 1970s and reached 94 percent of GDP in 2024, places an enormous burden on EMDEs. This debt burden complicates some governments' ability to meet their debt obligations and maintain fiscal stability. Additionally, the evolving landscape of creditors, with an increased share of commercial debt and Non-Paris Club lenders, adds complexity to managing fiscal policies and debt restructuring processes. In a large number of EMDEs, record-high debt levels, elevated interest rates, and weak growth prospects further restricts the fiscal space available to support economic development and respond to environmental shocks.

Given these fiscal constraints, most EMDEs cannot rely solely on limited national public funds to finance substantial clean energy investments. A significant portion of future investments must come from external sources, with an estimated USD 1 trillion per year in private capital needed in EMDEs, excluding China, by 2030 (IHLEG 2023). This represents an incremental external funding requirement of USD 850 billion, a more than fivefold increase, per year from current levels. However, many EMDEs struggle with poor sovereign credit ratings and exchange rate volatility, hindering their ability to attract necessary private investment. Regulatory constraints, counterparty credit quality, and transparency issues pose significant barriers to project development and investment in EMDEs.

To address these challenges, it is crucial for EMDEs to develop strategic plans and foster international cooperation. Enhancing financial stability, improving sovereign credit ratings, and creating a conducive environment for private investment are essential steps. By doing so, EMDEs can better manage their debt sustainability and attract the necessary investments to meet their climate and SDGs.

7.3 MOBILIZING CLIMATE FINANCE IN EMDES

7.3.1 *Overcoming Barriers to Private Investment*

Despite private interest in funding net-zero projects, financial, technological, and structural barriers often prevent capital from reaching the sectors and projects that need it most. Many EMDEs suffer from high funding costs, credit margins, and swap rates, particularly in high-risk, low-income regions. This environment, combined with insufficient returns and high-risk profiles, may discourage

Table 7.2 *Types of investors and return expectations*

Entity type	Returns spectrum
• Private companies of all sizes • Commercial banks • Institutional investors such as pension funds, sovereign wealth funds, and other asset managers	Market-rate returns
• Bilateral, multilateral, and national development banks (private sector arms) • Impact investors (seeking impacts and returns)	Quasi or blended returns
• Philanthropies and NGOs • Bilateral, multilateral, and national development banks (public sector arms) • Impact investors (not seeking market returns) • Governments	Below-market-rate returns by design

Source: IEA

private-sector investment. Table 7.2 outlines the different types of investors and their return expectations. Private companies, commercial banks, and institutional investors such as pension and sovereign wealth funds typically seek market-rate returns. By contrast, philanthropies, Non Governmental Organizations (NGOs), and the public arms of development banks act as impact investors, deliberately accepting below-market returns in pursuit of social and environmental goals. In EMDEs, many climate projects fail to meet the high return expectations of private investors, making public donors and NGOs crucial in improving the return profile of these projects. By accepting lower returns and providing funding, these public and philanthropic entities can de-risk investments and attract private capital, thereby enabling the successful implementation of climate initiatives in these regions.

In addition to low returns, clean energy and adaptation projects in EMDEs face a range of specific risks, which could be categorized into political, technical, and commercial barriers.

- *Political risks* include political and social risks such as corruption, governance issues, legal rights infringements, and social opposition, which can affect project development and cooperation with the public sector. Administrative risks involve permitting delays, denial or repeal, and forced relocation, particularly impacting site-specific renewable energy technologies. Policy and regulatory risks stem from changes in support levels or tariffs, which can affect less mature renewable energy technologies relying on public support.
- *Technical risks* encompass construction delays and risks related to the timing and quality of construction, which are heightened by the novelty of some technologies. Upstream resource-related risks involve the availability of materials and workforce, which is especially significant for geothermal exploration. Operational risks and other downstream output-related risks cover technical issues in the plant, environmental risks, and natural variability affecting output, which are increasing due to new technologies.
- *Commercial barriers* include access to capital, which is challenging due to unfamiliarity with new technologies and higher financing costs. Market-specific construction, financial, and operation cost increases relate to uncertainties specific to the technology. Currency risk involves unfavorable currency fluctuations when projects are financed with foreign loans but earn revenue in local currency. Counterparty/Offtaker/[1] Credit risk concerns the inability of parties to honor contracts due to unreliable counterparty credit quality. Lastly, investment horizon/liquidity risks, scale of investment, and lack of capacity at the local level further obstruct early-stage projects and clean energy companies from accessing necessary financing, with clean energy projects requiring large, long-term investments and specialized knowledge.

Overcoming barriers to climate investment involves enhancing and redesigning green financing instruments and platforms, such

---

[1] Offtaker risk in green energy investment is associated with the financial and operational risks tied to the entity, usually a state-owned utility, that agrees to buy the power produced by a renewable energy project under a power purchase agreement (PPA). Risks include the offtaker failing to purchase the agreed amount of electricity, delaying payments, or facing financial insolvency, which can jeopardize the project's revenue and financial stability. These risks are often heightened in EMs or less stable economies due to economic fluctuations and regulatory changes.

as green bonds, sustainability-linked loans, project aggregation platforms, and voluntary carbon markets (VCMs). Deepening capital markets and financial systems are also essential for scaling up domestic private investment in clean energy. Participation in global initiatives, such as green bonds and climate finance mechanisms in capital-scarce EMDEs would be pivotal for accessing new funding sources. The strategic use of blended finance, supportive policies, and institutional strengthening is critical to mobilizing the necessary resources to achieve clean energy and climate goals in EMDEs.

Attracting international funding relies heavily on improving transparency and governance, which builds investor confidence and reduces perceived risks. A stable and attractive investment climate emerges from strong regulatory frameworks, reliable contract enforcement, and active public-private partnerships. Effective policy actions and robust regulations would also enhance the viability of climate projects.

Comprehensive sector-wide reforms and strengthening key institutions, such as utilities, are essential for creating a robust pipeline of projects and laying the foundation for blended finance to mitigate remaining risks. Power sector reforms are particularly pivotal given the high reliance on state-owned utilities. Addressing these interrelated barriers requires a comprehensive, country-led approach to secure buy-in, support sectoral solvency, and boost medium- and long-term capacity. DFIs leverage their technical expertise, financial capacity, and risk mitigation tools to alleviate various macro, sectoral, and project-related risks, advancing development and climate objectives. In addition to financial support at below-market terms, DFIs offer project development support and advisory services for government tenders, assisting public authorities in creating effective clean energy policies. Collaborations between clean energy companies and governments help to leverage past experiences to address complex issues and tailor solutions to each country's specific needs.

7.3.2 What Energy Strategies and Policy Action to Overcome Climate Investment Barriers in EMDEs?

Technological innovation in clean energy has advanced globally, increasing capacity and reducing costs, but this progress is mainly concentrated in AEs and China. EMDEs typically need to adapt technologies developed elsewhere, which requires a supportive ecosystem rich in knowledge, capital, and favorable policies – resources more readily available in AEs.

Investments in clean energy generation depend on the timely expansion of grids, energy storage, and other solutions to integrate variable renewables. In many EMDEs, weak electricity infrastructure leads to unreliable access for users, posing a significant risk for investors. Over 90 percent of investments in EMDE grids fall under the responsibility of state-owned enterprises (SOEs), many of which are financially strained and lack access to capital. Private sector involvement in electrical grids is typically limited to the distribution sector, though private financing for energy storage projects is increasing. Early network investment planning, public support, public-private partnerships, and measures to strengthen the operational and financial performance of utilities are crucial to transforming grid infrastructure into an enabler, rather than a bottleneck, for renewable energy expansion.

Low-emission fuels are important in the clean energy transition, especially in sectors where direct electrification is not feasible or cost-effective. There is growing investor interest in low-emission hydrogen, particularly for production via electrolysis in countries with low-cost solar or wind potential. While commercial viability is in its early stages, supply-side initiatives in Africa, Latin America, and the Middle East are not yet matched by a comparable level of commitments from buyers, putting a premium on secure offtake arrangements to underpin investments. Sustainable biofuels and carbon capture, utilization, and storage (CCUS) are other main investment avenues. Policy incentives and mandates in Brazil, China,

India, and Indonesia have driven a strong rise in EMDE biofuel production, encompassing both liquid biofuels and biogases.

EMDEs can attract more international funding by leveraging several strategies. First, improving transparency and governance can build investor confidence and reduce perceived risks. Second, strengthening regulatory frameworks and ensuring the enforcement of contracts can create a stable investment climate. Third, developing public-private partnerships can mobilize private capital by sharing risks and benefits. Additionally, investing in education and skill development can enhance the local workforce's capabilities, making EMDEs more attractive to investors. International cooperation and participation in global initiatives, such as green bonds and climate finance mechanisms, can also provide access to new funding sources. Finally, creating targeted incentives for sustainable investments, such as tax breaks and subsidies for renewable energy projects, can further attract international capital to support climate action and economic growth in EMDEs.

To reduce investment risks, government policies play a crucial role by establishing clear energy transition plans, enhanced regulatory frameworks, and robust grid infrastructure development to balance supply and demand. Competitive tenders and auctions are also vital as they provide legal certainty and foster fair competition, which is essential to draw private investments. Robust regulations, public policies, strengthened institutions, and enhanced international support are essential to unlock significant private financing for clean energy in developing economies. These elements mitigate policy and regulatory barriers, creating an environment conducive to attracting and securing private investments in clean energy projects.

Strong market signals, such as a carbon price or similar regulatory measures, are fundamental to guiding investments toward cleaner technologies. Enhancing data quality is another critical factor; improved risk assessment tools can help decrease perceived risks and lower capital costs for private investors. Initiatives like the Global Emerging Markets Risk Database (GEMs) contribute to this by providing comprehensive risk statistics and enhancing data transparency, thereby widening investor access to crucial information. These efforts facilitate the effective channeling of private funds into climate action within EMDEs.

7.3.3 Critical Role of Concessional Finance in Scaling Up Climate Investments

DFIs provide credit, equity investments, and guarantees to support private sector development and economic growth in developing countries. Funded by national governments or private investors, DFIs have become increasingly crucial in providing climate finance to EMDEs, especially as rising global inflation in 2021 and 2022 has driven up capital costs.

To facilitate high-impact projects, DFIs offer concessional finance, which includes loans with lower interest rates, longer repayment periods, and more favorable terms than standard market loans. Concessional finance is essential for mobilizing additional private capital by mitigating risks and making investments more attractive. This type of financing often takes the form of grants, low-interest loans, equity investments, and guarantees. DFIs mitigate financial, technological, and geographical risks associated with climate investments through innovative de-risking instruments, making projects in challenging markets more attractive. By blending concessional funds with commercial financing, DFIs can rebalance the risk-reward profile of pioneering investments, enabling projects that would otherwise be too risky or unprofitable for private investors.

7.3.3.1 Need to Mobilize More Concessional Finance

While market-rate debt remains the primary global climate finance mechanism, concessional finance – accounting for less than 10 percent of total climate investment flows – is vital for climate investment in highly indebted and capital-scarce EMDEs. To reach the Paris Agreement targets and ensure sustainable development in

EMDEs, concessional finance for climate investments must be significantly scaled up.

The scarcity of concessional funds, aggravated by issues like food security, inflation, and geopolitical tensions, requires greater collaboration between existing donors and attracting new concessional finance. These funds must be used strategically to mitigate risk and crowd in private capital through well-designed instruments and structures. Developing financial architectures that merge public and private funds, tailored to local needs and risk profiles, is essential to catalyze climate finance. Increasing the lending capacity of MDBs and greater voluntary contributions from the corporate sector and philanthropy are key to mobilizing concessional finance.

The G20-mandated Independent Expert Group (IEG) on MDB Reform has called for a tripling of sustainable annual lending levels to USD 390 billion by 2030, with a significant portion directed toward climate initiatives. According to IFC (2023) and ETC (2023), an estimated USD 100 billion of concessional finance will be required annually until 2035 solely for the clean energy transition. Additionally, the International High-Level Expert Group (IHLEG) suggests that to meet the Paris Agreement targets and related development goals, concessional financing needs to increase to USD 150–200 billion annually by 2030, which is more than four times the current levels.

There is also a pressing need to boost financing through multilateral climate funds, which have been increasing and now provide USD 3.9 billion annually in concessional financing, mostly in the form of grants, to EMDEs. The four largest climate financial intermediary funds – the Global Climate Fund (GCF), Global Environment Facility (GEF), Climate Investment Fund (CIF), and the Adaptation Fund (AF) – have cumulative commitments exceeding USD 30 billion.

MDBs are IFIs created by multiple countries to provide financial support and professional advice for economic development projects in developing countries. The major MDBs include the World Bank (WB),

International Monetary Fund (IMF), Asian Development Bank (ADB), African Development Bank (AfDB), Inter-American Development Bank (IDB). Scaling up the lending capacity of MDBs can primarily come from three complementary and mutually reinforcing sources: more efficient utilization of existing capital, augmenting capital through voluntary contributions from shareholders and other contributors (including lending and portfolio guarantees as well as hybrid capital), and regular capital increases to provide the basis for the sustained expansion of lending. These combined efforts will enable the necessary growth in lending capacity to meet increasing financial demands. In addition, recent proposals on the incorporation of callable capital into the capital adequacy frameworks are promising as they have the potential to increase MDBs' risk tolerance (while maintaining their AAA credit rating), which would result in additional lending.

Rechanneling idle Special Drawing Rights (SDRs) held by AEs has become an effective way to boost concessional climate finance.[2] The IMF primarily rechannels SDRs to developing countries through the Poverty Reduction and Growth Trust (PRGT) and the Resilience and Sustainability Trust (RST). The PRGT offers low or zero-interest loans to low-income countries. At the same time, the RST, founded in 2022, supports countries in addressing long-term challenges such as climate change and pandemic preparedness. AEs can also enter into bilateral agreements with the IMF to lend their SDRs to developing countries.

Existing IMF mechanisms have already seen pledges of over USD 100 billion in SDRs, but disbursal has been slow. Expanding SDR rechanneling mechanisms and exploring the issuance of SDR-denominated, cash-settled bonds by MDBs or other public authorities could further mobilize concessional funds for climate finance in EMDEs.

---

[2] SDRs were created by the IMF in 1969 to supplement the international reserve assets of its member countries.

Despite the urgent need for increased climate action, there has been a slowdown in public climate financing growth, a reduction in private climate finance volumes, and a regression in climate blended finance (see section 7.3.4.2). This trend highlights the necessity for more concessional capital from donors and philanthropic sources to mobilize substantial commercial investment needed for global net-zero emissions targets. Philanthropy, including from the corporate sector, could significantly boost climate finance, as it currently accounts for only 2 percent of overall philanthropic giving. In 2022, USD 435 million, or about 20 percent of philanthropic giving by foundations, went to EMDEs (excluding China). Engaging the corporate sector and wealthy individuals presents a significant opportunity to expand the pool of philanthropic contributions for climate-related projects.

7.3.3.2 Innovative Financial Approaches of Development Institutions to Crowd in Private Capital

MDBs are essential for unlocking investment opportunities and mobilizing finance through lending and attracting private finance. They bridge the gap between necessary financial instruments and those currently available, particularly in risk mitigation (e.g., guarantees and insurance), local currency financing, early-stage risk financing, and aggregation vehicles for small projects. Tools like guarantees, equity positions, performance-based incentives, and viability gap funding are crucial for mobilizing private capital for otherwise unfeasible projects. Scaling up climate finance in EMDEs involves continuously revising and adapting MDB strategies and operations to better catalyze public and private finance for climate change, biodiversity, and infrastructure.

Public and philanthropic funding is critical when market financing is unavailable, boosting market confidence and demonstrating the viability of new technologies. By leveraging concessional finance, MDBs draw in private funds, managing risks associated with new technologies and markets. This creates a crowding-in effect, where public investment attracts further private capital, supported by innovative funding and financial risk management tools.

Development banks have increasingly used various innovative mechanisms to mobilize local currency financing to effectively meet climate finance needs, combining loans, swaps, and synthetic structures to de-risk investments. Enhancing local capital markets and increasing the capacity of local investors to provide direct project financing are crucial steps. By leveraging their balance sheets fostering partnerships with local and international investors, and promoting financial innovations like microfinance and digital finance, development banks can grow local investment pools and support climate-positive projects.

DFIs and some other international finance institutions have effectively used co-investment and syndication models to facilitate private investments in clean energy projects by sharing risks and leveraging their expertise. These models broaden the scope of manageable risks and encourage investment in new technologies and markets. Moreover, managed co-lending portfolio programs allow DFIs to mobilize significant capital by enabling institutional investors to participate in diversified portfolios of emerging market loans, boosting private sector involvement in climate finance. Insurance companies and other financial institutions enhance climate finance through products like credit insurance, which allows DFIs to transfer project risks to the private sector. However, the market for concessional guarantees remains limited, with only a handful of specialized institutions and development finance entities offering climate-focused instruments. Notable examples include the Green Guarantee Company, the US International Development Finance Corporation, and the World Bank's Multilateral Investment Guarantee Agency (MIGA).

Credit guarantee facilities have the potential to mobilize 6–25 times more financing than loans, particularly in developing economies and EMs where financial instability and geopolitical uncertainty can hinder investment.

There is a significant opportunity for MDBs to expand the number of climate-exclusive guarantees they offer, aligning more closely with global climate goals. The proposed Global Credit Guarantee Facility (GCGF), as outlined by the Climate Policy Initiative (2023), is a crucial step toward scaling up guarantees and reducing credit risk in EMDEs. This facility could help lower the cost of capital for countries with high solar and other renewable energy potential, thereby significantly increasing their installed renewable energy capacity. By leveraging guarantees, the GCGF could mobilize substantial capital. For instance, a conservative scenario with USD 4.1 billion in capital could achieve a leverage of 28 times the initial amount. In contrast, an optimistic scenario with USD 660 million could leverage up to 250 times. Additionally, the GCGF could reduce risk premia by 3 percent–6 percent on average and improve credit ratings by 2–6 notches, making it a transformative tool for financing climate action in EMDEs.

Project aggregation platforms and syndication vehicles address the mismatch between the small scale of many energy transition projects in EMs and the larger investment thresholds of institutional investors. By pooling numerous smaller projects, these platforms reduce transaction costs, diversify risks, and create standardized investment-grade portfolios, enhancing their attractiveness to large investors. Coupled with robust monitoring and impact measurement, these measures can significantly increase the effectiveness of public funds in mobilizing private finance for climate projects in EMs.

7.3.4 Blended Finance as a Key De-risking Instrument in EMDEs

Mobilizing private investment is a key goal of development finance. MDBs and DFIs aim to attract private capital into sustainable development projects in EMDEs. As EMDEs work toward rapid development and low-carbon transitions, blended finance becomes vital for bridging climate financing gaps, enabling critical yet commercially unviable projects to secure necessary funding (IMF, 2022b).

Blended finance is an investment strategy that combines concessional funds from public and philanthropic sources with commercial capital from private investors and DFIs. It aims to support high-impact projects in areas like climate change, where commercial viability may not yet exist. By reducing investment risks, particularly in high-risk sectors or regions, blended finance lowers barriers to entry for private investors. Blended finance addresses risks specific to emerging and developing markets, such as economic volatility, political instability, and regulatory uncertainties. Additionally, it mitigates currency mismatches between local revenue streams and hard currency financing, reducing costs associated with foreign exchange hedging and swaps.

Blended finance is essential for mobilizing the scale of investment needed in developing economies. These mechanisms are designed to maximize the impact of each dollar of public or philanthropic funding by attracting multiple dollars of private investment, thereby amplifying the reach and effectiveness of development initiatives.

Blended finance is instrumental in catalyzing private funds in sectors like clean energy, which, despite offering substantial environmental and social benefits, may not immediately yield the financial returns that attract traditional investments. While commercial-scale solar and onshore wind projects in many middle-income countries are already viable without subsidies, newer technologies like low-emission hydrogen, electric mobility solutions (e-mobility), and distributed generation with batteries still require blended finance due to their developmental stages and commercial uncertainty. In low-income countries, where macroeconomic and political risks are higher, even mature sectors like renewable power may require blended finance. The development of alternative clean fuels such as low-emission hydrogen, ammonia, and bioenergy, as well as emerging energy storage solutions, would particularly benefit from blended finance due to their nascent stages of development.

7.3.4.1 Blended Finance Instruments and Structures

Blended finance utilizes a range of financial tools, including guarantees, various forms of debt, equity investments, performance-based incentives, and viability gap funding (Table 7.3). Key blended finance instruments include concessional loans, which are senior or subordinated loans priced below market rates to lower the cost of capital. Guarantees provide first-loss coverage or liquidity support, mitigating risks for investors. Concessional equity involves lower-priced or subordinated equity to make investments more attractive. Investment grants offer performance-based incentives and viability gap funding to cover a portion of project costs that are not commercially viable. Bond investments can be privately or publicly traded, providing loan-like funding. Local currency support offers concessional funds or subsidized loans to manage currency risk, making investments in local currencies more feasible. The long-term objective of blended finance mechanisms is to achieve commercial sustainability, minimizing reliance on concessional support and expanding the pool of bankable projects. Leveraging these instruments is crucial in developing countries where projects encounter obstacles such as high upfront costs or the implementation of new, unproven technologies. Moreover, blended finance facilitates essential infrastructure development and encourages regulatory reforms, fostering an environment conducive to broader investment.

In blended finance projects, financial instruments are selected based on their ability to address specific investment risks or market failures, ensuring that only the necessary amount of concessional funding is used to achieve the desired outcomes. These tools adjust the risk-return profile of investments and provide incentives for investing in developmentally beneficial projects like clean energy transitions, thereby increasing private capital flows into climate projects in EMs. A typical blended finance structure involves multiple layers of funding and risk mitigation, designed to attract private sector investment to projects considered too risky or unprofitable under normal market conditions (Figure 7.2):

Table 7.3 Blended finance instruments

Instrument type	Description	Examples	Addresses which specific risks/barriers
Direct investment	Debt or equity instruments with direct contribution into a blended finance vehicle (e.g., project or fund)	Junior/subordinated capital Commercial capital	Multiple risks, including off-taker risks, construction risks, revenue attractiveness, etc. Access to capital risk
Guarantees	Three-party agreements, where a third party provides an extra layer of protection for the beneficiary of a service, for example, debt service, in case the entity that would typically provide a service fails to do so	Loan guarantees Performance guarantees	Access to capital, counterparty/off-taker/credit risk Technical risk
Hedging instruments, swaps, and derivatives	Contractual instruments to help manage different types of risks faced by an investor or borrower	Local currency hedges/swaps Securitization	Liquidity/time horizon, scale, counterparty/off-taker/credit risk
Insurance	Two-party contracts between the insurer and the policyholder. The insurance provider promises to provide financial compensation in the event of a financial loss.	Political risk insurance Performance insurance	Construction risks, operation and output risks, upstream resource-related risks
Commercially oriented preparation support	Grant or concessional funding specifically to address early-stage development risks	Project preparation funding or technical assistance	Administrative risks, access to capital, capacity at the local level

Source: IEA-IFC (2023)

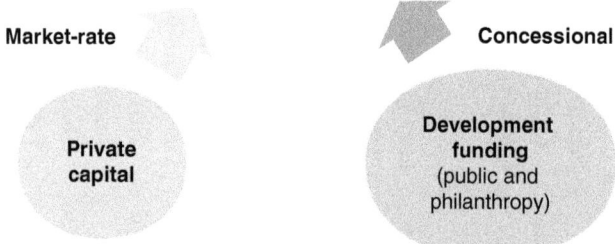

Blended finance structure
Examples: Private equity and debt funds with concessional finance to attract institutional investors; bond issuance with concessionally priced guarantees or insurance from development funders; grants from development funders to build capacity to achieve the expected returns or to design and structure projects to attract institutional investors

Market-rate   Concessional

Private capital   Development funding (public and philanthropy)

FIGURE 7.2 Blended finance structure
Source: State of Blended Finance, 2023

Concessional Capital Placement: Public or philanthropic entities invest capital at below-market rates, accepting a higher-risk profile. This concessional capital acts as a cushion or first-loss layer within the investment's capital structure, absorbing initial risks and potential losses, thus securing the investment for subsequent private investors.

Junior Equity Tranche: This involves providing equity that takes a subordinate position to other investments, absorbing losses first in case of default, which protects other investors and encourages their participation. Public finance institutions, backed by government resources, can take on initial losses in investment defaults, reducing the financial burden on private investors.

Risk Mitigation through Guarantees or Insurance: Public or philanthropic sectors may provide guarantees or risk insurance to enhance the investment's attractiveness. These guarantees serve as a credit enhancement tool, promising to cover part of the losses in case of default, thereby reducing perceived risk and aligning the investment's risk-return profile with market expectations. Products like guarantees or insurance can cover specific risks such as currency fluctuations, political instability, or default, making the investment more secure for private investors.

Performance-Based Incentives: Project developers are rewarded if they achieve predetermined targets, which encourages efficiency and effectiveness in project implementation.

Cross-Currency Swaps: These are used to manage currency risks for investments in foreign countries, ensuring that investors can manage their exposure to currency fluctuations, which might affect the returns on their investments.

Use of Grants for Transaction Design and Technical Assistance (TA): The structure often includes a grant-funded TA facility to enhance the project's commercial viability and developmental impact. This facility can be used before or after the investment is made and helps cover crucial upfront costs during the project preparation or design stage.

Enhanced Commercial Viability: By integrating concessional funding, risk mitigation tools, and grant-funded support, blended finance structures effectively de-risk investments, making them more attractive to private investors who require risk-adjusted returns in line with market rates.

Assessing the effectiveness of blended finance in catalyzing private investment involves key concepts like private finance mobilization, often referred to as leverage. This entails mobilizing private finance directly, such as through co-financed projects, or indirectly via funds or enabling outputs. However, measuring effectiveness purely based on mobilized finance can be misleading because further upstream investments generally show higher mobilization, irrespective of their necessity.

Another critical factor in evaluating blended finance is *additionality*, which considers whether the investments would occur without the blended finance instrument. This criterion assesses if the initiative fills a crucial gap, even if it may not achieve high leverage.

Additionally, the *demonstration effect* of investment is also vital, showcasing the potential to guide further investments even if it has low direct leverage. These elements combined provide a more holistic view of the catalytic impact of blended finance.

7.3.4.2 Overall Landscape and Recent Trends in Climate Blended Finance

Despite their catalyzer role in financing climate investment, blended climate finance initiatives faced numerous challenges due to adverse recent global macroeconomic developments. Inflationary pressures, mounting debt burdens, and geopolitical instabilities profoundly influence the flow of climate-blended finance funds. Despite maintaining a similar deal count in 2022 compared to 2021, total deal volume in climate blended finance decreased by approximately 55 percent, reaching a ten-year low.

Critically, the supply of concessional capital to climate blended finance deals has stagnated since 2017, with only a minor increase from USD 967 million annually between 2017 and 2019 to USD 1.08 billion between 2020 and 2022. This level is far below what is required to meet key mobilization targets, such as the United Nations Conference on Trade and Development's (UNCTAD) estimate that USD 6 trillion in climate finance to developing economies is needed by 2030 to reach just half of their Nationally Determined Contributions (NDCs). The OECD has observed similar trends, noting little change in the proportion of Official Development Assistance (ODA) disbursement to climate-related investment since 2017. The DFI Working Group on Blended Concessional Finance also reports that DFI market rate and concessional allocations to climate finance deals have shown no real growth since 2019.

From 2020 to 2022, just over half of the commitments to climate blended finance transactions came from public sector investors. Within this group, development agencies accounted for 49 percent of commitments during this period and increasingly acting as the primary suppliers of concessional capital.

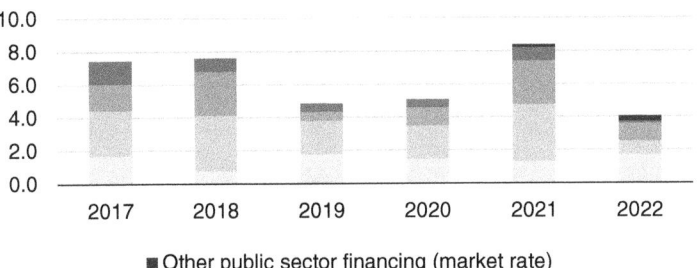

FIGURE 7.3 Sources of financing to climate blended finance (USD billion)
Source: State of Blended Finance, 2023

Based on investment amounts captured by Convergence from 2017 to 2022, private-sector investors were the largest source of capital for climate-blended finance transactions by volume (Figure 7.3). Private sector invested an average of USD 2.3 billion in commercial capital in these deals. However, private sector climate financing totals have plateaued, with aggregate financing flows decreasing by 45 percent between 2020 and 2022 compared to 2017 and 2019, declining from USD 7.13 billion to USD 5.87 billion.

DFIs and MDBs are also key suppliers of capital to climate-blended finance, with the majority of investment deployed on market terms. Between 2017 and 2022, DFIs/MDBs supplied USD 2.2 billion of commercial capital per year to climate-blended finance deals. These transactions have been concentrated in Sub-Saharan Africa (SSA), which accounted for 48 percent of transactions between 2020 and 2022, followed by Latin America and the Caribbean at 24 percent (Figure 7.4). The proportion of transactions focused on SSA grew 14 percentage points between 2017–2019 and 2020–2022, representing an absolute increase of nearly 90 percent. Conversely, there was a decrease in the proportion of deals targeting East Asia and the Pacific, dropping from 20 percent to 13 percent over the same period.

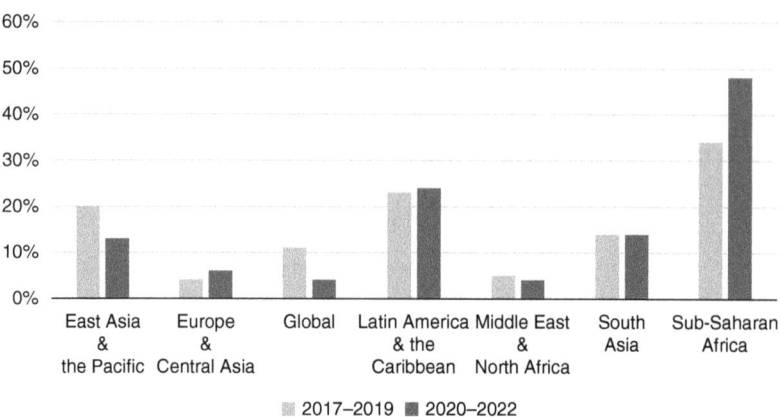

FIGURE 7.4 Climate blended finance deals by regional breakdown (%)
Source: State of Blended Finance, 2023

Adaptation blended finance continues to be underrepresented, with only 15 percent of deals since 2013 having a pure adaptation focus.[3] This equates to USD 7.5 billion in total financing, compared to USD 64.2 billion for pure mitigation and USD 18.5 billion for hybrid transactions. Hybrid transactions, which address both climate mitigation and adaptation goals, represent an area of opportunity for the private sector to invest with an adaptation lens. Overall, the total value of hybrid transactions amounts to USD 18.5 billion. These transactions span various sectors, including infrastructure, financial services, housing, and real estate. However, the largest share of hybrid deals (27 percent) is concentrated in agricultural inputs and farm productivity. This sector is particularly well-suited to deliver both mitigation and adaptation benefits, making it a focal point for hybrid investments.

Recent trends in climate-blended finance indicate a shift in institutional investor activity from equity to debt (Figure 7.5). While 80% of institutional commitments were in equity during 2017–2019, this changed to 50% in debt instruments by 2022. This shift presents a promising opportunity for institutional investors to become a more

---

[3] Institutional investments in climate finance are divided as follows: 45% in hybrid solutions, 35% in mitigation, and 20% in adaptation.

7 CHALLENGES IN EMDEs AND WAYS TO OVERCOME THEM 283

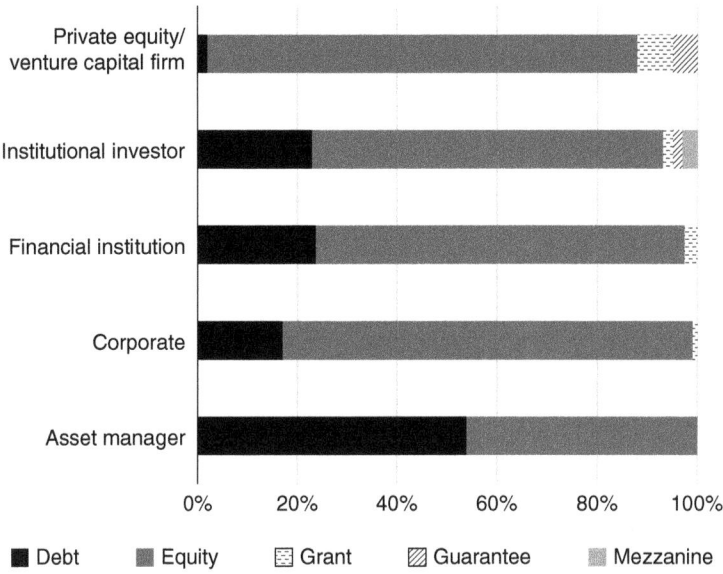

FIGURE 7.5 Breakdown of private sector investor commitments by instrument type (%)
Source: State of Blended Finance 2023
Note: A mezzanine instrument refers to a hybrid of debt and equity financing, ranking below senior debt but above equity. It helps to bridge financing gaps with higher returns while including equity-like features.

reliable source of debt capital, particularly as traditional lenders, like banks, face challenges. Bringing institutional investors into project finance can lower debt spreads significantly, almost comparable to the impact of securing a DFI/MDB guarantee. However, liquidity and credit risk requirements are critical considerations, as most institutional investors avoid noninvestment-grade jurisdictions or securities. Blended finance instruments, such as concessional guarantees and loans, can mitigate these risks, aligning perceived risks with higher-rated opportunities and reducing capital costs for borrowers. With their longer-term investment horizons, pension funds and insurance companies are particularly well-positioned to invest in climate finance, navigating the longer timelines required to realize the full value of climate projects.

7.3.5 Voluntary Carbon Markets (VCMs) as an Alternative Climate Finance Mechanism in EMDEs

7.3.5.1 Structure, Potential, and Current State of Play in VCMs

AEs have been experimenting over the past decade with carbon finance mechanisms such as carbon taxes and emissions trading systems (ETS) as alternative funding sources for climate projects (see Chapter 2). These compliance markets, where firms must pay for their emissions, are central to many countries' policies and serve as an important source of government revenue. While these markets are region-specific, voluntary carbon credits are more accessible across various sectors of the economy. Although currently small, VCMs have significant potential to expand climate finance, particularly in EMDEs. By trading verified emission reductions and removals, these markets could evolve into an important additional source of both climate and development finance. Unlike debt-generating capital flows, revenue from carbon credits covers costs without the need for borrowing, making them a crucial tool for managing unavoidable emissions during the transition to permanent decarbonization methods.

Despite its relatively small size, the carbon offsets market is rapidly growing, attracting increasing interest from investors and corporations. This market is projected to expand from approximately USD 2 billion in 2022 to about USD 250 billion by 2050, significantly boosting private sector investment in climate mitigation. This growth is fueled by the proliferation of net-zero commitments from governments and companies and climate-related disclosure policies aligned with frameworks like the Task Force on Climate-Related Financial Disclosures (TCFD), which encourage companies to internalize carbon prices (see Chapter 4). A growing complement to offsets in the voluntary carbon market is the use of insets – emissions reductions generated within a company's own supply chain. Insets directly target Scope 3 emissions, which account for up to 90 percent of total emissions in sectors like agri-food and fashion. Unlike offsets, insets are not typically traded but are used to meet a company's own climate goals. Their rise reflects a shift toward more integrated, supply chain-based decarbonization strategies.

The volume of transactions in the VCM has surged notably in recent years, driven by increasing climate commitments from private businesses. From 2017 to 2021, the issuance of carbon credits grew from 96 million tonnes of CO_2 to 282 million tonnes, while retired credits increased from 47 million to 161 million tonnes. In 2021 alone, trading totaled approximately USD 2 billion across 493 million tonnes of CO_2 equivalent.

However, the market has experienced setbacks and negative sentiment amid an uncertain regulatory and policy landscape. Future market potential for VCM remains difficult to gauge, with estimates for 2030 ranging from USD 10 billion to USD 100 billion, according to analyses by McKinsey (2021) and Morgan Stanley (2023). The IHLEG (2023) considers that the VCM could reach up to USD 50 billion in financing in the medium term with supportive policies and actions. While small compared to the trillions needed for clean energy investments in EMDEs, this still represents a significant alternative source of climate finance.

Increasing corporate and investor interest in carbon credits, alongside a shift from emission reduction and avoidance to more direct carbon removal methods (both nature-based and technological), will likely drive the expansion of the VCM.

Developing VCMs emerges as an effective strategy for transferring non-debt-generating financial flows from the Global North to the Global South, thereby financing climate mitigation and adaptation efforts. VCMs allow businesses and individuals to purchase carbon credits generated by projects that reduce or remove GHGs, often located in developing countries. This mechanism incentivizes emission reductions while contributing to sustainable development in the Global South. By directing capital toward renewable energy, reforestation, and other climate-friendly initiatives, VCMs help bridge the funding gap for climate action in regions most vulnerable to climate change. Additionally, VCMs can enhance local economies, create jobs, and promote technology transfer, contributing to broader socioeconomic benefits. As the demand for carbon credits grows, well-regulated and transparent VCMs can play a critical role in global climate finance, ensuring that mitigation and adaptation projects receive the necessary funding without increasing the debt burden on developing countries.

7.3.5.2 Voluntary versus Compliance Carbon Markets, Carbon Reduction versus Removal Credits, and Nature-Based versus Industrial Methods to Generate Carbon Credits

Voluntary and compliance carbon markets differ significantly in their structure and operation (Table 7.4). Voluntary markets, operating outside regulatory frameworks, trade in carbon offsets facilitated by project-based systems. Credits in these markets are generally cheaper, influenced by factors such as project type, size, location, co-benefits, and vintage. These credits are available to businesses, governments, NGOs, and individuals. Without a centralized trading system, project developers sell directly to buyers, brokers, exchanges, or retailers.

In contrast, compliance markets function within national, regional, or international regulatory regimes, such as the Kyoto Protocol, and use a cap-and-trade system for trading allowances. Credits in these markets are typically more expensive due to regulatory obligations. They are primarily purchased by companies and governments that must adhere to emission limits set by entities like the United Nations. Companies that exceed their emission targets can sell their surplus credits to those needing to offset emissions within this regulated market framework.

Carbon credit corresponds to one metric tonne of reduced, avoided, or removed CO_2 or equivalent GHG reduced/avoided emissions and removed emissions. While carbon credits are tradeable units representing certified reductions or removals of CO_2, carbon offsets are specific credits generated from these activities. Carbon allowances issued by governments within emissions trading programs

Table 7.4 Voluntary versus compliance carbon markets

	Voluntary market	Compliance market
Exchanged commodity	Carbon offsets. Facilitated by the project-based system.	Allowances. Facilitated by the cap-and-trade system.
How is the market regulated?	Functions outside of the compliance market.	National, regional, or international carbon reduction regimes (e.g., Kyoto Protocol, California Carbon Market).
What is the price?	Voluntary credits tend to be cheaper because they cannot be used in compliance markets. Several factors, such as project type, size, location, co-benefits, and vintage, impact the price.	Compliance credits tend to be more expensive because regulatory obligations drive them.
Who can purchase credits?	Businesses, governments, NGOs, and individuals.	Companies and governments have adopted emission limits established by the United Nations Convention on Climate Change.
Where do credits trade?	There is currently no centralized voluntary carbon credit market. Project developers can sell credits directly to buyers through a broker or an exchange or sell to a retailer, who then resells them to a buyer.	Companies that surpass their emission targets can sell their surplus credits to those looking to offset emissions. Credits can be sold under the Kyoto Protocol's emissions trading scheme.

Source: https://carboncredits.com/what-is-the-voluntary-carbon-market/

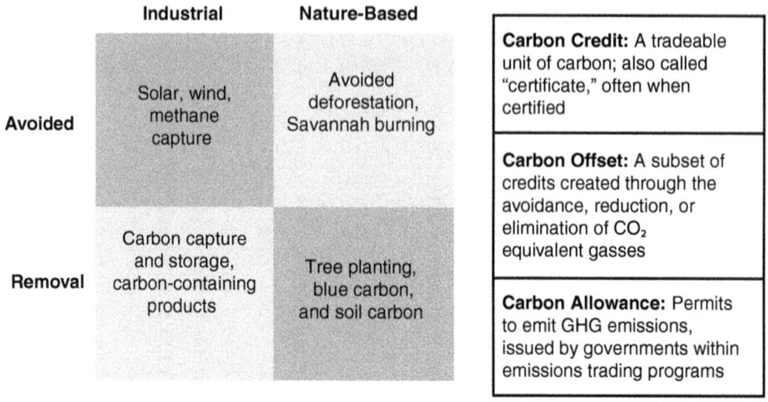

	Industrial	Nature-Based
Avoided	Solar, wind, methane capture	Avoided deforestation, Savannah burning
Removal	Carbon capture and storage, carbon-containing products	Tree planting, blue carbon, and soil carbon

Carbon Credit: A tradeable unit of carbon; also called "certificate," often when certified

Carbon Offset: A subset of credits created through the avoidance, reduction, or elimination of CO_2 equivalent gasses

Carbon Allowance: Permits to emit GHG emissions, issued by governments within emissions trading programs

FIGURE 7.6 Carbon removal versus avoidance solutions
Source: www.csrwire.com/press_releases/749971-ab-are-carbon-offsets-next-esg-investing-frontier

permit the holder to emit a certain amount of GHGs, thus creating a regulated market to control overall emissions (Figure 7.6).

These credits are verified instruments representing these reductions and come in two main types:

Reduction or Avoidance Credits are generated from actions that reduce emissions compared to a baseline, such as adopting low-carbon technologies or conservation efforts (Box 7.1). They currently make up the majority of the carbon markets, helping to prevent future emissions by maintaining forest cover or opting for renewable energy sources over fossil fuels.

Avoided emissions can be categorized into two types: industrial and nature-based. Industrial projects, such as solar, wind, and methane capture, avoid emissions by replacing fossil fuel-based energy sources with renewable energy or capturing methane that would otherwise be released into the atmosphere. Nature-based activities, such as avoided deforestation and savannah burning, prevent the release of carbon stored in forests and savannahs by avoiding deforestation and uncontrolled burning practices.

These credits are crucial for bridging the gap until the transition to a low-carbon economy is complete. Currently, projects focusing on avoiding or reducing atmospheric carbon dioxide emissions account for over 80 percent of the carbon offsets market.

BOX 7.1: **Nature-Based versus Technology-Based Solutions to Meet Net-Zero Targets**

Nature-based solutions (NbS) generate carbon credits by reducing, avoiding, and removing GHGs through activities such as afforestation, wetland restoration, and sustainable soil management. These projects harness natural processes to capture carbon dioxide, enhancing carbon sinks in forests, oceans, and soils, while also improving biodiversity, ecosystem health, and climate resilience. Despite their benefits, financial backing for NbS is insufficient. Current annual investments stand at USD 133 billion, far below the USD 536 billion needed to meet climate, biodiversity, and land degradation goals. Projected investments need to more than triple by 2030 to effectively limit global temperature rises and halt biodiversity loss. Key challenges for NbS include accurate measurement and verification of carbon benefits, ensuring long-term permanence, preventing leakage, managing costs, and securing regulatory support. Enhanced financing mechanisms, such as debt-for-nature swaps (See Chapter 4 Section 4.3.2) and the expansion of the VCM, are crucial to scale up investments and support NbS projects but they require better coordination and greater availability of risk mitigation instruments.

Industrial and tech-based solutions hold strong potential for boosting carbon credit generation through Carbon Dioxide Removal (CDR) in the future. CDR involves technologies and practices that extract CO_2 from the atmosphere and sequester it. Key methods include Direct Air Capture (DAC), which uses machines to capture CO_2 directly from the air and store it underground or use it in various applications. An extension of this method, Direct Air Carbon Capture and Storage (DACCS), securely sequesters CO_2 in deep geological formations. Bioenergy with Carbon Capture and Storage (BECCS) involves burning biomass for energy and capturing the resulting CO_2, preventing it from re-entering the atmosphere.

Despite their potential, these technologies face significant challenges. For example, DAC is currently costly, ranging between USD 125 and USD 335 per metric tonne of CO_2 captured, with only

> 18 operational plants worldwide. Scaling up to the necessary levels by 2050 will require substantial growth and investment.
>
> Tech-based solutions are expected to increasingly complement nature-based methods post-2030, with projections suggesting that tech-based carbon removal could account for upwards of 5 gigatonnes of CO_2 annually by 2050. This shift will involve expanding renewable technologies, enhancing methane capture, and introducing carbon capture in everyday applications. While CDR is crucial for hard-to-decarbonize sectors like steel, cement, and petrochemicals, it is not a substitute for reducing emissions across all sectors. Significant research and development are needed to make these technologies technically and financially viable.

- *Removal Credits* involve the direct extraction of CO_2 from the atmosphere and are growing in importance. Although they currently account for only a small fraction of the market, around 5 percent,[4] they are critical for offsetting emissions from sectors that are difficult to decarbonize, such as steel and cement.
- Removal of emissions relies on two major approaches: nature-based and industrial. Nature-based projects, such as tree planting, *blue carbon*, and soil carbon, focus on increasing the natural absorption of CO_2 through activities like reforestation, restoring coastal and marine ecosystems that capture carbon, and improving soil carbon content through sustainable land management practices. Industrial methods, including Carbon Capture and Storage (CCS) and carbon-containing products, involve capturing carbon dioxide directly from industrial processes and storing it underground or using it to create carbon-containing products. These technology-driven methods, such as direct air capture (DAC), sequester or capture carbon directly from industrial processes and fossil-fuel-powered stations.
- Carbon removal is a crucial strategy to achieve net-zero and climate goals. However, the investment in removal projects must not detract global efforts from the urgency of drastically reducing GHG emissions.

---

[4] The remaining 13 percent of the total offsets market relates to a mix of avoidance/reduction and removal projects.

The Science-Based Targets initiative (SBTi) suggests that companies should limit these credits to no more than 10 percent of their portfolio by 2030, focusing increasingly on removal-based credits thereafter. While removal projects are likely to gain importance in the long term, current challenges in scaling and cost are constraining their supply. These challenges include the extensive land, energy, and investment needed to make these methods viable and effective.

7.3.5.3 Challenges in Standardization and Credibility of VCM and Suggestions for Improvement

The VCM has faced setbacks and growing skepticism, amplified by an uncertain regulatory and policy environment. Despite their small size relative to the vast financing needs of climate action, voluntary carbon markets hold significant potential to advance global mitigation efforts – highlighting the need for integrity and strong supporting measures.

To maintain market integrity, emissions related to these transactions undergo rigorous monitoring, reporting, and verification by independent third parties. Credibility is ensured through a set of established standards, each with distinct methodologies. The most widely recognized standards include Verra (The Verified Carbon Standard), Plan Vivo, The Gold Standard, The American Carbon Registry, and Climate Action Reserve. These standards are essential for maintaining trust in carbon emission reduction projects globally, ensuring that emission reductions, avoidance, or removals are authentic.

Despite their growing importance in global climate action, VCMs face critical challenges that threaten their credibility and long-term impact. On the supply side, ensuring the credibility and quality of carbon credits is essential. Continuously updating standards like the Verified Carbon Standard and the Gold Standard is crucial for addressing baseline setting, permanence, and additionality to ensure that credits lead to real carbon reductions. On the demand side, the effectiveness of VCMs can be undermined by reputational risks, particularly greenwashing. Companies may use carbon credits to project environmental responsibility without making substantial reductions in their emissions. Initiatives like the Voluntary Carbon Market Integrity Initiative (VCMI) aim to establish clear guidelines and standards to ensure carbon credits supplement genuine emission reductions.

For companies engaging in VCMs, understanding the nuances of carbon credits is crucial:

1. *Quality of Offsets:* It is challenging to source high-quality offsets that deliver the same climate benefits as direct emission reductions. Many available offsets may only facilitate short-term carbon removal, not aligning with the long-term benefits of emission reductions.
2. *Role of Carbon Credits:* Forward-thinking companies view carbon credits as a secondary tool to boost their climate impact beyond robust internal decarbonization measures, not as the primary method of addressing their emissions.
3. *Supplementary Use:* Carbon credits should complement, not replace, deep decarbonization efforts. This approach helps ensure that companies are actively contributing to climate mitigation, enhancing their operational strategies with offsets to achieve broader environmental goals.

Currently, there is regulatory uncertainty regarding the relationship between VCMs and the mechanisms established by Article 6 of the Paris Agreement. Convergence between the rules governing voluntary and compliance markets would enable high-integrity finance to flow to EMDEs. Article 6 allows countries to meet their climate goals by trading carbon emission reductions and removals internationally, preventing double-counting through *corresponding adjustments*. These adjustments ensure accurate emissions accounting by deducting internationally transferred mitigation outcomes (ITMOs) from the seller's totals and adding them to the buyer's.

Implementing Article 6.4, which regulates these trades, will demand substantial effort, with differences across countries in institutional capacity, regulatory frameworks, and the readiness of domestic carbon markets. Nations must establish robust systems for tracking and validating emissions and decide on regulations for exporting carbon credits. For example, Indonesia and Papua New

Guinea have temporarily halted the export of VCM credits to evaluate their impact on national climate objectives. Differentiating between credits under Article 6 and those from VCMs is crucial for countries strategizing their carbon reduction financing.

EMDEs need strategies to access carbon credit markets, including developing pipelines of projects or programs that can generate high-quality credits compatible with their broader climate commitments and development plans. For companies, integrating VCMs into a comprehensive climate strategy involves more than just purchasing offsets; it requires embedding these mechanisms into broader, impactful actions that prioritize significant emission reductions alongside offset usage for overall environmental gains. MDBs and donors can assist EMDE governments in investing in their capability to attract high-integrity carbon finance and ensure that benefits are shared fairly, including by supporting Indigenous Peoples and local communities.

MDBs play a key role in advancing carbon markets by promoting unified standards, improving monitoring, reporting, and verification systems, and supporting the development of digital frameworks for carbon markets. They help countries establish carbon pricing mechanisms that reflect their developmental goals and encourage the private sector to engage in low-carbon technologies and projects that prevent deforestation. By linking credible buyers with projects that generate high-quality carbon offsets, MDBs facilitate genuine climate action. Completing guidelines and standards by authoritative bodies is expected to enhance market practices and efficiency.

7.3.6 *Promoting Domestic Capital Markets and Local Currency Financing to Unlock Private Capital*

Leveraging domestic markets is crucial to unlocking private capital in EMDEs. Approximately USD 17 trillion of domestic financial capital exists in these regions, consisting of household savings, pension funds, and corporate and local bank finance (IHLEG 2023). Deploying this capital is vital for investing in low-carbon infrastructure, climate-positive technologies, and transitioning companies. For major projects like infrastructure or renewable energy, capital markets are crucial, providing funding through instruments such as bonds and securitization, often supported by institutional investors like mutual funds, pension funds, and insurance companies. On the other hand, smaller climate initiatives, such as adopting solar panels and EVs by SMEs and households, typically rely on domestic banks for funding. These banks are pivotal in supplying stable, long-term financing, especially in well-developed markets, and are instrumental in balancing short-term financial needs with sustainable, long-term capital solutions.

Increasing the use of green finance products like green bonds and sustainability-linked loans, which are currently underused in EMDEs compared to developed economies, is essential. Well-developed capital markets improve resource allocation by enhancing information flow and governance, facilitating the funding of innovative and higher-risk projects that traditional banking sectors might overlook.

Equity markets are especially important for financing new businesses reliant on intangible assets like research and development (R&D) and human capital. Robust domestic capital markets also attract climate-related foreign direct investment, including through mergers and acquisitions focused on climate solutions. The greatest potential for such financing exists in environments where supportive policies and regulatory frameworks ease local fundraising and lower barriers for foreign investors. DFIs and MDBs often bring their support by helping implement policy and regulatory reforms that deepen and strengthen capital markets.

In EMDEs, the heavy reliance on dollar-denominated debt presents significant challenges for financing climate projects. These difficulties have been compounded by post-COVID financial volatility, monetary tightening in advanced economies, and rising geopolitical tensions, which have weakened EMDE currencies, dampened investor confidence, and heightened aversion to exchange rate risk. To mitigate these challenges, it is essential to develop robust local currency markets and financial systems that can drive private investment in clean energy, as demonstrated by countries like China and India.

In EMDEs with less developed capital markets, cross-currency swaps are vital for securing local currency financing for energy transition projects. These swaps often face limited availability and high costs, stalling investments. DFIs help overcome these obstacles by leveraging blended finance and partnering with entities like the Currency Exchange Fund (TCX), which offers long-term hedging against currency fluctuations in over 100 emerging market currencies. Enhancing initiatives like TCX can significantly boost access to local currency financing, align international funding with local needs, support debt sustainability, and attract private capital for climate-related investments.

7.3.7 *Scaling Up Adaptation Finance*

7.3.7.1 *Current Status of Adaptation Finance and the Gap between Needs and Available Funding*

Mobilizing financial resources for adaptation in EMDEs is crucial to address the escalating impacts of climate change and prevent severe economic and social setbacks. Despite this urgency, the proportion of adaptation finance within the overall climate finance framework has recently diminished, exacerbating the adaptation finance gap. Current adaptation costs are estimated to be 10–18 times higher than the current flows of international public adaptation finance.

Enhancing adaptation finance in EMDEs is essential to mitigate losses in lives and livelihoods, reduce financial costs, create meaningful jobs, and bolster security and stability. Investing in adaptation helps vulnerable communities better prepare for and respond to climate-related threats, fostering sustainable economic growth and resilience. Greater adaptation efforts also strengthen the capacity to preserve development gains against the detrimental impacts of climate change.

Establishing clear terminology and asset classifications, along with a consensus on what constitutes finance for adaptation and resilience, as well as loss and damage, is essential. This clarity will strengthen the business case for adaptation investments and encourage scaling adaptation financing strategies against climate impacts.

Adaptation finance, mainly managed by public sectors, faces challenges in mobilizing private contributions and overcoming barriers that inhibit private sector engagement. Boosting private sector adaptation efforts is essential, as each dollar invested can yield economic benefits ranging from USD 2 to USD 10 through risk reduction, productivity enhancement, and innovation. According to "Adapt Now: A Global Call for Leadership on Climate Resilience" by the Global Commission on Adaptation, a hypothetical investment of USD 1.8 trillion in five key areas of adaptation could result in USD 7.1 trillion in total net benefits. Digital climate advisory services can produce returns for African farmers – on average, productivity can increase by 30 percent, and average income can increase by 23 percent.

Although there was a 30 percent increase in adaptation funds from 2019 to 2020, the USD 63 billion allocated in 2021–2022 for developing countries is far below the estimated USD 212 billion required annually by 2030. Specifically, the agriculture, forestry, and land use sectors, despite their high vulnerability, received only USD 7 billion, accounting for 11 percent of all adaptation finance. Commercial interest in adaptation finance remains subdued, particularly in Africa, where private sector funding comprises less than 3 percent of the total. This is stark in contrast to the needs of sub-Saharan Africa, which received 31 percent (USD 11 billion) of international adaptation finance in 2021/2022 but requires at least USD 52 billion annually by 2030 to meet its adaptation goals. The challenge is compounded by a fragmented private finance landscape and a lack of incentives for engaging in large-scale projects.

In 2015, the Paris Agreement set a global goal for adaptation, prompting nine MDBs to commit to doubling their adaptation finance to USD 18 billion annually by 2025 – a target they surpassed by 2021 with USD 19.2 billion in adaptation finance delivered. Adaptation finance remains underrepresented in the blended finance market. The investment barriers facing adaptation have been well-documented, with a fundamental issue being the lack of a clear taxonomy defining climate adaptation parameters. Currently, adaptation and physical risk disclosures have not been widely integrated within robust regulatory frameworks like the TCFD.

Effective and inclusive investments in climate adaptation can minimize the impacts of climate change and, in some cases, even prevent them. Climate adaptation efforts – such as early warning systems, improved disaster risk management, climate-resilient infrastructure, alternative water storage, and climate-tolerant crops – can reduce the severity of climate impacts and enable quicker recovery for people, communities, businesses, and governments.

7.3.7.2 Strategies to Increase the Flow of Adaptation Finance, with a Focus on Blending Mechanisms

Investors generally find mitigation transactions more attractive, as they are easier to quantify regarding GHG emission reductions and often linked to revenue-generating activities, providing clearer returns on investment. Data deficiencies and inconsistent National Adaptation Plans (NAPs) hinder efforts to enhance adaptation strategies, often failing to address region-specific needs. The Lima Adaptation Knowledge Initiative has identified critical data gaps, especially in water-related hazards. Technical assistance is crucial for improving NAP development, with efforts to increase investment in data collection and management being vital. Blended finance in adaptation transactions is increasing, with entities like the Adaptation Fund leveraging concessional financing to attract additional resources, signaling a trend toward integrating blended finance in adaptation efforts.

Tracking adaptation finance in the private sector and local governments presents challenges due to the unique nature of adaptation, the difficulty of linking climate risks to specific actions, unclear impact metrics, and confidentiality concerns. There is a pressing need for a unified tracking method. In addition to closing data and information gaps, solutions to boost adaptation finance include integrating climate adaptation and resilience into financial systems for sectors like agriculture, coastal real estate, and water infrastructure that face significant climate risks. For instance, in Indonesia, mangrove restoration not only addresses climate change through carbon sequestration but also enhances flood protection, supports fisheries, and creates jobs, particularly empowering women through financial independence.

Blended finance exemplifies the *crowd-in* effect, where USD 1 of concessional donor funding can leverage nearly USD 7 of additional finance. Hybrid Mitigation-Adaptation Blended Finance, integrating both mitigation and adaptation elements, is particularly effective in sectors like sustainable agriculture, enhancing climate resilience while increasing carbon sequestration. This approach has attracted significant institutional investment, with 45 percent of climate finance flowing into hybrid solutions.

Projects like Brazil's Planting Climate Resilience Project, which incorporates low-emission technologies to promote climate-resilient agricultural practices, highlight the effectiveness of hybrid finance in advancing both climate adaptation and mitigation. Such initiatives strengthen the business case for investing in adaptation and resilience, fostering more robust and informed financial strategies against climate impacts.

7.4 CONCLUSION

Financing climate initiatives and advancing the SDGs are among the greatest challenges of our time, especially for many developing economies that face significant barriers to accessing capital and managing high costs. Closing the financing gap for climate mitigation and adaptation is crucial for achieving the Paris Agreement goals and ensuring sustainable growth.

To address this challenge, prioritizing the mobilization of private investment must become an explicit goal of development finance, led by MDBs and DFIs within their operating models. Additionally, scarce concessional capital must be deployed efficiently and judiciously to maximize its leverage.

A collective, global response beyond the capacity of local governments alone is essential to meet the climate finance needs of EMDEs. Policy coordination between AEs and EMDEs is crucial for ensuring climate justice. Effective policy coordination guarantees that financial resources are efficiently allocated where most needed, enhancing the resilience of vulnerable populations and ecosystems. By working together, AEs and EMDEs can share knowledge, drive innovation, and accelerate the transition to a low-carbon economy. Coordinated policies can also prevent carbon leakage, where stringent regulations in one country lead to increased emissions in others with less stringent controls, undermining global efforts to reduce GHG emissions and creating economic disparities.

Building resilient financial ecosystems requires strong partnerships among governments, international financial institutions (IFIs), philanthropic organizations, and private sector actors. Public budgetary resources play a pivotal role by de-risking investments in EMDEs, mitigating non-diversifiable risks such as country risk, and unlocking private capital that would otherwise remain sidelined. Increasingly, public entities are shifting their focus from greening individual projects to transforming entire economies toward sustainability.

Multilateral development banks (MDBs) are central to this process. By leveraging their balance sheets, MDBs can unlock investment opportunities, crowd in private finance, and direct resources toward climate, biodiversity, and infrastructure goals. Scaling up climate finance in EMDEs will require MDB strategies to evolve continuously, ensuring that public and private investment is catalyzed at the necessary scale.

To achieve this, risks must be reduced through clear long-term transition strategies, stronger regulatory frameworks, and well-planned grid infrastructure that aligns energy supply with demand. Only then can EMDEs mobilize the unprecedented volumes of finance required to meet development and climate objectives.

References

Aboumahboub, T., Auer, C., Bauer, N., et al. (2020). REMIND – Regional Model of Investments and Development – Version 2.1.0, www.pik-potsdam.de/research/transformation-pathways/models/remind

Acemoglu, D., Aghion, P., Bursztyn, L., et al. (2012). "The environment and directed technical change," *American Economic Review*, 102(1), 131–166.

Acemoglu, D., Aghion, P. and Zilibotti, F. (2006). "Distance to frontier, selection, and economic growth," *Journal of the European Economic Association*, 4(1), 37–74, March.

ACPR-Banque de France (2021). A first assessment of financial risks stemming from climate change: The main results of the 2020 climate pilot exercise, Analyses et syntheses No. 122–2021.

Aghion, P., Dechezleprêtre, A., Hémous, D., et al. (2016). "Carbon taxes, path dependency, and directed technical change: Evidence from the auto industry," *Journal of Political Economy*, 124(1), 1–51, https://doi.org/10.1086/684581

Ahnert, T. and Georg, Co-P. (2018). "Information contagion and systemic risk," *Journal of Financial Stability*, 35(C), 159–171.

Aldasoro, I., Delli Gatti, D. and Faia, E. (2017). "Bank networks: Contagion, systemic risk and prudential policy," *Journal of Economic Behaviour & Organization*, 142, 164–188.

Aldy, J. E. and Pizer, W. A. (2009). "Alternative metrics for comparing domestic climate change mitigation efforts and the emerging international climate policy architecture," *Review of Environmental Economics and Policy*, 10(1), 3–24.

Alestra, C., Cette, G., Chouard, V., et al. (2022). "Growth impact of climate change and response policies: The advanced climate change long-term (ACCL) model," *Journal of Policy Modeling*, 44(1), 96–112, https://doi.org/10.1016/j.jpolmod.2021.10.001

Allen, T., Boissinot, J., Clerc, L., et al. (2022). Developing climate transition scenarios to manage financial risks. *Bulletin de la Banque de France*, Banque de France, Issue 237/9.

Allen, T., Boullot, M., Dées, S., et al. (2023). Using Short-Term Scenarios to Assess the Macroeconomic Impacts of Climate Transition, Banque de France WP #922.

Alogoskoufis, S., Dunz, N., Emambakhsh, T., et al. (2021). ECB economy-wide climate stress test: Methodology and results, Occasional Paper Series No 281 European Central Bank.

Alp, H., Klepacz, M. and Saxena, A. (2023). "Second-Round Effects of Oil Prices on Inflation in the Advanced Foreign Economies," FEDS Notes. Washington: Board of Governors of the Federal Reserve System, December 15, 2023. https://doi.org/10.17016/2380-7172.3401

Ambec, S., Cohen, M., Elgie, S., et al. (2013). "The Porter hypothesis at 20: Can environmental regulation enhance innovation and competitiveness?" *Review of Environmental Economics and Policy*, 7(1), 2–22.

Andersson, M., Baccianti, C. and Morgan, J. (2020). Climate change and the macro economy, Occasional Paper Series 243, European Central Bank.

Anthoff, D., and Tol, R. S. J. (2013). The climate framework for uncertainty, negotiation and distribution (fund), tables, version 3.7. Available from www.Fund-Model.Org

Aon (2023). Weather, Climate and Catastrophe Report Weather. Available at: www.aon.com/getmedia/f34ec133-3175-406c-9e0b-25cea768c5cf/20230125-weather-climate-catastrophe-insight.pdf

Apel, H., Aronica, G. T., Kreibich, H., et al. (2009). "Flood risk analyses – How detailed do we need to be?" *Natural Hazard*, 49, 79–98.

BaFin (2019). Merkblatt zum Umgang mit Nachhaltigkeitsrisiken. www.bafin.de/SharedDocs/Downloads/DE/Merkblatt/dl_mb_Nachhaltigkeitsrisiken.pdf;jsessionid=792CF270EAF606C3F0F684A0551BE8C5.internet011?__blob=publicationFile&v=2

BaFin (2020). Guidance Notice on Dealing with Sustainability Risks. Available at: www.bafin.de/SharedDocs/Downloads/EN/Merkblatt/dl_mb_Nachhaltigkeitsrisiken_en.pdf?__blob=publicationFile&v=3

Baker, M. P., Bergstresser, D., Serafeim, G., et al. (2018). Financing the Response to Climate Change: The Pricing and Ownership of U.S. Green Bonds (October 12), http://dx.doi.org/10.2139/ssrn.3275327

Bank of England (2022). Results of the 2021 Climate Biennial Exploratory Scenario (CBES), www.bankofengland.co.uk/stress-testing/2022/results-of-the-2021-climate-biennial-exploratory-scenario

Baranović, I., Busies, I., Coussens, W., et al. (2021). "The challenge of capturing climate risks in the banking regulatory framework: Is there a need for a macroprudential response?," *Macroprudential Bulletin*, European Central Bank, 15.

Barbera, A. J. and McConnell, V. (1986). "Effects of pollution control on industry productivity: A factor demand approach," *Journal of Industrial Economics*, 35(2), 161–172.

Barbera, A. J. and McConnell, V. (1990). "The impact of environmental regulations on industry productivity: Direct and indirect effects," *Journal of Environmental Economics and Management*, 18(1), 50–65.

Basel Committee on Banking Supervision (2015). Corporate governance principles for banks, www.bis.org/bcbs/publ/d328.pdf

Basel Committee on Banking Supervision (2021a). Climate-related risk drivers and their transmission channels, April 2021, www.bis.org/bcbs/publ/d517.pdf

Basel Committee on Banking Supervision (2021b). Climate-related financial risks – Measurement methodologies, April 2021, www.bis.org/bcbs/publ/d518.pdf

Basel Committee on Banking Supervision (2023). The Effects of Climate Change-Related Risks on Banks: A Literature Review, Working Paper 40.

Batini, N., di Serio, M., Fragetta, M., et al. (2021). Building Back Better: How Big Are Green Spending Multipliers? IMF Working Paper 21/87.

Batten, S. (2018). "Climate Change and the Macro-economy: A Critical Review," Staff Working Paper No. 706. Bank of England.

Battiston, S., Mandel, A., Monasterolo, I., et al. (2017). "A climate stress-test of the financial system." *Nature Climate Change*, 7(4), 283–288.

Bellora, C. and Fontagné, L. (2023). EU in search of a Carbon Border Adjustment Mechanism, *Energy Economics*, 106673. https://doi.org/10.1016/j.eneco.2023.106673

Black, S., Minnett, D. N., Parry, I. W. H., et al. (2022). "A Framework for Comparing Climate Mitigation Policies across Countries," IMF Working Paper No. 2022/254.

Black, S., Parry, I. and Vernon, N. (2022). Methane Emissions Must Fall for World to Hit Temperature Targets, IMF Blog, International Monetary Fund.

Boer, L., Pescatori, A. and Stuermer, M. (2021). Energy Transition Metals, IMF Working Paper No. 2021/243.

Boettle, M., Kropp, J. P., Reiber, L., et al. (2011). "About the influence of elevation model quality and small-scale damage functions on flood damage estimation," *Natural Hazards and Earth System Sciences*, 11, 3327–3334.

Böhringer, C., Fischer, C., Rosendahl, K. E., et al. (2022). "Potential impacts and challenges of border carbon adjustments," *Nature Climate Change*, 12, janvier, 22–29.

Boirard, A., Payerols, C., Overton, G., et al. (2022). Climate scenario analysis to assess financial risks: Some encouraging first steps, Bulletin de la Banque de France 241/1.

Bollen, J., Guay, B., Jamet, S., et al. (2009). Co-benefits of Climate Change Mitigation Policies: Literature Review and New Results, No. 693, OECD Economics Department Working Papers, OECD Publishing.

Bolton, P. and Kacperczyk, M. (2021). "Do investors care about carbon risk?" *Journal of Financial Economics*, 142(2), 517–549. https://doi.org/10.1016/j.jfineco.2021.05.008

Bolton, P., Despres, M., Pereira da Silva, L. A., et al. (2020). *The Green Swan*. Bank for International Settlements, Basel.

Boneva, L., Ferrucci, G. and Mongelli, F. P. (2022). "Climate change and central banks: What role for monetary policy?"*Climate Policy*, 22(6), 770–787. https://doi.org/10.1080/14693062.2022.2070119

Bosetti, V., Carraro, C., Galeotti, M., et al. (2006). WITCH: A World Induced Technical Change Hybrid model. Energy J., Hybrid Modeling, Special Issue #2: https://doi.org/10.5547/ISSN0195-6574-EJ-VolSI2006-NoSI2-2

Boston Consulting Group (2025). Global Asset Management 2025: A Critical Turning Point, BCG, Boston, www.bcg.com/press/29april2025-global-asset-management-record-high-critical-turning-point

Botzen, W. J., W., Deschenes, O. and Sanders, M. (2019). "The economic impacts of natural disasters: A review of models and empirical studies." *Review of Environmental Economics and Policy*, 13(2), 167–188. https://doi.org/10.1093/reep/rez004

Bowen, A. (2021). *Green Public Investment (English)*. Washington, DC: World Bank Group. http://documents.worldbank.org/curated/en/567431636143644443

Bretschger, L., and Pattakou, A. (2019). "As bad as it gets: How climate damage functions affect growth and the social cost of carbon." *Environmental and Resource Economics*, 73(1), 135–165. https://doi.org/10.1007/s10640-018-0219-y

Brownlees, C. and Engle, R. F. (2017). "SRISK: A conditional capital shortfall measure of systemic risk," *The Review of Financial Studies*, 30(1), 48–79. https://doi.org/10.1093/rfs/hhw060

BSG (2022). Climate finance funding flows and opportunities: What gets measured gets financed, https://web-assets.bcg.com/df/f4/95a9ca6d4af4a51c6bc542c66c4d/what-gets-measured-gets-financed-nov-2022.pdf

Buchele, B., Kreibich, H., Kron, A., et al. (2006). "Flood-risk mapping: Contributions towards an enhanced assessment of extreme events and associated risks," *Natural Hazards and Earth System Sciences*, 6, 485–503. https://doi.org/10.5194/nhess-6-485-2006.

Buchanan, J. M. (1965). "An economic theory of clubs," *Economica*, 32(125), 1–14.

Burke, M., Hsiang, S. M. and Miguel, E. (2015). "Global non-linear effect of temperature on economic production." *Nature*, 527(7577), 235–239. https://doi.org/10.1038/nature15725.

Calel, R. and Dechezleprêtre, A. (2014). "Environmental Policy and Directed Technological Change: Evidence from The European Carbon Market," *Revue d'Économie Statistique*.

Calvin, K., Patel, P., Clarke, L., et al. (2019). "GCAM v5.1: Representing the linkages between energy water, land, climate, and economic systems," *Geoscientific Model Development*, 12(2), 677–698. https://gmd.copernicus.org/articles/12/677/2019/

Campiglio, E., Daumas, L., Monnin, P. and von Jagov, A. (2023). Climate-related risks in financial assets. *Journal of Economic Survey*, 37(3), 950–992.

Carbon Tracker Initiative (2015). The $2 trillion stranded assets danger zone: How fossil fuel firms risk destroying investor returns. www.carbontracker.org/wpcontent/uploads/2015/11/CAR3817_Synthesis_Report_24.11.15_WEB2.pdf

Carhart, M., Litterman, B., Munnings, C., et al. (2022). "Measuring comprehensive carbon prices of national climate policies," *Climate Policy*, 22(2), 198–207, https://doi.org/10.1080/14693062.2021.2014298.

Carleton, T. and Greenstone, M. (2021). Updating the United States Government's Social Cost of Carbon, No. 2021-04, Working Papers, Becker Friedman Institute for Research in Economics.

CBI (2023). Green bond pricing in the primary market H1 (Q1-Q2) 2023. www.climatebonds.net/files/reports/cbi_pricing_h1_2023_01f.pdf

Cheung, A., Yushan, Z., Meredith, A., et al. (2025). *Energy Transition Investment Trends 2025*, BloombergNEF, https://about.bnef.com/energy-transition-investment

Christiansen, G. B. and Haveman, R. H. (1981). "The contribution of environmental regulations to the slowdown in productivity growth," *Journal of Environmental Economics and Management*, 8(4), 381–390.

Ciccarelli, M., Kuik, F. and Martínez Hernández, C. (2023). "The Asymmetric Effects of Weather Shocks on Euro Area Inflation," Working Paper Series, No 2798, ECB, March.

Ciccarelli, M. and Marotta, F. (2024). "Demand or supply? An empirical exploration of the effects of climate change on the macroeconomy," *Energy Economics*, 129, 107163. https://doi.org/10.1016/j.eneco.2023.107163

Congressional Budget Office (2011). *Reducing the Deficit: Spending and Revenue Options*. Washington, DC: Congressional Budget Office. www.cbo.gov/publication/22043

Convergence (2023). The state of Blended Finance, Overall landscape and recent trends in climate blended finance. www.convergence.finance/resource/state-of-blended-finance-2023/view

CPI (2023a). Proposal for a Global Credit Guarantee Facility (GCGF), www.climatepolicyinitiative.org/wp-content/uploads/2023/10/Discussion-Paper-Proposal-for-a-Global-Credit-Guarantee-Facility-GCGF-Oct-2023.pdf

CPI (2023b). Global landscape of climate finance, www.climatepolicyinitiative.org/wp-content/uploads/2023/11/Global-Landscape-of-Climate-Finance-2023.pdf

Crassous, R., Hourcade, J. C. and Sassi, O. (2006). "Endogenous structural change and climate targets modeling experiments with imaclim-R," *The Energy Journal*, SI2006. https://doi.org/10.5547/issn0195-6574-ej-volsi2006-nosi1-13

Criqui, P. (2023). *Les coûts d'abattement en France, Note de synthèse*. France Stratégie, Paris.

Daumas, L. (2024). "Financial stability, stranded assets and the low-carbon transition: A critical review of the theoretical and applied literatures," *Journal of Economic Surveys*, 38, 601–716. https://doi.org/10.1111/joes.12551

de Serres, A. and Murtin, F. (2014). "Your money or your life: Green growth policies and welfare in 2050," *Environmental & Resource Economics*, 63(3), 571–590.

Dechezleprêtre, A. and Kruse, T. (2022). The Effect of Climate Policy on Innovation and Economic Performance along the Supply Chain: A Firm- and Sector-level Analysis, OECD Environment Working Paper No. 189.

Dées, S. and Weber, P.-F. (2020). "Les conséquences du changement climatique pour la politique monétaire," *Revue d'économie financière, Association d'économie financière*, 0(2), 243–257.

Del Negro, M., di Giovanni, J. and Dogra, K. (2023). Is the Green Transition Inflationary? FRB of New York Staff Report No. 1053, http://dx.doi.org/10.2139/ssrn.4359216

Dell, M., Jones, B. F. and Olken, B. A. (2012). "Temperature shocks and economic growth: Evidence from the last half century," *American Economic Journal: Macroeconomics*, 4(3), 66–95. https://doi.org/10.1257/mac.4.3.66.

Dell, M., Jones, B. F. and Olken, B. A. (2014). "What do we learn from the weather? The new climate-economy literature," *Journal of Economic Literature*, 52(3), 740–98. https://doi.org/10.1257/jel.52.3.740.

Dietrich, J. P., Bodirsky, B. L., Humpenöder, F., et al. (2019). "MAgPIE 4: A modular open-source framework for modeling global land systems," *Geoscientific Model Development*, 12(4), 1299–1317. https://gmd.copernicus.org/articles/12/1299/2019/

Dietz, S., and Stern, N. (2015). "Endogenous growth, convexity of damage and climate risk: How Nordhaus' framework supports deep cuts in carbon emissions," *Economic Journal*, 125(583), 574–620. https://doi.org/10.1111/ecoj.12188

Dikau, S. and Volz, U. (2021). "Central bank mandates, sustainability objectives and the promotion of green finance," *Ecological Economics*, 184, 107022. https://doi.org/10.1016/j.ecolecon.2021.107022

DiLeo, M., Rudebusch, G. D. and van't Klooster, J. (2023). Why the Fed and ECB Parted Ways on Climate Change: The Politics of Divergence in the Global Central Banking Community, Hutchins Center Working Paper #88, The Brookings Institution.

Dolphin, G., Pollitt, M. G. and Newbery, D. G. (2020). "The political economy of carbon pricing: A panel analysis," *Oxford Economic Papers*, 72(2), 472–500.

Drudi, F., Moench, E., Holthausen, C., et al. (2021). "Climate Change and Monetary Policy in the Euro Area," Occasional Paper Series 271, European Central Bank.

Dupraz, S., Lisack, N., Marx, M., et al. (2022). Greenflation: Price Stability and the decarbonization of the economy, Mimeo. Available at: https://drive.google.com/file/d/1ppj6FEgM4Lwru-NqvnJMkEIciJqfTgKt/view?usp=drive_link

Dutta, D., Herath, S. and Musiake, K. (2003). "A mathematical model for flood loss estimation," *Journal of Hydrology*, 277, 24–49.

ECB/ESRB (2022). The macroprudential challenge of climate change, ECB/ESRB Project Team on climate risk monitoring.

ECB-Banking Supervision (2022). 2022 climate risk stress test. www.bankingsupervision.europa.eu/ecb/pub/pdf/ssm.climate_stress_test_report.20220708~2e3cc0999f.en.pdf

Ehlers, T. and Packer, F. (2017). Green Bond Finance and Certification (September 17). BIS Quarterly Review September 2017, https://ssrn.com/abstract=3042378

EIOPA (2022). European Insurers' Exposure to Physical Climate Change Risk. Potential implications for non-life business. EIOPA-22/278.

Emambakhsh, T., Fuchs, M., Kördel, S., et al. (2023). "The Road to Paris: Stress testing the transition towards a net-zero economy," Occasional Paper Series, No 328, European Central Bank, Frankfurt am Main, September.

Engle, R., Giglio, S., Kelly, B., et al. (2020). Hedging climate change news," *The Review of Financial Studies*, 33(3), 1184–1216.

ETC (2023). Energy Transition Commission, Financing the Transition: How to Make the Money Flow for a Net-Zero Economy March 2023. www.energy-transitions.org/wp-content/uploads/2023/08/ETC-Financing-the-Transition-MainReport_update.pdf

Everett T., Ishwaran M., Ansaloni G.P., et al. (2010). "Economic Growth and the Environment," Defra Evidence and Analysis Series Paper 2. Department for Environment Food and Rural Affairs, March.

Faccia, D., Parker, M. and Stracca, L. (2021). Feeling the Heat: Extreme Temperatures and Price Stability. Working Paper No. 2626, European Central Bank.

Farmer, J. D., Hepburn, C., Mealy, P., et al. (2015). "A third wave in the economics of climate change," *Environmental and Resource Economics*, 62, 329–357.

Fatica, S., Panzica, R. and Rancan, M. (2021). "The pricing of green bonds: Are financial institutions special?" *Journal of Financial Stability*, 54, 100873, ISSN 1572-3089. https://doi.org/10.1016/j.jfs.2021.100873

Fischer, C., and Fox, A. K. (2012). Climate policy and fiscal constraints: Do tax interactions outweigh carbon leakage? *Energy Economics* 34(Supplement 2): S218–S227 (December).

Flammer, C. (2021). "Corporate green bonds," *Journal of Financial Economics*, 142(2), 499–516. https://doi.org/10.1016/j.jfineco.2021.01.010

Fontagné, L., Bouët, A., Perego, E., et al. (2023). Les incidences économiques de l'action pour le climat. Compétitivité. France Stratégie; Banque de France.

Forslid, R. and Sanctuary, M. (2023). Climate Risks and Global Value Chains: The Impact of the 2011 Thailand Flood on Swedish Firms, CEPR DP17855.

Foster, M. J. (1993). "Scenario planning for small businesses," *Long Range Planning*, 26(1), 123–129. https://doi.org/10.1016/0024-6301(93)90240-G

Frondel, M., Horbach, J. and Rennings, K. (2007). "End-of-pipe or cleaner production? An empirical comparison of environmental innovation decisions across OECD countries," *Business Strategy and the Environment*, 16, 571–584. https://doi.org/10.1002/bse.496

Frondel, M., Ritter, N., Schmidt, C. M., et al. (2010). "Economic impacts from the promotion of renewable energy technologies: The German experience," *Energy Policy*, 38, 4048–4056.

Fujimori, S., Hasegawa, T., Masui, T., et al. (2017). "SSP3: AIM implementation of shared socioeconomic pathways." *Global Environmental Change*, 42, 268–283. https://doi.org/10.1016/j.gloenvcha.2016.06.009

Ganopolski, A., Winkelmann, R. and Schellnhuber, H. J. (2016). "Critical insolation-CO_2 relation for diagnosing past and future glacial inception," *Nature*, 529, 200–203.

Gatzert, N. and Özdil, O. (2003). "The impact of dependencies between climate risks on the asset and liability side of non-life insurers," *European Actuarial Journal*, 14, https://doi.org/10.1007/s13385-023-00364-2

Gifford, L. and Knudson, C. (2020). "Climate finance justice: International perspectives on climate policy, social justice, and capital." *Climatic Change*, 161, 243–249. https://doi.org/10.1007/s10584-020-02790-7

Girard, P.-L., Le Gall, C., Meignan, W., et al. (2022). Croissance et décarbonation de l'économie, Trésor Eco N° 315.

Glenn, J. C. (2009). Scenarios. In Glenn, J. C. and Gordon, T. J., editors, Futures Research Methodology – Version 3.0. The Millenium Project.

Gray, W. B. and Shadbegian, R. J. (1993). "Environmental Regulation and Manufacturing Productivity at the Plant Level," NBER Working Papers 4321, National Bureau of Economic Research, Inc.

Gray, W. B. and Shadbegian, R. J. (1995). "Pollution Abatement Costs, Regulation, and Plant-Level Productivity," NBER Working Papers 4994, National Bureau of Economic Research, Inc.

Greaker, M. (2006). "Spillovers in the development of new pollution abatement technology: A new look at the Porter-hypothesis," *Journal of Environmental Economics and Management*, 52/1, 411–420.

Grubb, M., Wieners, C. and Yang, P. (2021). "Modeling myths: On DICE and dynamic realism in integrated assessment models of climate change mitigation." *WIREs Climate Change*, 12, e698. https://doi.org/10.1002/wcc.698

Hachenberg, B., Schiereck, D. (2018). "Are green bonds priced differently from conventional bonds?" *Asset Management*, 19, 371–383. https://doi.org/10.1057/s41260-018-0088-5

Hallegatte, S. (2023). Du bon usage du coût d'abattement pour piloter la transition, Billet d'analyse, I4CE.

Hallegatte, S. and Rozenberg, J. (2017). "Climate change through a poverty lens." *Nature Climate Change*, 7(4), 250–256.

Hallegatte, S. (2015). The Indirect Cost of Natural Disasters and an Economic Definition of Macroeconomic Resilience. World Bank Policy Research Working Paper No. 7357.

Havlík, P., Valin, H., Herrero, M., et al. (2014). "Climate change mitigation through livestock system transitions," *Proceedings of the National Academy of Sciences*, 111, 3709–3714.

Heyes, A. and Kapur, S. (2011). "Regulatory attitudes and environmental innovation in a model combining internal and external R&D," *Journal of Environmental Economics and Management*, 61/3, 327–340.

Holm-Hadulla, F. and Hubrich, K. (2017). Macroeconomic Implications of Oil Price Fluctuations: A Regime-switching Framework for the Euro Area, European Central Bank Working Paper No. 2119.

Hope, C. (2011). The Social Cost of CO_2 from the Page09 Model. Economics Discussion Paper No. 2011-39. https://doi.org/10.2139/ssrn.1973863

Hope, C., Anderson, J. and Wenman, P. (1993), "Policy analysis of the greenhouse effect: An application of the PAGE model," *Energy Policy*, 21, 327–338.

Horbach, J., Rammer, C., Rennings, K., et al. (2013). Determinants of Eco-innovations by Type of Environmental Impact, the Role of Regulatory Push/Pull, Technology Push and Market Pull, ZEW Discussion Paper 11-027.

Hottenrott, H. and Rexhäuser, S. (2013). Policy-Induced Environmental Technology and Inventive Efforts: Is There a Crowding Out? ZEW Discussion Paper No. 13-115.

Hunt, A. (2011). *Policy Interventions to Address Health Impacts Associated With Air Pollution, Unsafe Water Supply and Sanitation, and Hazardous Chemicals.* OECD Environment Directorate, Paris.

Huppmann, D., Gidden, M., Fricko, O., et al. (2019). "The MESSAGEix Integrated Assessment Model and the ix modeling platform (ixmp): An open framework for integrated and cross-cutting analysis of energy, climate, the environment, and sustainable development," *Environmental Modelling & Software*, 112, 143–156. https://doi.org/10.1016/j.envsoft.2018.11.012

ICMA (2024). Sustainability-Linked Bond Principles Voluntary Process Guidelines, International Capital Market Association. Available at: www.icmagroup.org/assets/documents/Sustainable-finance/2024-updates/Sustainability-Linked-Bond-Principles-June-2024.pdf

IEA (2014). Capturing the Multiple Benefits of Energy Efficiency, International Energy Agency Report. Available at: Capturing the Multiple Benefits of Energy Efficiency.

IEA (2017). World Energy Outlook 2017, International Energy Agency Report. Available at: World Energy Outlook-2017.

IEA (2021). The importance of focusing on jobs and fairness in clean energy transitions, International Energy Agency Commentary. Available at: www.iea.org/commentaries/the-importance-of-focusing-on-jobs-and-fairness-in-clean-energy-transitions

IEA (2023). Net Zero Roadmap: A Global Pathway to Keep the 1.5 °C Goal in Reach, International Energy Agency Report. Available at: www.iea.org/reports/net-zero-roadmap-a-global-pathway-to-keep-the-15-0c-goal-in-reach

IEA (2023). Tripling renewable power capacity by 2030 is vital to keep the 1.5°C goal within reach, International Energy Agency Commentary. Available at: www.iea.org/commentaries/tripling-renewable-power-capacity-by-2030-is-vital-to-keep-the-150c-goal-within-reach

IEA-IFC (2023). Joint Report Calls for Ramping Up Clean Energy Investments in Emerging and Developing Economies, International Energy Agency-International Finance Corporation Report. Available at: www.iea.org/news/iea-ifc-joint-report-calls-for-ramping-up-clean-energy-investments-in-emerging-and-developing-economies

IFC (2023). Biodiversity Finance Reference Guide, International Finance Corporation Report. Available at: www.ifc.org/en/insights-reports/2022/biodiversity-finance-reference-guide

IFC (2021). Climate Investment Opportunity Report, International Finance Corporation Report. Available at: www.ifc.org/content/dam/ifc/doc/mgrt/3503-ifc-climate-investment-opportunity-report-dec-final.pdf

IFC (2021). A Green Reboot for Emerging Markets. Available at: https://documents1.worldbank.org/curated/en/560761621495404959/pdf/Ctrl-Alt-Delete-A-Green-Reboot-for-Emerging-Markets-Key-Sectors-for-Post-COVID-Sustainable-Growth.pdf

IFRS (2023). Effects of climate-related matters on financial statements, International Financial Reporting Standards educational material. Available at: www.ifrs.org/content/dam/ifrs/supporting-implementation/documents/effects-of-climate-related-matters-on-financial-statements.pdf

IHLEG (2023). A climate finance framework: Decisive action to deliver on the Paris Agreement, Second report of the Independent High-Level Expert Group on Climate Finance, November 2023. Available at: www.lse.ac.uk/granthaminstitute/wp-content/uploads/2023/11/A-Climate-Finance-Framework-IHLEG-Report-2-SUMMARY.pdf

ILO (2023). Achieving a just transition towards environmentally sustainable economies and societies for all, International Labor Organisation Report. Available at: www.ilo.org/media/254901/download

IMF (2020). Policies for the Recovery, IMF Fiscal Monitor October 2020. Available at: www.imf.org/en/Publications/FM/Issues/2020/10/27/Fiscal-Monitor-October2020-Policies-for-the-Recovery-49642

IMF (2022a). Near-Term Macroeconomic Impact of Decarbonization Policies, IMF World Economic Outlook 2022. www.imf.org/en/Publications/WEO/Issues/2022/10/11/world-economic-outlook-october-2022

IMF (2022b). Scaling Up Private Climate Finance in Emerging Market and Developing Economies: Challenges and Opportunities, IMF Global Financial Stability Report October 2022 Chapter 2. www.imf.org/-/media/Files/Publications/GFSR/2022/October/English/ch1.ashx

IMF (2023a). Gita Gopinath's Introductory Remarks for the Conference "Fiscal Policy in an Era of High Debt." Available at: www.imf.org/en/News/Articles/2023/11/17/sp-fdmd-gopinath-remarks-at-fiscal-forum-era-of-high-debt

IMF (2023b). List of LIC DSAs for PRGT-Eligible Countries as of August 31, 2023. Available at: www.imf.org/external/pubs/ft/dsa/dsalist.pdf

IPCC (2012). Managing the Risks of Extreme Events and Disasters to Advance Climate Change Adaptation. A Special Report of Working Groups I and II of the Intergovernmental Panel on Climate Change Cambridge University Press, Cambridge, UK, and New York, NY, USA, 582 pp.

IPCC (2014). Climate Change 2014: Impacts, Adaptation, and Vulnerability. Part A: Global and Sectoral Aspects. Contribution of Working Group II to the Fifth Assessment Report of the Intergovernmental Panel on Climate Change [Field, C. B., V. R. Barros, D. J. Dokken, K. J. Mach, M. D. Mastrandrea, T. E. Bilir, M. Chatterjee, K. L. Ebi, Y. O. Estrada, R. C. Genova, B. Girma, E. S. Kissel, A. N. Levy, S. MacCracken, P. R. Mastrandrea, and L. L. White (eds.)]. Cambridge University Press, Cambridge, United Kingdom and New York, NY, USA, 1132 pp.

IPCC (2018). Summary for Policymakers. In: Global Warming of 1.5°C. An IPCC Special Report on the impacts of global warming of 1.5°C above pre-industrial levels and related global greenhouse gas emission pathways, in the context of strengthening the global response to the threat of climate change, sustainable development, and efforts to eradicate poverty [Masson-Delmotte, V., P. Zhai, H.-O. Pörtner, D. Roberts, J. Skea, P. R. Shukla, A. Pirani, W. Moufouma-Okia, C. Péan, R. Pidcock, S. Connors, J. B. R. Matthews, Y. Chen, X. Zhou, M. I. Gomis, E. Lonnoy, T. Maycock, M. Tignor, and T. Waterfield (eds.)]. World Meteorological Organization, Geneva, Switzerland, 32 pp.

IPCC (2021). Climate Change 2021: The Physical Science Basis. Contribution of Working Group I to the Sixth Assessment Report of the Intergovernmental Panel on Climate Change [Masson-Delmotte, V., P. Zhai, A. Pirani, S. L. Connors, C. Péan, S. Berger, N. Caud, Y. Chen, L. Goldfarb, M. I. Gomis, M. Huang, K. Leitzell, E. Lonnoy, J. B. R. Matthews, T. K. Maycock, T. Waterfield, O. Yelekçi, R. Yu, and B. Zhou (eds.)]. Cambridge University Press, Cambridge, United Kingdom and New York, NY, USA, https://doi.org/10.1017/9781009157896.

IPCC (2022). Climate Change 2022: Impacts, Adaptation, and Vulnerability. Contribution of Working Group II to the Sixth Assessment Report of the Intergovernmental Panel on Climate Change [H.-O. Pörtner, D.C. Roberts, M. Tignor, E. S. Poloczanska, K. Mintenbeck, A. Alegría, M. Craig, S. Langsdorf, S. Löschke, V. Möller, A. Okem, B. Rama (eds.)]. Cambridge University Press. Cambridge University Press, Cambridge, UK and New York, NY, USA, 3056 pp., https://doi.org/10.1017/9781009325844.

IPCC (2022). Climate Change 2022: Mitigation of Climate Change, Chapter 5: Demand, services and social aspects of mitigation, figure 5.7, p. 530 et Supplementary Material II, tableau 5.SM.2, p. 4.

IRENA (2017). Stranded assets and renewables: how the energy transition affects the value of energy reserves, buildings and capital stock, International Renewable Energy Agency (IRENA), Abu Dhabi, www.irena.org/remap

Issing, O. (2019). The Problem with "Green" Monetary Policy. Project Syndicate. Available at: www.project-syndicate.org/commentary/central-banks-no-to-green-monetary-policy-by-otmar-issing-2019-11

Jaffe, A. B. and Palmer, K. (1997). "Environmental regulation and innovation: A panel data study," *The Review of Economics and Statistics, MIT Press,* 79(4), 610–619.

Jaffe, A. B., Peterson, S. R., Potney, P. R., et al. (1995). "Environmental regulation and the competitiveness of US manufacturing: What does the evidence tell us?," *Journal of Economic Literature,* 23, 132–163.

Jaison, A., Sorteberg, A., Michel, C., et al. (2023). Windstorm damage relations – Assessment of storm damage functions in complex terrain, Natural Hazards and Earth System Sciences. https://doi.org/10.5194/nhess-2023-90

Jorgenson, D. W. and Wilcoxen, P. J. (1990). "Environmental regulation and U.S. economic growth," *The RAND Journal of Economics,* 21–2, 314–340.

Jung, H., Engle, R. F. and Berner, R. (2021). CRISK: Measuring the Climate Risk Exposure of the Financial System. FRB of New York Staff Report No. 977, Rev. March 2023. http://dx.doi.org/10.2139/ssrn.3931516

Kalkuhl, M. and Wenz, L. (2020). "The impact of climate conditions on economic production: Evidence from a global panel of regions," *Journal of Environmental Economics and Management,* 103, 102360, ISSN 0095-0696, https://doi.org/10.1016/j.jeem.2020.102360

Känzig, D. R. (2023). "The Unequal Economic Consequences of Carbon Pricing," National Bureau of Economic Research, Working Paper No. 31221. doi:10.3386/w31221

Kapraun, J., Kapraun, J., Latino, C., et al. (2021). (In)-Credibly Green: Which Bonds Trade at a Green Bond Premium? (April 29). Proceedings of Paris December 2019 Finance Meeting EUROFIDAI – ESSEC, http://dx.doi.org/10.2139/ssrn.3347337

Karpf, A. and Mandel, A., (2017). Does it pay to be green? (February 24). http://dx.doi.org/10.2139/ssrn.2923484

Keen, S., Lenton, Timothy, M., Godin, Antoine, et al. (2021). "Economists' erroneous estimates of damages from climate change," Papers 2108.07847, arXiv.org.

Kelly, D. L. and Kolstad, C. D. (1999). "Integrated assessment models for climate change control," in Henk Folmer and Tom Tietenberg (eds), *International Yearbook of Environmental and Resource Economics 1999/2000: A Survey of Current Issues.* Cheltenham, UK: Edward Elgar.

Khoo, F. and Yong, J. (2023). Too hot to insure – avoiding the insurability tipping point, FSI Insights on policy implementation No 54, Bank for International Settlements.

Kim, S. K., Shin, J., An, S. I., et al. (2022). "Widespread irreversible changes in surface temperature and precipitation in response to CO_2 forcing." *Nature Climate Change*, 12, 834–840. https://doi.org/10.1038/s41558-022-01452-z

Klawa, M. and Ulbrich, U. (2003). "A model for the estimation of storm losses and the identification of severe winter storms in Germany," *Natural Hazards and Earth System Sciences*, 3, 725–732. https://doi.org/10.5194/nhess-3-725-2003

Koléda, G. and Pillu, H. (2011). "Déterminants de l'innovation dans les technologies énergétiques efficientes et renouvelables," *Économie et Prévision, Programme National Persée*, 197(1), 105–128.

Kolstad, C. D. and Moore, F. C. (2019). "Estimating the Economic Impacts of Climate Change Using Weather Observations," NBER Working Papers 25537, National Bureau of Economic Research, Inc.

Konradt, M. and Weder di Mauro, B. (2023). "Carbon taxation and greenflation: Evidence from Europe and Canada," *Journal of the European Economic Association*, 21(6), 2518–2546. https://doi.org/10.1093/jeea/jvad020

Kosuke, A. (2001). "Optimal monetary policy responses to relative-price changes," *Journal of Monetary Economics*, 48(1), 55–80. https://doi.org/10.1016/S0304-3932(01)00069-1

Kotz, M., Kuik, F., Lis, E., et al. (2024). "Global warming and heat extremes to enhance inflationary pressures," *Communications Earth & Environment*, 5, 116. https://doi.org/10.1038/s43247-023-01173-x

Kousky, C. (2014). "Informing climate adaptation: A review of the economic costs of natural disasters," *Energy Economics*, 46(C), 576–592.

Kozluk, T. and Zipperer, V. (2014). "Environmental policies and productivity growth: A critical review of empirical findings," *OECD Journal: Economic Studies, OECD Publishing*, 2014(1), 155–185.

Kraemer, M. and Negrila, L. (2014). Climate Change is a global mega-trend for sovereign risk. Credit Week Special Report: Climate Change, Preparing for the Long Term. Standard and Poor's Rating Services McGraw Hill Financial. Copyright © 2014 Standard & Poor's Financial Services LLC, a part of McGraw Hill Financial. All rights reserved.

Kreibich, H., Bubeck, P., Kunz, M., et al. (2014). "A review of multiple natural hazards and risks in Germany," *Natural Hazards*, 74, 2279–2304, https://doi.org/10.1007/s11069-014-1265-6.

Lange, S., Volkholz, J., Geiger, T., et al. (2020). Projecting exposure to extreme climate impact events across six event categories and three spatial scales. Earth's Future, 8, e2020EF001616. https://doi.org/10.1029/2020EF001616

Larcker, D. F. and Watts, E. (2020). "Where's the Greenium?" *Journal of Accounting and Economics*, 69(2–3), April–May 2020, 101312, http://dx.doi.org/10.2139/ssrn.3333847

Leckebusch, G. C., Ulbrich, U., Fröhlich, L., et al. (2007). "Property loss potentials for European mid-latitude storms in a changing climate," *Geophysical Research Letters*, 34, L05703, https://doi.org/10.1029/2006GL027663.

Lenton, T. M., Rockström, J., Gaffney, O., et al. (2019). "Climate tipping points – too risky to bet against," *Nature*, 575, 592–595. https://doi.org/10.1038/d41586-019-03595-0.

Leonard, M., Westra, S., Phatak, A., et al. (2014). A compound event framework for understanding extreme impacts. Wiley Interdisciplinary Reviews: Climate Change. 5. https://doi.org/10.1002/wcc.252.

Lesk, C., Rowhani, P. and Ramankutty, N. (2016). "Influence of extreme weather disasters on global crop production." *Nature*, 529(7584), 84–87. https://doi.org/10.1038/nature16467. PMID: 26738594.

Mallampalli, V. R., Mavrommati, G., Thompson, J., et al. (2016). "Methods for translating narrative scenarios into quantitative assessments of land use change." *Environmental Modelling & Software*, 82, 7–20.

Marcantonini, C. and Ellerman, A. D. (2013). "The Cost of Abating CO_2 Emissions by Renewable Energy Incentives in Germany," EUI Working Paper, RSCAS 2013/05.

Mattauch, L., Hepburn, C., Spuler, F., et al. (2022). "The economics of climate change with endogenous preferences," *Resource and Energy Economics*, 69. 101312. https://doi.org/10.1016/j.reseneeco.2022.101312

McKibbin, W. J., Konradt, M. and Weder di Mauro, B. (2021). "Climate policies and monetary policies in the euro area," in ECB Forum on Central Banking, Conference Proceedings. European Central Bank Frankfurt am Main.

McKibbin, W., Morris, A., Panton, A. J., et al. (2017). "Climate Change and Monetary Policy: Dealing with Disruption," Centre of Applied Macroeconomic Analysis (CAMA) Working Paper 77/2017, December.

McKibbin, W. J., Morris, A. C. and Wilcoxen, P. J. (2012a). "Pricing carbon in the United States: A model-based analysis of power sector only approaches," *Resource and Energy Economics*, 36(2014), 130–150.

McKibbin, W. J., Morris, A. C., Wilcoxen, P. J., et al. (2012b). The Potential Role of a Carbon Tax in U.S. Fiscal Reform. Brookings. Climate and Energy Economics Discussion Paper.

McKinsey & Company (2021). A blueprint for scaling voluntary carbon markets to meet the climate challenge. Available at: www.mckinsey.com/~/media/mckinsey/business%20functions/sustainability/our%20insights/a%20blueprint%20for%20scaling%20voluntary%20carbon%20markets%20to%20 meet%20the%20climate%20challenge/a-blueprint-for-scalingvoluntary-carbon-markets-to-meet-the-climate-challenge.pdf?shouldIndex

McKinsey & Company (2022). The net-zero transition report: What it would cost, what it would bring, www.mckinsey.com/capabilities/sustainability/our-insights/the-net-zero-transition-what-it-would-cost-what-it-could-bring

Meadowcroft, James and Rosenbloom, Daniel (2023). "Governing the net-zero transition: Strategy, policy, and politics," *Proceedings of the National Academy of Sciences*, 120, 47.

Meinshausen, M., Raper, S. C. B. and Wigley, T. M. L. (2011). "Emulating coupled atmosphere-ocean and carbon cycle models with a simpler model, MAGICC6 – Part 1: Model description and calibration," *Atmospheric Chemistry and Physics*, 11(4), 1417–1456, https://acp.copernicus.org/articles/11/1417/2011/

Merz, B., Kreibich, H., Schwarze, R., et al. (2010). "Review article "Assessment of economic flood damage," *Journal Natural Hazards and Earth System Sciences*, 10, 1697–1724, https://doi.org/10.5194/nhess-10-1697-2010

Meyers, J. G. and Nakamura, L. (1980). "Energy and Pollution Effects on Productivity: A Putty-Clay Approach," in John W. Kendrick (ed.) *New Developments in Productivity Measurement and Analysis*. University of Chicago Press, Chicago.

Moessner, R. (2022). "Effects of Carbon Pricing on Inflation," CESifo Working Paper Series 9563, CESifo.

Moore, F. C. and Diaz, D. B. (2015). "Temperature impacts on economic growth warrant stringent mitigation policy," *Nature Climate Change*, 5, 127–131.

Morgan Stanley (2023). www.morganstanley.com/ideas/carbon-offset-market-growth#:~:text=The%20voluntary%20carbon%2Doffset%20market,help%20meet%20net%2Dzero%20targets

Morris, A. (2015). *Why the Federal Government Should Shadow Price Carbon*. Commentary, The Brookings Institution, Washington, DC.

Mukherjee, K. and Ouattara, B. (2021). "Climate and monetary policy: Do temperature shocks lead to inflationary pressures?"*Climatic Change*, 167(3), 1–21.

Nachtigall, D., Lutz, L., Rodríguez, M. C., et al. (2022). "The Climate Actions and Policies Measurement Framework: A Structured and Harmonised Climate Policy Database to Monitor Countries' Mitigation Action," OECD Environment Working Papers, No. 203, OECD Publishing, Paris, https://doi.org/10.1787/2caa60ce-en

Nascimento, N., Machado, M. L., Baptista, M., et al. (2007). "The assessment of damage caused by floods in the Brazilian context," *Urban Water Journal*, 4, 195–210.

Network for Greening the Financial System (2019). Macroeconomic and financial stability implications of climate change, Technical supplement to the First comprehensive report.

Network for Greening the Financial System (2020). Climate Change and Monetary Policy: Initial takeaways.

Network for Greening the Financial System (2022a). Final report on bridging data gaps. Technical document.

Network for Greening the Financial System (2022b). Physical Climate Risk Assessment: Practical Lessons for the Development of Climate Scenarios with Extreme Weather Events from Emerging Markets and Developing Economies. Technical document.

Network for Greening the Financial System (2023). Conceptual note on short-term climate scenarios. Technical document.

Network for Greening the Financial System (2024). Improving Greenhouse Gas Emissions Data – NGFS Information Note. www.ngfs.net/en/improving-greenhouse-gas-emissions-data-ngfs-information-note

Neumann, J. E., Willwerth, J., Martinich, J., et al. (2020). "Climate damage functions for estimating the economic impacts of climate change in the United States," *Review of Environmental Economics and Policy*, 14(1), 25–43. https://doi.org/10.1093/reep/rez018.

Nordhaus W. (2020). "The Climate Club: How to fix a failing global effort," Foreign Affairs, May–June, 10–17.

Nordhaus, W., and Sztorc, P. (2013). DICE 2013R: Introduction and user's manual. Available from www.econ.yale.edu/~nordhaus/homepage/homepage/documents/DICE_Manual_100413r1.pdf

Nordhaus, W. D. (2017). "Revisiting the social cost of carbon," Proc. Natl. Acad. Sci. U.S.A., 114(7): 1518–1523.

Nordhaus, W. D. (2018). "Evolution of modeling of the economics of global warming: Changes in the DICE model, 1992–2017," *Climatic Change, Springer*, 148(4), 623–640, June.

Nordhaus, W. D. (2018). "Climate change: The ultimate challenge for economics," *American Economic Review*, 108(6), 1283–1307. https://doi.org/10.1257/aer.108.6.1283.

Nordhaus, W. D. (1992). "The 'DICE' Model: Background and Structure of a Dynamic Integrated Climate-Economy Model of the Economics of Global Warming," Cowles Foundation Discussion Papers 1009, Cowles Foundation for Research in Economics, Yale University.

Nowzohur, L. and Dees, S. (2024). On the near-term macro-financial risks of the low-carbon transition and climate change. SUERF Policy Brief | No. 876 | May 10, 2024.

OECD (2013). *Effective Carbon Prices*. Paris: OECD Publishing, https://doi.org/10.1787/9789264196964-en

OECD (2022). *Pricing Greenhouse Gas Emissions: Turning Climate Targets into Climate Action, OECD Series on Carbon Pricing and Energy Taxation.* Paris: OECD Publishing. https://doi.org/10.1787/e9778969-en

Parker, M. (2018). "The impact of disasters on inflation," *Economics of Disasters and Climate Change*, 2(1), 21–48, April.

Parry, I. W. H. (2012). Chapter 1. "What is the best policy instrument for reducing CO_2 emissions?," in Ruud A. de Mooij, Mr. Michael Keen, and Ian W. H. Parry (eds.), *Fiscal Policy to Mitigate Climate Change*, International Monetary Fund.

Pietsch, A. and Salakhova, D. (2022). "Pricing of Green Bonds: Drivers and Dynamics of the Greenium", ECB Working Paper No. 2022/2728, http://dx.doi.org/10.2139/ssrn.4227559

Pommeret, A., Oliu-Barton, M., Robinet, A., et al. (2023). Sobriété, Rapport thématique, in Pisani-Ferry and Mahfouz, Les incidences économiques de l'action pour le climat, France Stratégie.

Popp, D. (2006). "International innovation and diffusion of air pollution control technologies: The effects of NOX and SO_2 regulation in the US, Japan, and Germany," *Natural Hazards and Earth System Sciences*, 51(1), 46–71.

Popp, D. and Newell, R. (2012). "Where does energy R&D come from? Examining crowding out from energy R&D," Energy Economics, 34(4), 980–991.

Popp, D. (2002). "Induced innovation and energy prices," *American Economic Review*, 92(1), 160–180. https://doi.org/10.1257/000282802760015658

Prahl, B. F., Rybski, D., Boettle, M., et al. (2016). "Damage functions for climate-related hazards: Unification and uncertainty analysis," *Natural Hazards and Earth System Sciences*, 16, 1189.

Prahl, B. F., Rybski, D, Burghoff, O, et al. (2015). "Comparison of storm damage functions and their performance," *Natural Hazards and Earth System Sciences*, 15, 769.

Quilcaille, Y., Gudmundsson, L., Schumacher, D. L., et al. (2025). "Systematic attribution of heatwaves to the emissions of carbon majors." *Nature*, 645, 392–398.

Rausch, S. and Reilly, J. (2015). "Carbon taxes, deficits, and energy policy interactions," *National Tax Journal*, 68(1), 157–178. http://dx.doi.org/10.17310/ntj.2015.1.07

Revesz, R. L., Howard, P. H., Arrow, K., et al. (2014). "Global warming: Improve economic models of climate change," *Nature*, 508, 173–175.

Roncoroni, A., Battiston, S., D'Errico, M., et al. (2021a). "Interconnected banks and systemically important exposures," *Journal of Economic Dynamics and Control*, 133, 104266.

Roncoroni, A., Battiston, S., Escobar-Farfán, L. O., et al. (2021b). "Climate risk and financial stability in the network of banks and investment funds," *Journal of Financial Stability*, 54, 100870.

S&P Global (2022). Weather Warning: Assessing Countries' Vulnerability to Economic Losses from Physical Climate Risks. Available at: www.spglobal.com/esg/insights/weather-warning-assessing-countries-vulnerability-to-economic-losses-from-physical-climate-risks

Schnabel, I. (2023). "Monetary policy tightening and the green transition," Speech to the International Symposium on Central Bank Independence Sveriges Riksbank, Stockholm, January 10, 2023.

Schnabel, I. (2022). A new age of energy inflation: Climateflation, fossilflation and greenflation, Speech at a panel on "Monetary Policy and Climate Change" at The ECB and its Watchers XXII Conference, Frankfurt am Main, 17 March 2022.

Semieniuk, G., Holden, P. B., Mercure, J. F. et al. (2022). "Stranded fossil-fuel assets translate to major losses for investors in advanced economies," *Nature Climate Change*, 12, 532–538.

Smith, J. B., and Sims, W. A. (1985). "The impact of pollution charges on productivity growth in Canadian brewing," *Rand Journal of Economics*, 16(3), 410–423.

Stavins, R. N. (1997). "Policy instruments for climate change: How can national governments address a global problem?" *University of Chicago Legal Forum*, 1997, Article 10. Available at: http://chicagounbound.uchicago.edu/uclf/vol1997/iss1/10

Steffen, W., Rockström, J., Richardson, K., et al. (2018). "Trajectories of the Earth system in the anthropocene," *Proceedings of the National Academy of Sciences*, 115(33) 8252–8259. https://doi.org/10.1073/pnas.1810141115

Stehfest, E., van Vuuren, D., Bouwman, L., et al. (2014). Integrated assessment of global environmental change with IMAGE 3.0: Model description and policy applications. Netherlands Environmental Assessment Agency (PBL).

Stenek, V., Amado, J. C. and Connell, R. (2011). Climate risk and financial institutions: Challenges and opportunities. IFC.

Stern, N. (2007). *The Economics of Climate Change: The Stern Review*. Cambridge: Cambridge University Press.

Stiglitz, J., Sen, A., Fitoussi, J. P. (2009). Commission on the measurement of economic performance and social Progress. Making Globalization Work: Stiglitz, Joseph E.: 9780393330281: Amazon.com: Books

Stiglitz, J. E. (2006). *Making Globalization Work*. New York: W. W. Norton & Company.

Stolbova, V., Monasterolo, I. and Battiston, S. (2018). "A financial macro-network approach to climate policy evaluation," *Ecological Economics*, 149, 239–253. https://doi.org/10.1016/j.ecolecon.2018.03.013

Tagliapietra, S., Wolff, G. B. and Zachmann, G. (2022). Greening Europe's post-COVID-19 recovery, BRUEGEL BLUEPRINT SERIES 32.

Thinking Ahead Institute (2023). The World's Largest 500 Asset Managers. Available at: www.thinkingaheadinstitute.org/research-papers/the-worldslargest-asset-managers-2023

Tang, D. Y. and Zhang, Y. (2018). Do Shareholders Benefit from Green Bonds? Available at: http://dx.doi.org/10.2139/ssrn.3259555

TCDF (2021). Task Force on Climate-related Financial Disclosures Guidance on Metrics, Targets, and Transition Plans. https://assets.bbhub.io/company/sites/60/2021/07/2021-Metrics_Targets_Guidance-1.pdf

Tol, R. S. J. (1997). "On the optimal control of carbon dioxide emissions: An application of FUND," *Environmental Modeling & Assessment*, 2(3), 151–163. https://doi.org/10.1023/A:1019017529030

Tol, R. S. J. (2009). "The economic effects of climate change." *Journal of Economic Perspectives*, 23(2). 29–51.

Tol, R. S. J. (2022). A Meta-analysis of the Total Economic Impact of Climate Change, Working Paper Series 0422, Department of Economics, University of Sussex Business School.

Tsan, M., Totapally, S., Hailu, M., et al. (2019). "The Digitalisation of African Agriculture Report 2018–2019." Wageningen, The Netherlands: CTA / Dalberg Advisors.

UNFCCC (2025). Introduction to Climate Finance, UNFCCC Secretariat (UN Climate Change). Available at: https://unfccc.int/topics/introduction-to-climate-finance#:~:text=Climate%20finance%20refers%20to%20local,that%20will%20address%20climate%20change

United Nations (2025). Renewable energy – powering a safer future. Available at: www.un.org/en/climatechange/raising-ambition/renewable-energy

United Nations Office for Disaster Risk Reduction (UNDRR) (2023). Closing climate and disaster data gaps: New challenges, new thinking, UNDRR Working Paper. Closing climate and disaster data gaps: New challenges, new thinking | UNDRR.

Van der Heijden, K. (2005). *Scenarios: The Art of Strategic Conversation*. John Wiley & Sons, Hoboken, New Jersey.

van der Ploeg, F. and Rezai, A. (2020). "Stranded assets in the transition to a carbon-free economy," *Annual Review of Resource Economics*, 12(1), 281–298.

Verdolini, E., and Gaelotti, M. (2011). "At home and abroad: An empirical analysis of innovation and diffusion in energy-efficient technologies," *Journal of Environmental Economics and Management*, 61, 119–134.

Viscusi, W. K. (1983). *Risk by Choice: Regulating Health and Safety in the Workplace*. Cambridge, MA: Harvard University Press.

Vogt-Schilb, A., Meunier, G. and Hallegatte, S. (2018). "When starting with the most expensive option makes sense: Optimal timing, cost and sectoral allocation of abatement investment," *Journal of Environmental Economics and Management*, 88, 210–233, https://doi.org/10.1016/j.jeem.2017.12.001

Walther, U. (2023). Climate stress tests: Are banks fit for the green transition? *SUERF Policy* Note No. 305. www.suerf.org/wp-content/uploads/2023/11/f_4 515167f9a463006c21cd66f2ab2cd73_63709_suerf.pdf

Weche, J. P. (2019). "Does green corporate investment crowd out other business investment?"*Industrial and Corporate Change*, 28(5), 1279–1295.

Weitzman, M. L. (2007). "A review of the stern review on the economics of climate change," *Journal of Economic Literature*, 45(3), 703–724. https://doi.org/10.1257/jel.45.3.703

Weitzman, M. L. (2010). "GHG targets as insurance against catastrophic climate damages," *Journal of Public Economic Theory*, 12(2), 197–219. https://doi.org/10.1111/j.1467-9779.2009.01441.x

Weitzman, M. L. (2012). "GHG targets as insurance against catastrophic climate damages," *Journal of Public Economic Theory*, 14(2), 221–244.

World Bank (2022). What is results-based climate finance and how is it different from most international public climate finance? Available at: www.worldbank.org/en/news/feature/2022/08/17/what-you-need-to-know-about-results-based-climate-finance

World Bank (2025). Climate-smart agriculture (CSA). Available at: www.worldbank.org/en/topic/climate-smart-agriculture

Zerbib, O. D. (2019). "The effect of pro-environmental preferences on bond prices: Evidence from green bonds," *Journal of Banking & Finance*, 98, 39–60. ISSN 0378-4266, https://doi.org/10.1016/j.jbankfin.2018.10.012

Zhao, C., Liu, B., Piao, S., et al. (2017). "Temperature increase reduces global yields of major crops in four independent estimates," *Proceedings of the National Academy of Sciences of the United States of America*, 114(35), 9326–9331. https://doi.org/10.1073/pnas.1701762114

Index

abatement cost, 55, 60–63, 67, 70
adaptation, 2, 5, 11–12, 20, 29–30, 49–50, 57, 110, 130–32, 134–35, 137–38, 140–42, 148, 154, 156, 163, 169, 186, 213, 220, 250–51, 253, 255–56, 260–61, 264, 282, 285, 295–98
anthropocene, 7–8, 15
Avoid, Shift, Improve (ASI), 109

Basel framework, 247
behavioral shifts, 110, 136
biodiversity, 155–56
blended finance, 2–3, 168, 253, 266, 272, 274–77, 279–82, 295, 297
blue bonds, 154

Carbon Border Adjustment Mechanism (CBAM), 84, 122–25
carbon budget, 3, 51–55, 62–63, 72
carbon capture and storage, 83, 85, 267, 289–90
carbon credits, 137, 292
carbon leakage, 3, 84, 118, 122, 124–28, 254, 299
carbon market, 136, 286, 288, 293
    compliance, 137
    voluntary (VCM), 82, 137, 266, 284, 293
carbon price, 57–60, 62–63, 73, 82, 91, 113–114, 121, 123, 125–26, 128, 176, 179–80, 237, 238, 268
carbon shadow price, 58, 121
carbon tax, 17, 30, 73, 78, 82, 114, 121–25, 179–80, 187, 196, 200
Climate Bonds Initiative, 150
Climate Club, 126–27
climate finance, 132–42
    activity-based, 135
    outcome-based, 136
    results-based, 136
climate Minsky moment, 222
concessional funds, 2, 135, 253, 266, 269–71, 275–76

cost-benefit, 55, 57, 68, 70
cost-effectiveness, 55–56, 88
counterparty risks, 220–21
credit risks, 220–21, 225, 239, 242–43, 247, 253–54, 265, 274, 283
critical minerals, 172, 177
Currency Exchange Fund (TCX), 295

damage functions, 35–42
data gaps, 149, 202, 217, 238, 297
debt-for-nature swaps, 159
deflation, 178, 188, 194, 197
de-risking, 264, 269, 273, 279
DICE model, 39, 56–57, 65–71
disasters, climate-related, 22–29
disclosures, 143–45, 149, 203–5, 216, 218, 221, 230, 247, 297

effective lower bound (ELB), 195–96
emissions trading system, 73, 77, 82, 90–91
EU Green Deal, 148

feebates, 80
feed-in tariffs (FITs), 80
financial stability, 1, 3, 21, 72, 182, 207–8, 210, 212, 214, 221, 224, 229, 244, 247, 250, 252, 263, 265
fiscal policy space, 131, 236, 263
fossilflation, 171, 176

Global Credit Guarantee Facility (GCGF), 274
Green Bond Principles (GBP), 150, 152
green bonds, 150, 152, 154, 294
    GSS+, 142–44, 151, 164
    transition bonds, 156
green bubble, 179
green innovation, 94, 99, 113, 128, 179
greenflation, 1, 171, 193
greenhouse effect, 6–8
greenium, 161, 164–67
greenwashing, 147, 149, 153, 217, 226, 291

INDEX

inflation, 5, 31–32, 162, 171, 169–201
    expectations, 31, 171, 176, 181–82, 184, 187–88, 190–94, 198, 200
    target, 199, 201
    targeting, 169, 198, 200
insurance companies, 24, 212, 214, 224, 227, 244–46, 283, 294
insurance protection gap, 224–25, 227, 245, 251
Integrated Assessment Models (IAMs), 57, 60, 65–66, 69–71
internationally transferred mitigation outcomes (ITMOs), 292
investment gap, 129, 253, 257

labor, 106, 134, 170, 173, 177, 186, 188, 196
liability risks, 221
look-through monetary policy, 187–94
loss and damage, 48, 132, 256, 261–62, 296

market risks, 107, 220–21, 225
migration, 1, 29–30, 185–86, 219
monetary policy, 3, 169–71, 173, 180–85, 187–89, 191–99, 202, 205, 207, 209–11, 294
    conventional, 20, 59, 161, 164–67, 183, 187, 196, 241
    operational framework, 202–3, 207, 210
    space, 183, 185–86, 196, 207, 210, 212
    unconventional, 196–97

National Adaptation Plans (NAPs), 297
Nationally Determined Contributions (NDCs), 49, 119, 126, 137, 149, 280
Natural (Neutral) Interest Rate (NIR) or R*, 185–86, 196, 201
Network for Greening the Financial System (NGFS), 16–17, 19, 43, 60, 71, 129–30, 182–83, 186, 206, 213, 216–17, 230, 233, 239, 246

operational risks, 213, 220–21, 265

physical risks, 5, 16–17, 21, 29, 38, 33–45, 66, 147, 173, 212–13, 215, 220, 226, 229, 231, 237, 240–41, 243, 246, 249, 251
Pillar 1, 247
Pillar 2, 247
Porter hypothesis, 96, 98
Poverty Reduction and Growth Trust (PRGT), 271

price stability, 3, 82, 167, 169–71, 178, 181–82, 187–89, 192–93, 198–99, 208, 212
prudential policy, 246–51
    macroprudential, 230, 248–49
    microprudential, 230, 248
public-private partnerships (PPPs), 250

regulatory standards, 78
reinsurance, 227, 246, 250
representative concentration pathways (RCP), 12
Resilience and Sustainability Trust (RST), 271

scenarios, 10–12, 16–17, 19–21, 33, 39–40, 43, 53, 60, 66, 68–70, 72, 84, 102–3, 124, 130, 144, 178, 222, 230–35, 237, 239, 241–43, 246, 252
shared economic pathways (SSP), 11–12
social cost of carbon (SCC), 57–58, 68
stagflation, 178, 188
standards, 142, 150, 218, 291
stranded assets, 1, 105–8, 178, 221–22, 225, 235
stress test, 223, 229–46, 247
supervisory expectations, 247
supply shock, 178, 187–89, 200
sustainability-linked bonds, 149, 156–58, 162, 168, 294
Sustainable Development Goals (SDGs), 149, 258, 263, 298
Sustainable Finance Disclosure Regulation (SFDR), 143

Task Force on Climate-related Financial Disclosures (TCFD), 143, 145, 216, 284, 297
taxonomies, 142, 147–48, 217, 254
tipping points, 2, 14–16, 40–41, 45, 53, 243
trade-off, output-inflation, 181, 187–88, 192–94, 197
transition plans, 132, 144, 146–47, 254, 268
transition policy, 1–2, 17, 19, 21, 52, 60, 64, 67, 73–91, 93–94, 101, 104, 113, 169–70, 177–80, 184, 187, 196, 199, 212, 216
transition risks, 21, 54, 66, 171, 178, 180, 183, 188, 213, 215, 216, 221, 223, 229, 231, 237, 239–46, 249, 252
transition, just, 253, 256, 260–61

well-being, 5, 23, 46, 51, 93–94, 101, 115, 128

For EU product safety concerns, contact us at Calle de José Abascal, 56–1°, 28003 Madrid, Spain or eugpsr@cambridge.org.

www.ingramcontent.com/pod-product-compliance
Ingram Content Group UK Ltd.
Pitfield, Milton Keynes, MK11 3LW, UK
UKHW022248220326
469255UK00019B/413